Busy Woman's Cookbook

Other titles in the
Women's Edge Health Enhancement Guide
series:

Fight Fat
Food Smart
Growing Younger
Herbs That Heal
Natural Remedies
Total Body Toning

Women's Edge
HEALTH ENHANCEMENT GUIDE™

Busy Woman's Cookbook

*Delicious, Healthy Recipes
in 30 Minutes or Less*

By the Editors of

RODALE®

© 2000 by Rodale Inc.
Illustrations © by Shawn Banner, Tom Ward

Prevention Health Books for Women and Women's Edge Health Enhancement Guide are trademarks of Rodale Inc.

Printed in the United States of America on acid-free ∞, recycled paper ♻

Library of Congress Cataloging-in-Publication Data

    Busy woman's cookbook : delicious, healthy recipes in 30 minutes or less / by the editors of Prevention Health Books for Women.
         p.   cm. — (Women's edge health enhancement guides)
    Includes index.
    ISBN 1–57954–238–7 hardcover
    1. Quick and easy cookery.   I. Prevention Health Books for Women.   II. Women's edge health enhancement guides.
    TX833.5 .B874   2000
    641.5'55—dc21   00–022011

Distributed to the book trade by St. Martin's Press

2   4   6   8   10   9   7   5   3   1   hardcover

Visit us on the Web at www.rodalebooks.com, or call us toll-free at (800) 848-4735.

WE INSPIRE AND ENABLE PEOPLE TO IMPROVE THEIR LIVES AND THE WORLD AROUND THEM

Busy Woman's Cookbook Staff

EDITORS: Matthew Hoffman, Carol J. Gilmore
SERIES EDITOR: E. A. Tremblay
WRITERS: Betsy Bates, John Forester, Winnie Yu
ART DIRECTOR: Darlene Schneck
SERIES ART DIRECTOR: Lynn N. Gano
COVER AND INTERIOR DESIGNER: Lynn N. Gano
ILLUSTRATOR: Shawn Banner, Tom Ward
ASSOCIATE RESEARCH MANAGER: Shea Zukowski
PRIMARY RESEARCH COORDINATOR: Anita C. Small
BOOK PROJECT RESEARCHER: Carol J. Gilmore
RODALE TEST KITCHEN MANAGER: JoAnn Brader
RODALE TEST KITCHEN STAFF: Nancy Zelko
EDITORIAL RESEARCHERS: Lori Davis, Paula Rasich, Elizabeth Shimer
SENIOR COPY EDITORS: Kathy D. Everleth, Amy K. Kovalski
EDITORIAL PRODUCTION MANAGER: Marilyn Hauptly
LAYOUT DESIGNER: Donna G. Rossi
ASSOCIATE STUDIO MANAGER: Thomas P. Aczel
MANUFACTURING COORDINATORS: Brenda Miller, Jodi Schaffer, Patrick T. Smith

Rodale Healthy Living Books

VICE PRESIDENT AND PUBLISHER: Brian Carnahan
VICE PRESIDENT AND MARKETING DIRECTOR: Karen Arbegast
EDITORIAL DIRECTOR: Michael Ward
PRODUCT MARKETING MANAGER: Guy Maake
BOOK MANUFACTURING DIRECTOR: Helen Clogston
MANUFACTURING MANAGERS: Eileen Bauder, Mark Krahforst
RESEARCH MANAGER: Ann Gossy Yermish
COPY MANAGER: Lisa D. Andruscavage
PRODUCTION MANAGER: Robert V. Anderson Jr.
OFFICE MANAGER: Jacqueline Dornblaser
OFFICE STAFF: Julie Kehs, Mary Lou Stephen, Catherine E. Strouse

In all Rodale cookbooks, our mission is to provide delicious and nutritious recipes. Our recipes also meet the standards of the Rodale Test Kitchen for dependability, ease, practicality, and, most of all, great taste. To give us your comments, call (800) 848-4735.

Contents

Introduction ix

PART ONE
Starting Out Smart

The Busy Cook's Credo:
Quick and Healthy 2

Stocking Up 10

Quick and Healthy
Techniques 19

PART TWO
Healthy Cooking in 30 Minutes or Less

Main-Meal Salads 28

Lots o' Pasta 37

Talkin' Turkey and Chicken 46

Fresh and Divine Seafood 56

Meat Treats 64

Vegetarian Specialties 72

Great Grills 81

Freestyle Stir-Fries 91

Rapid Wraps 94

Super Sides 100

Did You Say Dessert? 108

PART THREE
Make-Ahead Meals

Casseroles: Lovin' from
the Oven 120

Sensational Soups
and Stews 127

Crock-Pots: Hands-Off
Cooking 134

Index 141

Conversion Chart 150

Introduction

Cooking can be great fun! What an opportunity to be creative, try new things, and put our personalities into something we make. Why, with grocery store bins overflowing with exotic foods, cookbooks of every cuisine known to woman calling out to us from their shelves, and all the computer-age conveniences of today's kitchens at our fingertips, we can put together meals that would pass muster at a four-star restaurant.

Only one question: Who has the time?

Between holding down a job, running kids to sports and band practice, getting to parent-teacher meetings, doing volunteer work, keeping up with household finances, and maintaining relationships with our spouses, what we need more than anything is to be able to put something on the table that's nutritious, good-tasting, and *fast*.

A fantasy? Not anymore. This volume of the *Women's Edge* series was created for—and by—*real* busy women. Women who are pressed for time but who still care about good food, who want to eat well without eating expensively, and who care about nutrition but also demand exciting tastes.

Here you'll find dozens and dozens of recipes, specially designed for fantastic flavor and total nutrition, that you can make in almost no time at all. Soups (fresh, not canned) that are ready in 15 minutes. Seafood secrets that take the fuss out of cooking fish and shellfish. Ways to use seasonings that don't require a shelf full of spices. Sinfully rich desserts that are ready in 5 minutes or less. Every recipe is fast, is easy to prepare, and can be completed—beginning to end—without hard-to-find ingredients.

In preparing this book, we talked with dozens of chefs, nutritionists, and other food experts. This book is packed with hundreds of their insightful, behind-the-scenes tips that tell you which timesaving kitchen gadgets you can't live without, the fastest (and lowest-fat) cooking techniques, how to create salads that double as main meals, and how to make canned vegetables taste just as good as fresh.

Finally, you'll find a fascinating array of answers to all the questions you've ever asked about cooking and health. Is butter healthier than margarine? Why are you hungry after eating Chinese food? Why does cooking cabbage smell so strong? Why does eating soup make your nose run?

As you'll discover in this book, having a busy lifestyle doesn't mean spending time in fast-food lines or putting your tastebuds to sleep. So pick a recipe. Give it a try. And have fun!

Anne Alexander
Editor-in-Chief
Prevention magazine

PART ONE

Starting Out Smart

The Busy Cook's Credo: Quick and Healthy

It's 5:00 P.M. Do you know where your sanity is?

For most women today, the dinner hour might as well be called the witching hour. It's the breaking point of a busy day, when deadlines, stress, exhaustion, and family duties converge. A generation ago, many women stayed home. They had time to shop carefully, prepare nice meals, and make the dinner hour the high point of the family's day. Women today are more likely to rush from offices to pick up children, go to aerobics class, or anxiously mark time in traffic as they try to get to the dry cleaner's before it closes.

At times like these, who has time to cook, much less cook healthy?

Guess what. You do.

"Cooking often seems like a huge amount of work. What women don't know is that they can develop a small repertoire of things that are easily prepared—and I mean in 15 minutes to half an hour," says Deann Bayless, chef and owner of the Frontera Grill, an acclaimed Chicago restaurant.

In addition to her work in the restaurant, Bayless is a wife, mother to an 8-year-old, and a cookbook author. She describes her life as being harried beyond belief. Yet she has developed tricks and shortcuts that enable her to prepare healthy meals that also taste great. She always keeps things simple. Maybe she'll boil some pasta and toss in a few colorful and enticing vegetables and season the dish with herbs from windowsill pots. Her daughter helps wash vegetables and mix ingredients. Her husband, a chef himself, pitches in as well.

True, their evening ritual is more time-consuming than pulling up to the drive-thru window. But only slightly. What they gain is precious time of togetherness along with meals that will strengthen and protect their bodies rather than merely add unwelcome pounds.

"Some women have lost the sense of joy that cooking can bring to their lives," Bayless says. "Putting a simple meal on the table and sharing delicious food with my family and my friends brings me an almost spiritual pleasure."

The Power of Good Food

It's easy to idealize the days when women actually had time to cook elaborate meals. And there's no question that today's high-speed lifestyles have put dents in our ability to eat well. But overall, we are actually eating better than we used to. We've learned a lot about the dangers of fat and cholesterol and the health benefits of grains, fruits, and other wholesome foods. Still, nearly all of us could use some improvements.

The U.S. Department of Agriculture has created a report called the Healthy Eating Index. It's essentially a report card that takes stock of how Americans are eating. In the years from 1994 to 1996, for example, women ages 19 to 50 scored just 62 on a 100-point scale. Women 51 and older did a little better, scoring 67. According to the Index, a score of 80 is a "good" diet, while scores in the 60s are nothing to write home about.

Where have we fallen short the most? Most dramatically, in the fruit category. Researchers have found that only 17 percent of women eat two to four servings of fruit a day, the amount recommended by experts. We didn't do so well with grains and dairy foods either. Barely one in four women surveyed got the amounts needed for optimal health.

Apart from the fact that our health may be paying the price, these findings are disappointing because the simplest changes in diet can have powerful results. Look at it this way: Assuming that you have three meals a day (and most of us have more, counting snacks), you eat nearly 1,100 times a year. That's

WOMAN TO WOMAN

Health Brought Her Back to Cooking

With three kids in diapers and a hectic job as a writer, Sabrina Nelson of Chatsworth, California, appreciated the convenience of frozen vegetarian meals, especially because she didn't like to cook very much anyway. But then, out of the blue, she became gravely ill. At age 33, she found herself back in the kitchen learning new tricks and nervously waiting for the payoff.

When we first got married, my husband and I used to eat out a lot. We both work as writers at home and we liked getting out at the end of the day. Then we had kids, twin girls, and that was the end of that.

Between raising the twins and working, I felt that I didn't have time to cook, much less clean up the mess afterward. So we started relying more and more on frozen foods, like pizza and veggie burgers.

Three years ago, I became pregnant with my son. At the same time, I developed a rare disease called relapsing polychondritis. Basically, my connective tissue was becoming inflamed, which resulted in the destruction of my bone cartilage. No one knows for sure what causes this disease, but one doctor I saw suggested that my diet might be involved. That's when I started reading about nutrition and the effects of food on health.

The more I learned, the more interested I became in healthy eating and cooking. I became an avid label reader, a regular consumer of fruits and vegetables, and a big fan of basmati brown rice. For a long time, I wasn't sure if my new diet was going to have any effect on the disease, but I could tell right away that I had more energy and was feeling better.

My illness finally did go into remission. So that's behind me. And I've become hooked on cooking. My husband has lost some weight. The children hardly ever get sick. And cooking doesn't seem like a chore the way it used to, partly because I take advantage of timesaving gadgets, like the microwave, bread machine, and food processor.

Lately, I've begun making Indian, Chinese, and Mexican dishes from scratch. Even though I'm still a novice, the recipes taste better than what we used to eat in restaurants. They're a lot healthier, too.

1,100 chances to have a positive influence on your health. And that's in just one year.

More is involved than an expanding waistline. Nearly every major disease is influenced by what we eat. In some cases, in fact, diet is the main factor that determines whether we stay healthy or get sick.

- The link between diet and heart disease is especially strong. Researchers have found that taking steps to lower your cholesterol and blood pressure with diet is the best way to reduce your risk for heart disease. Heart disease is the leading cause of death for American men and women, so cooking healthy is the most important gift you can give yourself and your family.

- Research shows that if everyone in this country ate more of the right foods—fruits, vegetables, whole grains, and beans—and less of the wrong ones, the incidence of all cancers would be reduced by 30 percent.

- Osteoporosis is among the most common and potentially serious conditions women get. Often caused by getting too little calcium in the diet, osteoporosis causes bones to become thin and brittle. It's usually preventable. In one study, for example, women who got at least 1,000 milligrams of calcium a day—about the amount in three glasses of milk—were able to reduce their bone loss by 43 percent.

- Diabetes, stroke, high blood pressure . . . many serious illnesses can be eased, pre-

REAL-LIFE SCENARIO
Spending Time to Make Time

With long hours on the job, a 2-hour daily commute, and a hungry, athletic husband who doesn't know how to cook, June has to struggle every night just to get dinner on the table. She usually doesn't get home until 7:00 or 8:00 P.M., and it's often 10:00 before they sit down to eat. She has tried cooking big Sunday dinners and saving the leftovers, but she and her husband, Joe, get bored eating the same thing 3 nights in a row. They both enjoy grilling, but that's too time-consuming for weeknight meals. Lately, they've started depending on low-fat frozen entrées. That's fast and they enjoy them, but Joe always leaves the table hungry. June can tell this latest plan isn't going to last very long, but she has run out of ideas. How can she fit healthy weeknight meals into their busy lives with little inconvenience?

June's problem is clearly time—she doesn't have enough of it. The only solution is going to be for her to get ahead of herself somehow, to prepare meals in advance so that she and Joe can eat well without actually having to cook something new every night.

It's too bad that she got discouraged with cooking extras on Sundays. That's clearly going in the right direction, and she should consider starting again. It's true that no one wants to eat the same meals for 3 days running, but that's not necessary. June could cook extras on Sunday and freeze them. Then, rather than eating the same thing every night, they could space it out, having frozen meals in between.

Store-bought frozen dinners are made for average people, not for people with big appetites like Joe's. What they could do is make the frozen meal just part of the dinner and round it out with side dishes and a salad. It will hardly take them any time at all to prepare the extras. For example, June could buy a week's worth of washed and packaged salad

vented, or even reversed by eating healthier foods. Most of us know this already, yet we continue to depend on fat- and calorie-laden convenience foods rather than greens at the supermarket. While a frozen dinner is heating in the microwave, they could just pour some salad greens into a bowl.

For Joe especially, it might be worth making the salads more filling. One way to do that would be to add 2 tablespoons of nuts. Salads with crunch—from pecans, hazelnuts, or walnuts—taste really good, and the nuts provide a lot of protein and other nutrients. Raw nuts are fine, but they taste even better when they've been toasted for 3 minutes in the microwave.

Adding side dishes doesn't have to be any more time-consuming than using instant salad. When June is at the store, she could buy vegetables ready-cut, then lightly steam or microwave them on Sunday. Steamed vegetables such as carrots, onions, and potatoes keep well for a few days in the refrigerator. Each night, they could scoop some out of a bowl and microwave them for a few minutes.

If they like grilling, there's no reason not to do it year-round, especially if they have a gas grill and a covered area outside. Grilling doesn't have to be fancy, and it doesn't have to take a lot of time. Grilling vegetables is very fast. Meats cook quickly when they're cut into slices less than a ½ inch thick. To make them more tender, June could put them in a marinade the night before.

Cooking ahead always seems like such a hassle at first because it does take time, and time is the one thing that Joe and June don't have. But by investing ½ hour or an hour on the weekend, they could easily save several hours during the week.

Expert Consulted
Susan Adams, R.D.
Cooperative Extension Agent
Washington State University
Seattle

▶ It's true that taste can be an issue. After all, when you remove large amounts of fat and sugar from food, the intensity of taste may go down. But as Bayless can attest, there are plenty of ways to pump more flavors into foods. It takes a lot less time to add extra spices than it does to edge across three lanes of interstate in order to grab a burger, and it's more pleasant than breathing exhaust fumes from the 16 cars ahead of you. And once you know a few tricks, cooking healthy doesn't take any longer than preparing foods that are bad for you.

Quick and Easy Changes

Research has shown that women who eat in restaurants more than six times a week consume at least 288 additional calories a day compared with their eat-at-home counterparts. It's not that restaurant food is always bad for you or that women who are concerned about their health should never eat out. It's simply that cooking at home puts you in control. It allows you to eat more foods that are good for you and less of those that contain a lot of saturated fat, sugar, and cholesterol.

The term *healthy cooking* sometimes seems confusing because it means different things to different people. In one family, a healthy improvement might be eating eggs once or twice a week instead of every morning. In another, it might involve adding a grain dish to the weekly menu or serving smaller portions of steak. Add to this the

making the switch. Many people believe that healthy foods take too long to fix, that they don't taste good, and that nutrition guidelines are too confusing to follow.

alphabet soup of expert recommendations—from the American Cancer Society, the American Heart Association, and others—and it's easy to see why many women find it easier to program a VCR than to keep up with the latest healthy-cooking guidelines.

Put your calculator away. Ultimately, it all comes down to a simple principle: Using less fat and sugar and using more unprocessed fruits, vegetables, whole grains, and beans will lower your health risks and give you plenty of natural flavors. There's no extra time involved. Sounds easy, doesn't it? It is. Here's how.

Focus on the "fabulous four." People who eat a lot of vegetables, fruits, whole grains, and beans tend to be healthy. Research has shown, for example, that those who eat five or more servings of fruits and vegetables a day are less likely to get cancer. Picture how much food this really is: a banana, an apple, a carrot, a couple of broccoli stalks, and a few fingers-full of green beans. Not much at all.

All fruits and vegetables are good, but cruciferous vegetables such as broccoli and cauliflower are especially good because they have been shown to reduce the risk for a variety of cancers, including cancers of the colon, stomach, and lungs.

It's just as easy to eat more grains. A slice of bread counts as a serving. So does half a cup of rice. Or half a bagel. Or half a cup of pasta. As long as the grains you eat are whole grains, like whole wheat bread, you'll be getting dietary fiber as well as nutrients such as B vitamins, zinc, magnesium, copper, and vitamin E. A study of 38,740 women found that those who ate more

WOMEN ASK WHY

Why are organic foods so expensive? Are they healthier?

Gold costs a fortune because there's less of it than, say, salt. The law of supply and demand dictates that the less there is of something and the more people want it, the higher the price is going to be. A lot of health-conscious people are demanding organically grown produce, and currently, there aren't enough growers to supply them. Economics being what it is, farmers, wholesalers, and retailers can charge a premium for a pound of organic onions.

Another reason for the high price of organics is the relatively high cost of producing them. Organic growing methods aren't as efficient as those that rely on synthetic fertilizers and pesticides. It may take more work to grow crops without these chemical shortcuts, and this is reflected in the higher price.

Some people suggest that organically grown foods are better for your health. So far, however, there's not a lot of evidence to support this. Scientists haven't been able to show that crops grown under nonorganic conditions, which may contain trace amounts of some chemicals, are a hazard to people's health.

Nor do organics necessarily contain a richer nutritional

whole grain foods had substantially lower risks for cancer and cardiovascular disease than those eating less.

Take down the fat. It wasn't so many years ago that "healthy" cooking meant filling the kitchen with vegetables and whole grains, then slathering every recipe with butter or cheese. People didn't know it then, but fat is *the* worst thing when you're trying to have a healthful diet.

♦ Fat raises levels of cholesterol in the blood, and high levels of cholesterol—especially LDL, or low-density lipoprotein cholesterol—can lead

payload than nonorganic produce. Plants growing in the field take what they need from the soil. They can't tell the difference between inorganic and organic fertilizers. They simply absorb whatever it is they need to grow. Then they convert it into their own tissues. The end result, when scientists look at the different plants in the laboratory, is virtually the same.

One thing you may get when you buy organic is better freshness. Most organic farmers have small operations, and they're often able to get their crops to market—especially farmers' markets—more quickly than the mega-operators do. A carrot that spent 2 weeks on the road isn't going to be as nutritious as one that was picked 2 days ago. This is true of all fruits and vegetables, regardless of how they're grown.

From a health perspective, it probably doesn't matter whether you buy organics or not. Taste is another issue. Some people swear that organically grown produce tastes better, and that's as good a reason as any to choose it. Most nutritionists are less demanding. They'd be happy if people would simply eat more produce, regardless of how it's grown.

Expert Consulted
Audrey Maretzki, Ph.D.
Professor of food science and nutrition
Pennsylvania State University
University Park

to stroke, heart disease, and high blood pressure. Researchers have found that for each 1 percent that you lower your total cholesterol, you lower your heart attack risk by 2 percent.

‣ People who cut way back on fat and eat a lot of fruits and vegetables can actually reverse the course of coronary heart disease.

‣ People who eat less fat have a much lower risk of cancer than those who eat more. One study found that women who got 10 fewer grams of fat a day cut their risk of ovarian cancer by 20 percent.

‣ A single gram of fat has about double the calories as a similar amount of carbohydrate or protein, so reducing the amount of fat in your diet is among the most important things you can do.

‣ Fat in the diet even affects the eyes. A high-fat diet may be linked with an increased chance of early macular degeneration, the leading cause of legal blindness among people over age 65 in the United States.

Fats aren't all the same, of course. Saturated fat, the kind found in red meats, whole milk, and butter, and trans fatty acids, like those found in shortening and certain margarines, are the ones most closely linked to coronary heart disease in women.

Fats called monounsaturated fats, on the other hand, are far healthier. Swedish researchers found that women who got a lot of monounsaturated fats (olive and canola oils are very high in this fat) had half the risk of being diagnosed with breast cancer than those who mainly consumed other types of fat.

All fats have the same amount of calories, and you don't want to get too many of any of them. But when you're cooking healthy, a change as simple as cutting back on meat or other sources of saturated fat and substituting a splash of olive oil can have substantial benefits.

Eat a little more dairy. Milk, sour cream, and cheese offer much more than just wonderful tastes and textures. They also provide abundant calcium, the mineral that's essential for protecting the bones. Women age 50 and younger need 1,000 milligrams of calcium a day. Those over 50 who are not taking estrogen need 1,500 milligrams of calcium a day. That sounds like a

HEALTH FOOD
VERSUS HEALTHY FOOD

It would seem self-evident that anything called health food is going to be good for you, but that health food label may be deceptive. Sometimes, the only thing that's healthy about so-called health food is the manufacturer's bottom line.

Just because something is labeled "health food" does not necessarily mean that it is healthy or low in fat, says Deborah Slawson, R.D., Ph.D., a nutrition coordinator for the Prevention Center at the University of Memphis. She remembers looking at a box of "healthy" whole wheat puffed cheese snacks. "When I really looked at the label, it was pretty shocking," she says. "There were 3 grams of fat in each serving, and a serving size was two little crunchies."

Marketing hype aside, many people are genuinely confused about what healthy food really is. A good example is soy. Many people are convinced that soy foods are the healthiest foods imaginable as well as superior sources of protein. Yet full-fat tofu may get as much as 60 percent of its calories from fat.

This doesn't mean that you shouldn't eat soy, or that all foods marketed as "health foods" are bad for you. Quite the contrary. As long as they're low in fat, soy and many other health foods may be among the healthiest foods you can eat. But you always want to be careful about what you buy, whether the label says "healthy" or not, says Dr. Slawson. Sea salt may be sold as a health food, but it's really no healthier than salt that's mined on land. Whole wheat pizza may be very high in fat. And saturated fat is saturated fat; whether it comes from vegetable oil or butter, it's still going to have a lot of calories, and it won't be very good for your health.

The real health foods—whole grains, fruits, vegetables, low-fat dairy, and yes, soy—are often the ones without the "Healthy!" labels, and you don't have to go to health food stores to get them.

Cooking Fast, Cooking Healthy

Women already know that they should make the switch to healthier cooking. But no one looks forward to spending time and energy unlearning old habits and making a U-turn in the kitchen. Here's what a lot of us don't realize: Cooking healthy doesn't take one second longer than cooking "old style." It isn't more expensive; in fact, it's often less expensive because natural, wholesome foods usually cost less than their processed counterparts. And it doesn't mean unlearning all the techniques that you've spent a lifetime developing. Here are a few ways to make the change easily and get the tastes that you want.

Shop for convenience. Some of the best salad recipes call for as many as three or four different greens. Even if you decide to buy them all, you'll make one meal, and the rest will go soggy in the produce drawer. Supermarkets have finally caught on to the fact that cooks want convenience. They now carry all sorts of bagged vegetables and salad greens, alone and in fun combinations. They're fresh, washed, and cut. All you have to do is open the bag and pour them into a bowl or steamer.

Here's another great time-saver: minced garlic in a jar. No one enjoys peeling garlic, and no one has to. Most markets stock jars of minced garlic, and it lasts almost forever. Spoon out only as much as you need, and you don't have to clean a garlic

lot, but by focusing on the right foods, you can get all the calcium your bones need almost automatically. A cup of 1 percent milk, for example, has 300 milligrams of calcium.

press afterward. Just put the jar back in the refrigerator when you're done.

Let someone else do the preparation. A wonderful way to save time and still cook healthy is to buy lean chicken breast that's already cooked. It's usually kept near the lunchmeats, and it comes plain as well as flavored. You can toss the pieces into a stir-fry, salad, or casserole.

Practice some "half-scratch" cooking. People think that cooking from scratch is a badge of freshness, but even professional chefs use prepared foods when they can. Bayless practices what she calls half-scratch cooking. She makes the foundation of meals herself—the pasta, potatoes, or meat—then jazzes them up with high-quality sauces. "There are lots of decent prepared sauces for pasta, especially in whole foods markets," she says. You can make the sauces even better by adding a little sautéed onion and garlic, a handful of herbs, and maybe some fresh green beans or snow peas. It's still

quicker than cooking from scratch, and it allows you to customize dishes for your family.

Using a combination of fresh and prepared foods can be faster than heating up a frozen meal, says Jackie Newgent, R.D., a nutrition and culinary consultant in New York City and spokesperson for the American Dietetic Association. "It may also be tastier and more nutritious. Good health, taste, and timeliness can all go together."

HEALTH BONUS
The Perfect Plate

Nutritionists are always telling us that the best-balanced meals consist of this percentage of protein or that percentage of vegetables. Who can figure it all out? Here's an easy way to make sure that you're getting the right balance of meat, vegetables, and starches with every meal.

- Fill half your plate with vegetables.
- Fill a quarter of your plate with starchy foods like rice, pasta, or potatoes.
- Fill a quarter of your plate with meat, fish, or beans.

Stocking Up

How many times have you come home at the end of the day, tired and hungry, opened the refrigerator, and found—well, there's no telling what it was, but it obviously had been in there for too long. The pantry wasn't any more promising: A few sacks of dried beans, a lot of spices, a canister of flour, and a can of condensed milk. So much for having something fast. That's about the time when you do the one thing that you didn't want to do: wearily tug your shoes back on and drive to the nearest restaurant. Another few hours lost, and another lost chance to make something healthy.

Whether you're cooking for yourself or a family, having a well-stocked kitchen is the key to having quality quickly and with a minimum of fuss. Even if you live in an apartment and pantry space is tight, you can easily have everything you need to put dinner on the table in a hurry. Quantity isn't important. What matters is having the right ingredients. Take dried beans. They're good to keep around for when you're planning a meal in advance, but they won't do you any good when you want something *now*.

The best ingredients are those that are fast, versatile (why waste shelf space on something you'll only use once?), and convenient. Most healthy foods, as it turns out, qualify on all counts. A few cans of vegetables and beans on the shelf will allow you to have a nutritious meal 10 minutes after you get home. A frozen fish fillet cooks almost as quickly. Even those dried beans, which take forever to cook, require no real time on your part because you can put them on the back burner and forget them until you're ready to eat.

In the following pages, you'll find out about the ingredients that every busy cook needs. You won't find anything elaborate here—just wholesome foods that can be mixed and matched quickly and in an astonishing variety of ways. Once your shelves are stocked, you'll be reminded why you took up cooking in the first place. It's fun. It's easy. And, when you know a few tricks, it's fast.

Grains and Breads

If there's one indispensable ingredient, it has to be grains. They form the backbone of just about every cuisine in the world. For convenience, nothing is better: Put them in a pot, let them simmer, and read a magazine until they're done. From a health perspective, all foods made from grains—from Italian pasta to Mediterranean couscous—are among the best foods that you can eat because they're loaded with nutrients and fiber.

Grains stay fresh nearly forever, so long as they're kept in airtight containers. For taste as well as convenience, keep a variety of grains in the pantry, both the slow-cooking and fast-cooking varieties. Wheat berries, for example, are good as a hot cereal and as a side dish. They have to soak for at least 12 hours, however, so they're no good when you're in a hurry. Rolled oats, on the other hand, take only about 10 minutes from package to table. Keeping both slow and fast grains in the pantry means that you'll always have a choice, depending on your schedule and what you're in the mood for.

There are thousands of different grains worldwide, and supermarkets and health food stores stock at least one to two dozen types. Regardless of the variety, grains require nothing more than simmering water and maybe a bit of patience until they're done. Exotic grains like amaranth or quinoa will add exciting new elements to any meal, and standbys like rice and oatmeal are almost the ultimate in convenience.

Speed things up with cereals. When you're pressed for time, cereals made with whole grains can't be beat. And they're among the most nutritious foods you can find. Whether you have a taste for cold breakfast cereal or a bowl of hot oatmeal with milk on top, you can't top the convenience. Jackie Newgent, R.D., a nutrition and

> ### HEALTH BONUS
> #### Frozen Spinach Beats Fresh
>
> Chill out about frozen foods: Frozen spinach is even healthier than anyone realized. In one study, spinach that had been frozen for a year was found to contain more than twice the vitamin C of fresh spinach that had spent just 7 days in refrigeration. Both samples came from the same crop, too. This finding proves just how healthy frozen vegetables can be.

culinary consultant in New York City and spokesperson for the American Dietetic Association, says that when she's pressed for time, cereal is her favorite meal in a hurry.

Make life easy with rice. White rice is a nutritional lightweight, but brown rice contains so many nutrients that it's almost a stand-alone meal. The usual complaint about brown rice is that it takes twice as long to cook as the white variety. That's true of traditional brown rice, but now there are quick-cooking varieties. "You probably lose a little fiber by cooking the quick versions, so just throw some frozen chopped vegetables into the pot minutes before the rice is finished cooking," says Newgent. "Frozen peas are my favorite."

A quick way to pump more flavor into rice is to add a bouillon cube or two to the cooking water. It's easier than sautéing an onion or garlic, and it gives rice a delicate kick of flavor—without any extra cleanup.

Boil some pasta. It's a staple in kitchens worldwide and a savior when you're pressed for time and want something wholesome in a hurry. Ask any chef or dietitian what they have the most of in their cupboards, and you'll probably be told that it's pasta. All pastas are good sources of complex carbohydrates and

HEALTHY—OR NOT?
Peanut Butter

Tablespoon for tablespoon, peanut butter is outrageously high in fat. Worse, some of the fat is usually hydrogenated, meaning that it is chemically altered in order to increase the food's shelf life (peanut butter will keep for months when it's refrigerated) and make foods more spreadable. A side effect of this process is that hydrogenated fat can raise levels of harmful low-density lipoprotein (LDL) cholesterol while lowering the beneficial high-density lipoprotein (HDL) cholesterol.

If you're watching your weight, peanut butter shouldn't be the first thing you reach for. Because it contains so much fat, it packs 190 calories in just 2 tablespoons, says Connie Diekman, R.D., a spokeswoman for the American Dietetic Association.

Does this mean that you should junk the Jif? Not at all. For one thing, most people don't eat a lot of peanut butter at one time. And while most commercially prepared peanut butters contain hydrogenated fats, natural peanut butters usually don't. You can also buy reduced-fat versions, which have fewer calories than the full-fat kind.

No matter what type you choose, peanut butter contains fiber as well as muscle-building protein. It also provides niacin and magnesium. The body uses niacin to generate energy within the cells, and magnesium helps the muscles work properly.

As long as calories aren't a problem and you don't overindulge, peanut butter is perfectly healthy for adults as well as children. And because it's an instant source of energy, it's nearly the ultimate in convenience foods.

higher in fiber than pasta made with heavily processed semolina flour. But even basic pasta is enriched with thiamin, riboflavin, niacin, and iron, so you can't go wrong either way.

Shop for quick grains. While grains such as barley and rye berries are great sources of nutrients (and good taste), they're slow to cook. When Newgent is in a hurry, she generally prefers quicker-cooking grain-based foods, such as couscous.

Keep bread in the freezer. Women don't bake bread as much as they used to because good, wholesome bread is available almost everywhere these days. Large supermarkets usually have in-store bakeries where you can buy many types of bread, from dense pumpernickels to crusty French loaves. Most breads freeze well, so you can buy several loaves and put them in the freezer when you get home. Slice them first, which will make it easier to thaw the amount that you need when you're ready.

Taste the world's breads. One of the perks of living in an increasingly multicultural society is the variety of bread that has become available, such as tortillas and pitas. You have to be a little careful buying these breads because sometimes they contain lard. Check the labels, and when you find one that you like, stock up and freeze the surplus. They keep well and can be used as a base for everything from refried beans and salsa to crab salad.

protein, and they're very low in fat. They're also the foundation for literally hundreds of recipes, many of them spur-of-the-moment quick.

Whole-grain pasta is best because it's much

Fruits and Vegetables

What's more convenient than peeling a banana? Or eating snap peas, either raw or steamed for 3 minutes? Most fruits and vegetables are ready for eating in less time than it takes to order a pizza.

Why don't Americans eat more fruits and vegetables? "People think that they're not available at certain times of the year, or that they take too long to prepare," says Deborah Beall, R.D., manager of the California Department of Health Services' "Five a Day" program in Sacramento.

In today's world of advanced agriculture and high-speed transportation, most fruits and vegetables are available all the time, Beall explains. And while some vegetable recipes are time-consuming to prepare, most require nothing more complex than trimming off the tough parts, cutting them to size, and putting them in a steamer, a stir-fry, or a stew.

Stock up on canned vegetables. They taste good, they keep for a long time, and they're certainly fast. Open a lid, and you have a side dish or a stew or soup ingredient ready to go in a minute. Some of the best canned vegetables are corn, green beans, peas, and mixed vegetables. They retain a lot of their crispness, and you may get just as many nutrients as with fresh. In fact, you may get even more. Canned vegetables are packaged right at the peak of ripeness. This process sometimes captures vitamins that are lost in fresh vegetables as they get older.

Canned sauces are worth stocking up on, too. Take tomato sauce. It has nearly the same nutritional value as whole tomatoes, and you'll use it in everything from soups and casseroles to meat loaf. In fact, canned tomatoes and tomato sauces top fresh when it comes to lycopene, the compound in tomatoes that has been shown to reduce the risk of cancer.

Buy them frozen. Many people are suspicious of frozen vegetables because they suspect that they're not as wholesome as fresh or have given up their pleasing textures. You can certainly tell the difference between fresh and frozen, but the differences are marginal, especially when you're adding vegetables to a recipe rather than serving them as stand-alones. And they don't lose much, if any, of their nutrients or fiber during processing.

Newgent has a penchant for frozen berries. They're always available, and they're great sources of fiber. She brings them out of the freezer a handful at a time—sprinkling a little on top of her morning cereal, for example, or using blueberries as a refreshing snack on hot summer days.

Explore farmers' markets. Unlike grocery store produce, which is sometimes picked early in order to stay fresh during transport, the fruits and vegetables at farmers' markets are usually picked a day or two before you eat them. They're sometimes grown organically, so the flavors are richer and more complex than those in mass-produced produce.

Stock up on onions and garlic. Many main-dish recipes call for one or both of these ingredients. Even if you're not fond of onions and garlic in their raw, pungent states, they add depth and richness to any meal—an important consideration when you're cooking with less fat. Their strong flavors mellow as they cook. Both onions and garlic keep well, as long as they're stored at room temperature in a basket so that air can circulate.

Buy the brightest varieties. The vivid hues of many vegetables tell a lot about their contributions to your health. Consider the bright red tomato: The red comes from lycopene. And the yellow-orange in carrots and squash comes mainly from beta-carotene, an antioxidant that may protect against cancer and heart disease.

Beans

Great Northerns. Pintos. Black beans. Split peas. You'd need a long piece of paper to list every dried bean available on supermarket shelves. Regardless of their different tastes and textures, all beans are very high in fiber and a variety of nutrients. And they're a lot like rice, in that they provide a foundation for almost any meal. They add their own flavors to recipes without overwhelming other ingredients.

Dried beans are slow to cook, but don't let that slow you down. They freeze well, so you can make a large batch in advance, says Newgent. Even if you prefer to eat them freshly cooked, they don't require a whole lot of attention. Cover them with water and let them simmer for a few hours—no stirring required.

Canned beans are fine, too, says Newgent. They won't have the same al dente texture of freshly cooked beans, but they're fine nutritionally and are very convenient to add to salads or sauces.

A bean that you probably haven't experimented with is soy. Soy beans are very slow to cook and don't have a lot of flavor. What they do have is an enormous amount of protein, says Newgent. The easiest way to get the benefits of soy is to eat tofu, a versatile alternative for meat.

Fish and Meats

It's true that healthy recipes depend more on plant-based foods than on meats. But there's no reason not to include a variety of meats in your diet, Newgent says. Beef and pork add a tremen-dous amount of flavor to foods. As long as you're buying lean cuts and trimming fat before you cook them, you'll get the culinary and nutritional benefits without adding too much fat. Chicken and turkey are quite lean once you remove the skin. Fish is among the healthiest foods that you can eat as well as one of the fastest to cook, says Newgent.

The American Heart Association recommends eating no more than 6 ounces of meat or seafood a day. Imagine a piece of meat that's about the same size as a deck of cards—that's roughly 3 ounces.

Buy fish—any fish. Nearly all fish are perfectly healthful additions to your diet, although those with whiter flesh, such as cod, halibut, orange roughy, and sole, are generally the lowest in fat. This isn't really an issue, however. In fact, fatty fish contain more omega-3 fatty acids, which appear to be good for the heart. Fish with a lot of omega-3's include salmon, tuna, and flounder.

Canned fish is the ultimate in convenience, and ounce for ounce, it's cheaper than fresh. It's worth putting a few cans of salmon, tuna, or even anchovies on the shelf. "The healthy things we look for in fish—the omega-3 fatty acids and the protein—don't change much, if at all, during canning," says Kristine Napier, R.D., a nutrition consultant in Mayfield Village, Ohio. In fact, canned pink salmon (with the bones) is better than fresh because it provides additional calcium and vitamin B_6.

Most canned fish comes packed in either oil or water. Avoid oil-packed fish because it's much higher in fat than fish packed in water. Even if you drain the oil, the fish will have a lot more fat than fish packed in water, Napier says. For example, 3 ounces of tuna canned in oil has 7 grams of fat, while water-packed tuna has less than 1 gram.

FOUR GREAT BLENDS— QUICK AND FLAVORFUL

The right blends of herbs and spices can magically transform the simplest foods into culinary treats to remember. And since spice blends are prepared ahead of time, you don't have to fumble with half a dozen (or more) bottles at the last minute or worry about keeping individual spices on the shelf all the time. The right blend will always add exciting layers of flavor.

Throughout this book, you'll find recipes that call for one of these four blends. Nothing could be easier, although in some cases, you may decide to use one or more of the individual ingredients rather than the blend itself. And don't be timid. Use one of these blends in lieu of herbs and spices in other recipes.

Dried herbs and spices have long shelf lives, but they don't last forever. About a year is the upper limit. These blends will last longer if you keep them inside a cupboard, away from direct sunlight. Just mix the ingredients together and store.

Everyday Spice Blend

This simple blend works as well with vegetables as it does with beef, pork, and chicken. It brings out the flavors of foods without overpowering them, and it's a good choice for simple everyday recipes.

2¼ c onion powder
⅓ c garlic powder
⅓ c dried chives
¼ c dried oregano
⅓ c dried parsley
⅓ c dried rosemary

Poultry Seasoning

This savory blend brings out the best flavors of chicken and poultry without adding salt. It's also a good addition to stews, soups, casseroles, stuffings, and dumplings.

½ c dried sage
1 c dried parsley
¼ c dried rosemary
¼ c dried summer savory
1 Tbsp fresh marjoram or ¼ cup dried
½ tsp ground black pepper
½ tsp onion powder

Italian Herb Blend

This all-purpose blend perks up the flavor of tomato sauce, meat loaf, lasagna, pot roast, chicken cacciatore, and gravy. Or sprinkle it on baked potatoes and pizza.

⅓ c dried oregano
⅓ c dried basil
¼ c dried thyme
¼ c dried sage
2 Tbsp garlic powder

Mexican Spice Mix

This spicy, salt-free blend will wake up your tastebuds in a hurry. (For a milder mix, cut back on the ground red pepper.) It's the perfect blend for beans, sloppy joes, stews, and savory sauces.

½ c chili powder
2 Tbsp onion powder
2 Tbsp garlic powder
3 Tbsp dried oregano
8 tsp ground cumin
2 tsp ground red pepper
2 tsp ground black pepper

WOMEN ASK WHY

Why do low-fat recipes have so many ingredients?

Where there's fat there's flavor. Most of the flavor components in foods are fat-soluble. When you eat fat, you get all of those flavors at the same time. When you start taking fat out of recipes, you lose some of those tastes. Low-fat recipes make up the flavor by using a variety of "extra" ingredients, especially herbs and spices.

Some of the ingredients may seem strange if you're new to low-fat cooking. Instead of butter or margarine, for example, low-fat recipes may substitute prune puree. It adds richness to the recipe and replaces the creamy texture that normally would come from fat.

Many low-fat recipes are needlessly complex, however. Adding too many ingredients to a recipe can distract from the natural goodness of the food itself. You may want to browse the cookbook aisle at your favorite bookstore. Look at the recipes and actually count the ingredients. If there are more than a dozen, or if there are ingredients that you can't imagine using more than once, look for a different cookbook. There are plenty of good ones that don't have mile-long lists of ingredients.

Consider pasta with fresh tomato sauce. Apart from the pasta, all you need are a few tomatoes, some onion and garlic, and a fresh or dried herb such as basil. Nothing could be simpler, or more satisfying.

It doesn't make sense to tackle recipes that seem overly complicated or call for too many exotic ingredients. Experimenting is fun, and at some point, you may enjoy the challenge. But most people, including most chefs, believe that simpler is better.

Expert Consulted
Sheah Rarback, R.D.
Assistant professor
Department of pediatrics
University of Miami School of Medicine
Spokeswoman
American Dietetic Association

Of course, it's hard to beat the taste of fresh fish. It's best to buy fish the same day you plan to use it. Fish doesn't freeze as well as other foods because it gives up its flavor quickly. A month in the freezer is about the limit, and that's pushing it, Napier says. It will lose flavor even faster if it's not wrapped very well. She recommends wrapping fish in a layer or two of waxed paper, then sealing it in an airtight plastic bag.

Treat poultry properly. Most of the fat in poultry is in the skin. It's fine to cook poultry in the skin—dietitians often recommend doing this because it helps keep the meat moist and tender—as long as you don't eat the skin afterward, says Newgent. Dark meat has more fat than white meat, so you may want to stock up on chicken and turkey breasts or turkey cutlets, she says. Boning poultry is time-consuming, so look for boneless breasts or other poultry fillets.

Fresh poultry will keep in the freezer for about 3 months if it's carefully wrapped, says Newgent. With both turkey and chicken, breasts or cutlets are your best choice because the smaller pieces will defrost much more quickly than a whole bird.

Turkey is every bit as nutritious as chicken, but don't go near birds that have been pre-basted, says Newgent. The bastes add a lot of flavor, but they can be tremendously high in saturated fat.

Buy USDA "select" or "choice." The U.S. Department of Agriculture grades meat according to the amount of marbling. Marbled meats are the most tender, but they're also the fattiest. Select and choice grades are the leanest. Good cuts include round steak, sirloin tip, tenderloin, and flank steak. These do require slower cooking for tenderness, but the increase in cooking time is minor and worth the fat trade-off.

As with poultry, beef will stay fresh in the freezer for about 3 months. Pork isn't as hardy—a month in the freezer is the limit. You'll probably want to stock several different cuts. Flank steaks are good because the meat is lean and versatile, equally suitable for grilling, stewing, or stir-frying. You'll also want to lay in some lean ground beef. "I always make hamburger patties when I get home from the store, then wrap and freeze them individually," Napier says. "That way, they don't stick together and they defrost very quickly."

Dairy

Women need the calcium in milk, cheese, and yogurt in order to prevent the bone-thinning disease called osteoporosis. What they don't need is the fat and calories that come with full-fat dairy foods.

The solution is pretty simple: Always stock fat-free or low-fat dairy foods, including milk, coffee creamers, and cheeses. Not long ago, only a few cheeses were available in low-fat versions. Now, even specialty stores stock dozens of varieties.

Most dairy foods have a good refrigerator life. Milk will keep for at least a week, and yogurt is usually good for about a month. Cheese won't keep very long in the refrigerator once it's opened, but it freezes well, Napier says. She recommends buying as much as you plan to use in a month and freezing it in serving-size packages. It won't lose any of its taste or texture.

Canned milk is also good to have around. Apart from sweetened condensed milk, which is mainly used for baking, many people like to stock a few cans of fat-free evaporated milk just in case they run out of fresh. It's good for cereal and pouring in coffee. You can drink it, too, although many people dislike the taste. The clear advantage of using evaporated milk is that it has a lot of calcium—741 milligrams in 1 cup, compared with 301 milligrams in regular fat-free milk.

Dry milk is another option. It doesn't give up any of its nutrients during processing, and it's probably the best milk substitute in terms of taste, Napier says. "You can make it as strong as you like to get more calcium and protein. It tastes best when it's refrigerated, however. You don't want to mix it and drink it right away."

Oils

There's a lot of confusion about cooking oils these days. Some oils, like coconut oil, are quite high in saturated fat. Others contain monounsaturated or polyunsaturated fats. How do you balance the need for oils with a healthy diet?

Regardless of the type of oil you use, always use as little as possible. Even the so-called healthy oils, like olive and canola oils, are pure fat. They may not be as bad for your heart as saturated fats—many studies suggest they may be beneficial—but you still don't want to get too much of them.

Newgent recommends buying a variety of monounsaturated oils, including olive and canola oils. Use canola oil for processes such as sautéing, when the oil is used mainly to lubricate food and sear in the flavors. Use olive oil, particularly extra-virgin olive oil, when you want extra flavoring. Olive oil breaks down at high heats, so it's not a good choice for prolonged high-heat cooking.

Newgent also keeps a variety of flavored oils on hand: a dark sesame oil that lends hints of Asia to stir-fried vegetables, and a red chile oil for giving foods some spice. "You might only need a teaspoon to flavor a whole salad," she says.

Spices and Condiments

The secret to boosting the flavor of low-fat foods in the shortest possible time is to use an abundance of spices, vinegars, and other highly flavored condiments. Newgent, for example, keeps five types of mustard in her cupboard, including roasted red pepper mustard and garlic mustard with herbs.

You don't have to get fancy when it's time to boost flavors. In fact, you don't want to get too fancy, because spices are only meant to complement foods, not overwhelm them. You probably have most of the essential spices and herbs already: black pepper, basil, dill, paprika, and oregano. If you like things simple, this may be all that you'll need. Remember that all spices, even dried, give up their flavors in less than a year, so you don't want to buy more than you're going to use in a fairly short time.

Quick and Healthy Techniques

The beauty of healthy cooking is that it's both simple and fast. It doesn't require a lot of exotic ingredients. It often uses brief cooking times to enhance flavors and preserve vitamins and minerals. And you don't have to load your kitchen cabinets with a lot of expensive cookware.

At its most basic, healthy cooking doesn't need much more than a steamer basket, a wok, maybe a grill, a few sauté pans, and a couple of pots for boiling water. Add a slow cooker and a microwave, and there's nothing you won't be able to do.

Three of the most common techniques—stir-frying, sautéing, and poaching—are among the fastest. Grilling takes a little more time, but only because you have to wait for the grill to heat up. Once your meats and vegetables are prepared and the grill is hot, the actual cooking time is usually less than 10 minutes.

In the following pages, we take a look at these and a few other healthy-cooking techniques. (You'll find more information when you read the recipe sections.) You'll discover why certain foods are best cooked using these techniques and just how easy the methods are to master.

Stir-Frying

Stir-frying is among the simplest of all kitchen techniques. It doesn't require anything more than a wok or high-sided skillet, and it's fast. Once you've cut up the ingredients, most meals are done in 5 minutes or less.

There's a good reason why healthy cooks do a lot of stir-frying. This technique essentially "flash-cooks" food, so you don't need to add much cooking oil, says Deann Bayless, chef and owner of the Frontera Grill in Chicago. Fresh foods retain their natural colors, textures, and freshness. Meats are by no means excluded from stir-fries, but most recipes call for an abundance of vegetables, fresh as well as frozen. And because it's all cooked in one pan, there's very little clean-up time.

As with all fast-cooking methods, stir-frying isn't recommended for tough foods or foods in big pieces. Yet even tough foods can be made tender enough for stir-frying just by cutting them thin and cooking them quickly.

Begin with a wok. Although deep-sided skillets are adequate for stir-fries, woks are better

HEALTHY—OR NOT?

Microwave Cooking

Unlike conventional ovens, which heat up the food (and the house), microwave ovens don't generate their own heat. Instead, they emit short waves of energy called microwaves. These rays are absorbed by molecules in the food, causing the molecules to vibrate and rub against each other, creating friction and heat that cooks the food.

There's something a little scary about a kitchen device that works by emitting radiation, especially since research has shown that exposure to high levels of microwaves can damage the eyes, kill sperm, and even cause burns. What happens when a person stands near a microwave oven while it's in use?

Not much of anything, it turns out. The Food and Drug Administration, which has regulated microwave ovens since 1971, has found that most don't leak at all. Even those that do leak produce very low levels of microwaves, much too low to cause health problems. All of the evidence so far is that microwaves are entirely safe—safer, in fact, than conventional stoves, which cause thousands of injuries each year.

What you should be concerned about, however, are the containers that you put into the microwave to heat the food, says Christine M. Bruhn, Ph.D., director of the Center for Consumer Research at the University of California, Davis. Foam plates and empty margarine tubs are made from a soft plastic and cannot withstand high temperatures. Similarly, plastic wrap that isn't labeled as microwaveable could melt and possibly release chemicals into the food, says Dr. Bruhn. So use only wraps, plates, and containers that are labeled as being safe for microwave cooking.

As for the oven itself, experts advise that you not lean against it while the microwave is in operation. Should microwaves escape from the oven, they'll be strongest at close range. Moving back as little as 20 inches will reduce the amount of radiation to 1/100th of the maximum amount that's considered safe. And you certainly shouldn't use a microwave if the door doesn't latch properly or is otherwise damaged.

because the higher sides speed cooking time and allow more room for foods to cook, says Jackie Newgent, R.D., a nutrition and culinary consultant in New York City and spokesperson for the American Dietetic Association. The best woks cook on the stove top; electric models don't get hot enough for efficient stir-frying. Many cooks prefer flat-bottomed woks, which sit solidly on electric and gas heating elements. Round-bottomed woks are fine, but you'll need to use a metal ring (which may or may not be included when you buy the wok) to give them stability.

Prepare ingredients ahead of time. Stir-fry cooking is extremely fast, so you won't have time to prepare ingredients as you work.

Stir early and often. Stirring, as the name *stir-fry* suggests, is central to this cooking technique. Allowing food to stay in one place will cause it to absorb fluids and lose its fresh, crisp texture. While food is cooking in one place, the wok is getting hotter somewhere else. Frequent stirring moves food from hot spot to hot spot so that it cooks more quickly.

Marinate the meat. Since you'll be using lean meats when making stir-fries, it helps to slice them thin and marinate them for 10 to 15 minutes before you start cooking. To create a simple marinade, combine ¼ cup soy sauce; 2 tablespoons vinegar, such as red wine, white wine, or rice; 1 tablespoon honey, and a chopped clove of garlic.

Keep tofu firm. Tofu is a popular ingredient in stir-fries because it adds protein and other nutrients to meatless meals, and it soaks up the flavors of whatever it's cooked with. It's best to use the firm style of tofu, which holds its shape better.

Go for crisp textures. Stir-fry cooking is designed to sear the outer surfaces of food and heat the pieces through. It's not designed for long, slow cooking. So keep an eye on vegetables and other ingredients. "Don't overcook them," says Newgent. "You want them heated through, but you still want a bit of crispness."

Sautéing

The word *sautéed* is often followed by the phrase "with butter." While traditional sautés do in fact use butter, sometimes in artery-clogging amounts, fat isn't an integral part of this very healthy cooking process. In some ways sautéing is similar to stir-frying, in that fairly small pieces of food are cooked quickly. The pans used for sautéing are much smaller, though, and they're generally used to prepare a base for a meal and not the meal itself.

In professional kitchens, sautéed foods are prepared to order instead of ahead of time. The reason for this is that sautéing is very fast. Food is cooked at high temperatures, although generally not quite so hot as those used in stir-fries.

FIVE GREAT WAYS TO USE THE MICROWAVE

Advertisers would have you believe that you can make an entire Thanksgiving dinner in the microwave, but like every other kitchen tool, microwaves aren't good for everything. Roasting a turkey, for example, is best done in a conventional oven. And some jobs, such as boiling water for pasta, are just as fast on the stove top. But for many small tasks that take a lot of time, microwaves are the perfect shortcut, says Jackie Newgent, R.D., a nutrition and culinary consultant in New York City and a spokesperson for the American Dietetic Association.

1. Defrosting meats and vegetables. Microwaves will bring frozen foods to room temperature in a hurry. Don't cheat and use the high setting instead of defrost, however. That will leave you with food that's warm in some places and frozen in others.

2. Steaming vegetables. This is where microwaves excel. Many nutrients are water-soluble. Vegetables boiled the conventional way give up a lot of their goodness to the cooking water. With microwaves, you use only a tablespoon of water, so most of the nutrients stay in the food where they belong. Plus, vegetables cook very quickly in the microwave.

Don't forget, however, that steam is hot. When uncovering vegetables cooked in the microwave, open the edge away from you first. This safely releases scalding steam away from your face.

3. Baking potatoes. An oven-baked potato takes about 40 minutes to cook. In the microwave, the flesh is fork-tender in as little as 5 minutes. You won't get that crispy skin in the microwave, however. Many people microwave potatoes until tender, then place them in a hot oven for 10 minutes to crisp the skin.

4. Reheating. Whether you're preparing a meal of leftovers or reheating a bowl of soup that got cold, microwaves will get the job done in minutes. Large amounts of food sometimes heat unevenly, however, so you'll want to interrupt the microwave cycle at about the halfway point to stir them up.

5. Cooking fish. You can place fish fillets in a covered container and microwave them for a few minutes. The moist heat quickly cooks fish all the way through without drying it out.

Ingredients are often sautéed as part of a recipe. For example, onions, garlic, and mushrooms are typically sautéed, then added to other ingredients that will undergo further cooking. Boneless chicken breast and pork tenderloin, on the other hand, may be sautéed for the end result—a simple, easy-to-prepare meal that's browned and cooked all the way through.

Get a heavy sauté pan. Sautéing requires a bit of stirring, and pans that are too light will skate all over the stove and also cause scorching or uneven cooking. The best sauté pans are tin-lined copper skillets. They're heavy and they conduct heat quickly and evenly. They're very expensive, however, which is why many cooks choose cast-iron skillets, which also hold and conduct heat well.

Reduce fat by preparing the pan. Since healthy sautés use very little fat, you'll want to prepare the surface of cast-iron pans before cooking to make sure that food doesn't stick. It takes only a second. Pour some salt into the cool pan, scour it around with a paper towel, then pour it out. Follow this with a light film of oil, then wipe the pan well with a paper towel. The almost invisible sheen of oil will help food cook evenly without sticking.

Invest in nonstick pans. When you're really getting serious about reducing the amount of oil you cook with, you'll want to buy a set of nonstick pots and pans. These have slick, nearly impermeable surfaces. Even if you don't use any oil at all, the food glides across the surface rather than sticking in the

TIMESAVING GADGETS YOU CAN'T LIVE WITHOUT

Walk into any kitchenware store, and you'll see hundreds of specialized gizmos and doodads. Some of them are truly useful. Others, like inside-the-shell egg scramblers, are just silly. We talked to some of the country's top culinary experts and asked them which kitchen gadgets they'd never do without. Here are their top picks.

Bread machine. Few women have time to make bread the traditional way anymore. Automatic bread machines make it easy. These amazing devices mix and knead the dough, let it rise, and bake it to perfect freshness, and you don't have to do a thing except measure and insert the ingredients. Most bread machines have timers, so you can add ingredients before you go to bed, then wake up to fresh-baked bread.

Coffee grinder. Now that good, fresh coffee beans are sold everywhere, few chefs grind their own anymore. But they still use their portable coffee grinders—for mincing fresh herbs. Here's a neat trick: To clean grinders between uses, grind a few tablespoons of uncooked white rice. It scours the inside clean.

Food processor or mini-chopper. Even chefs who can chop by hand with woodpecker speed often use mini-choppers or high-powered processors to churn out bowlfuls of grated cheese and chopped vegetables.

Good knives. They're not gadgets in the usual sense, but cooking experts say that high-quality sharp knives are impossible to live without. At a minimum, you'll need two

microscopic pits that dot the bottoms of conventional cookware.

Older generations of nonstick pans had a fatal flaw: They scratched easily, and the marred surfaces allowed foods to stick. The newer nonstick pans are much more rugged. Some are guaranteed to maintain their special finish for decades, and they're designed to withstand high heats as

knives: a paring knife for small jobs and a larger chef's knife for everything else. Don't waste money on inexpensive knives. They won't hold an edge, they don't cut cleanly, and they're going to slow you down. Only buy top-quality knives. Heft them in your hand before buying to make sure that they feel comfortable. You'll keep them for the rest of your life.

Kitchen shears. You can do almost anything with a good kitchen knife, but sometimes, heavy-duty scissors or kitchen shears work even better for cutting through poultry joints or for mincing fresh sprigs of parsley or basil.

Salad spinner. The water that remains on lettuce after washing makes the leaves limp and lifeless. It also makes it impossible for dressings to adhere. To dry lettuce in a hurry, put the leaves in a salad spinner, a hand-cranked device that spins a plastic basket at lightening speed, throwing off water and leaving the lettuce crisp and dry.

Steamer basket. Vegetables cooked in steamers retain their crispness, fresh color, and nutritional payload. One type of steamer is the collapsible metal basket, which can be slipped inside a lidded saucepan. Chefs prefer stacked metal steamers, which have two or three levels for different foods. Dense, slow-cooking foods go in the bottom level nearest the heat. More delicate foods go in the top compartment, where the heat is less intense.

Zester. These slender little devices have razor-sharp cutting edges that quickly remove thin strips of peel, called zest, from lemons, limes, and oranges. Zest is used in thousands of recipes, and zesters make the job easy.

well as metal implements. These pans are expensive, but they're worth it because there's a good chance you'll never have to replace them.

Leave plenty of empty space. For sautés to cook quickly and evenly, it's important that there be extra room in the pan. Place pieces of meat or poultry in a single layer with lots of space in between.

Leave it alone. Unlike stir-frying, the point of sautéing is to let food cook to a perfect golden brown. Let it cook, undisturbed, for a few minutes in one place. Then move it to another part of the pan for further cooking. This has the added advantage of preventing sticking.

Poaching

The most gentle of cooking methods, poaching occurs when food is submerged in hot liquid and carefully simmered until it's done. It's often done as a prelude to further preparation. Chicken breasts may be poached before being sliced and added to cold chicken salad. Poaching can also be the main cooking method for delicate, tender foods such as fish.

Use a deep enough pan. You can poach in any skillet or pot as long as it's deep enough to allow the cooking liquid to completely cover the food. Don't use a cast-iron skillet, however, because iron absorbs flavors and may impart an "off" taste to mild foods.

Flavor the liquid. Since poached foods are naturally mild, it's important to add flavors to the cooking liquid itself. The easiest way to season poaching liquid is to combine reduced-sodium chicken broth or wine with lemon juice and rosemary. This works very well for chicken or fish.

Keep the water action gentle. Rigorous boiling will cause tender foods to toughen or fall apart. The liquid should be at a very gentle simmer.

Wrap delicate foods in cheese-cloth. It can be tricky to get a whole fish in and out of the poaching liquid without having it fall apart. Wrapping it once or twice in cheesecloth before submerging it in the liquid will help it hold its shape without interfering with the poaching.

Start fish cold and chicken hot. When poaching a whole fish, it's best to start it in cold liquid so that the skin won't split. For chicken or fish fillets, it's fine to add them to liquid that's already simmering.

Steaming

Cooking with moist heat is among the oldest and easiest cooking methods. Moist heat cooks food gently with no added fat. In addition, it allows foods to retain most of their original character. Vegetables taste fresh-picked and will keep their shape, texture, and brilliant colors. Fish and seafood maintain their delicate flavors. And poultry, even when you take off the skin, cooks up plump, juicy, and moist.

Steaming food has the added advantage of cooking very quickly because temperatures rise above 212°F, the boiling point of water. This helps tenderize food while locking in moisture and nutrients. And because cooking takes place over water rather than in it, vitamins are retained that might otherwise wash away.

Use any kind of steamer. All steamers work in roughly the same way. You can get as fancy or plain as you like. If you do a lot of steaming, you may want to invest in a bamboo or stainless steel multitiered steamer. For most

---

REAL-LIFE SCENARIO
She Can't Get Her Act Together

You'd never know that Nancy is a nutritionist by the way she feeds her family. On evenings when the family is home together, she finds herself throwing a meal on the table—turkey dogs, sloppy joes, or chicken from the freezer. She always tries to round out the meal nutritionally by serving broccoli or another green vegetable, plus a baked potato or rice that she zaps in the microwave. But no matter what she serves, the kids turn up their noses. Ironically, Nancy loves to cook, but her life is so frazzled (two part-time jobs, community activities, a workaholic husband, and three very busy teens) that she never has time to prepare what she considers a decent meal. To make matters worse, she knows that her family eats junk food when they're not at home together. Sunday is the only day she gets to show off her culinary talents by preparing a lovely French or Italian meal from scratch. Unfortunately, Nancy is the only one who appreciates it. When it comes to feeding the family, Nancy can't win—or can she?

Actually, Nancy is winning in many ways. She's being too hard on herself. She clearly enjoys cooking and she knows about nutrition. These are the kinds of influences that children take with them, whether they show it or not. That's important.

In the short run, all Nancy really needs is to plan a little more. Since she has time to cook on Sundays, why not stretch those meals to last the entire week? She could triple the amount of sauce and chicken when she's cooking Italian, for example, then freeze meal-size leftovers. The same with the salad greens. It takes almost the same amount of time to trim and wash a week's worth of salad as it does for one meal. Putting the extras in a bag would give her instant salads.

---

foods, however, inexpensive collapsible metal steamer baskets, which drop in any pan deep enough to hold them, work just as well.

Start your timing late. Once food is added

No one likes preparing menus, but in Nancy's case, it makes sense. She could plan simple meals (using leftovers) for each night of the week. This will allow her to get what she needs at the grocery store ahead of time and also to adjust her Sunday cooking to make the rest of the week easier. These meals don't have to be fancy. One night could be a one-skillet meal of fajitas. Another might be pasta using the sauce she made on Sunday.

What Nancy also needs to do is stop thinking like a nutritionist. Meals don't have to be perfect balances of meats, vegetables, and starches. Rather, she could be combining foods in ways that are both nutritious and easy to cook. Take soups. She could clean out the vegetable bin on Monday, cut up whatever's in there, then add a can of tomatoes. She'd have instant tomato-vegetable soup. Or, she could make a roast one night, then cut up the leftovers and put them in a salad, using highly flavored greens such as arugula. She wouldn't have to touch the stove.

Getting teenagers to eat well is a challenge under the best of circumstances. Nancy isn't home to supervise them, so she'll have to settle for giving them opportunities for healthy eating. She could cut up fresh fruit and leave it in a bowl in the refrigerator. Many kids won't choose fruit if they have a choice, but if it's already prepared and waiting, there's a good chance they'll eat it, especially when the alternative is having to make something themselves.

Expert Consulted
Edith H. Hogan, R.D.
Spokesperson for the American Dietetic
*   Association*
Nutrition consultant
Washington, D.C.

to a steamer, the temperature of the water drops, and it will need a minute or two to return to a boil. Start your timing from the moment the water begins boiling again.

Don't let curiosity slow you down. Steamers depend on trapped steam to cook food. Every time you open the lid, steam escapes and substantially slows the cooking time.

Add additional flavors. The moist environment inside a steamer will dilute herbs and spices, so you may want to add more than you usually do. Rather than spicing the food itself, you can add herbs or spices to the water to impart subtle flavors.

Protect yourself. Always open the steamer cover away from you to prevent burns.

Grilling

Grilling food is the opposite of steaming. It uses dry heat, not moist. It imparts a lot of its own flavors rather than merely bringing out a food's natural flavors. And for the most part, it works best with robust foods that can withstand the rigors of going on and off the grill.

The advantage of grilling over oven or stove-top cooking is that the process itself adds a lot of flavor that you just can't get on the broiler pan. For healthy cooks who don't have a lot of time, it has the advantage of cooking most foods very quickly without much additional fat. Plus, there's no messy broiler pan to clean.

Begin with a marinade. Because grilling is a dry process, most meats will benefit from a marinade or a basting liquid. The difference between the two is that foods soak in marinades, while you brush on bastes during cooking. Ideally, poultry and meat should marinate in the refrigerator for a few hours before cooking.

"Marinades do not need fat," Newgent adds. She recommends mixing herbs and spices in an acidic liquid—such as vinegar, citrus juice, or even wine—which will tenderize the meat.

Start with a hot grill. Putting meat, fish, or poultry on a cold grill makes the food more likely to stick. You can prevent this by cleaning the grill very thoroughly when it's cool, then adding the food once the grill is hot.

Grill chicken with the skin on. Grilling tends to dry foods out. Cooking chicken in the skin essentially makes it self-basting. The meat itself absorbs little of the fat, however, so you'll still have a healthy meal once you remove the skin after cooking.

Consider precooking poultry. Unless you're grilling thin strips, chicken can take a while to grill, so it's helpful to precook it by poaching, baking, or microwaving before putting it on the grill.

Add some smoke. Hardwood chips, dried herbs, or citrus rinds can all be added to the coals or lava rocks to impart a smoky flavor that complements most grilled foods. When using smoke chips, you'll want to close the grill lid to get the most intense flavors.

Combine grilling and steaming. Wrapping ears of corn, fish, or poultry in foil and adding seasoning and a little water makes it possible to get the fast-cooking benefits of steaming along with the flavors from the grill.

PART TWO

Healthy Cooking in 30 Minutes or Less

Main-Meal Salads

Salads have traditionally been accompaniments to meals, and not very interesting accompaniments at that. But lately, there's been a shift toward making the salad the main meal by adding ingredients such as chicken, canned beans, and an eclectic variety of greens.

Main-meal salads are incredibly fast to make. Plus, there's not much clean-up time, since all you use is a big bowl, a cutting board, a knife, and maybe a sauté pan if you decide to warm some meat or spinach leaves. Even preparing the ingredients is easy when you know a few shortcuts.

Let someone else do the grunt work. This is the secret to fast salads. Rather than preparing everything yourself, buy greens that have already been washed, cut, and put in a bag, says Deborah Beall, R.D., manager of the California Department of Health Services' "Five a Day" program in Sacramento. All you have to do is open the bag and pour. It's a great time-saver.

Shop for variety. Since leafy greens and lettuces form the foundation of most salads, look for bagged lettuce combinations, which mix varieties such as arugula, Romaine, curly endive, radicchio, and spinach, says Beall.

Add fresh vegetables. There's nothing wrong with having an all-leaf salad, but you'll need something more substantial when it's a stand-alone meal. Asparagus tips, broccoli florets, and snap peas add substance and textures to salads along with a lot of nutrients and dietary fiber. As with salad greens, you can buy vegetables prewashed and cut in the produce section of the supermarket, eliminating nearly all of the preparation time, says Beall.

Use canned ingredients. There's no faster way to make a main-meal salad than to combine fresh greens with canned artichoke hearts, green beans, or corn or with canned fish such as tuna or crab, says Beall. Canned ingredients retain nearly all of their natural textures and nutrients.

Throw in the tomatoes. Whether your salad is mainly meat or mainly greens, the slight acidity of tomatoes makes a great counterpoint to the flavors underneath. It's fine to use beefsteak tomatoes, but Beall recommends using cherry tomatoes, since all you have to do is give them a quick rinse and throw them into the bowl.

Thinly slice some meat. Strips of grilled or broiled boneless chicken breast or leftover beef

HEALTHY—OR NOT?
Vegetable Oil

Vegetable oils sound as if they should be healthy—they're made from vegetables, right? But it's not that simple. Some vegetable oils are in fact quite good for you. Others are about as wholesome as lard. The difference lies in the types of fats they contain.

The best oils by far are those that contain a high percentage of monounsaturated fats. These have been shown to reduce the amount of harmful low-density lipoprotein (LDL) cholesterol in the bloodstream. Olive and canola oils contain a lot of monounsaturated fats, and they're the ones that you should use most often, says Connie Diekman, R.D., a nutrition consultant in St. Louis and a spokeswoman for the American Dietetic Association.

Not quite as good, but still not bad, are oils containing a lot of polyunsaturated fats, says Diekman. Corn oil is the main one. Polyunsaturated fats also help lower the amount of LDL cholesterol in the body. Unfortunately, they also lower the amount of beneficial high-density lipoprotein (HDL) cholesterol at the same time.

The worst oils are those that contain a lot of saturated fats. These are the fats that play the biggest role in raising total cholesterol and clogging the arteries, says Diekman. Palm and coconut oils are extremely high in saturated fats. These oils aren't typically used in home cooking, however. Manufacturers commonly add them in snack foods to give their products richer tastes and textures.

All of these oils have one thing in common: You want to use them sparingly. All oils are pure fat, and fat has a lot of calories—about 120 calories per tablespoon. Americans are in the habit of using way too much oil. It's easy enough to cut back. Getting the oil good and hot, for example, will sear the surface of foods and help prevent excess oil from being absorbed, Diekman says. You can also use less oil by adding a little water to the pan when sautéing vegetables. The water helps prevent sticking, and the steam helps speed the cooking time, giving oil less time to soak in.

---

add important protein to salads without adding too much fat. You can save even more time by buying ready-cooked meats at the supermarket deli counter.

Pour in some crunch. Apart from their high fat content, shelled pecans, walnuts, or almonds make perfect salad ingredients, says Jackie Newgent, R.D., a nutrition and culinary consultant in New York City and spokesperson for the American Dietetic Association. They don't get soggy from the dressing, and the crunchiness adds a pleasing accent to the softer greens.

Keep dressings simple. Another way to save time with main-meal salads is to skip the traditional dressings, says Newgent. You won't need them. The ingredients provide all of the main flavor. A splash of balsamic or herb-infused vinegar and a drizzle of olive oil may be all you need. No mixing required.

Keep the processor on the counter. When you're making only small salads, food processors or mini-choppers are more trouble than they're worth. But when you're making large salads—and making extras for leftovers—food processors can save a tremendous amount of time when slicing onions, chopping vegetables, or mincing fresh herbs, says Newgent.

HEALTHY— OR NOT?

Avocados

The avocado has the dubious distinction of packing more calories, ounce for ounce, than almost any other fruit on the planet—about 323 calories per fruit, on average. It's also one of the few fruits that actually has a measurable fat content—about 31 grams each.

It's hard to imagine that any food this sinfully rich could possibly be good for you, but avocados mainly contain monounsaturated fat, the same kind that's in olive oil and the one that can help improve cholesterol. In one study, two groups of people were put on low-fat diets. The diets were the same, except that those in one group were also given avocados to eat. Those in both groups saw drops in their levels of harmful low-density lipoprotein (LDL) cholesterol. Those eating avocados, however, also had a rise in their levels of healthful high-density lipoprotein (HDL) cholesterol.

In addition, one avocado has 124 micrograms of folate, a B vitamin that's essential for preventing birth defects. Avocados are also rich in vitamin E, potassium, iron, and magnesium.

Some people avoid avocados because they don't want the extra calories. But California avocados have about 10 percent fewer calories than those grown in Florida. Also, avocados harvested between November and March may have only one-third the fat of those picked in September or October.

Avocados are fine as long as you don't eat a lot of them. Healthy or not? "They aren't magic, but they're fine," says Connie Diekman, R.D., a nutrition consultant in St. Louis and a spokeswoman for the American Dietetic Association.

Couscous Salad Niçoise

Salad

  1 can (14½ oz) chicken broth
  1 tsp olive oil
  1 c whole wheat couscous
1½ lb small new potatoes, quartered
  8 oz green beans, halved
    Romaine lettuce leaves
  1 can (13 oz) water-packed tuna, drained
  2 tomatoes, cut into thin wedges
  1 small red onion, sliced

Dressing

⅔ c reduced-sodium chicken broth
  3 Tbsp grainy mustard
  3 Tbsp red wine vinegar
  2 Tbsp + 2 tsp olive oil
    Ground red pepper

To make the salad: In a medium saucepan over high heat, bring the broth and oil to a boil, then stir in the couscous. Remove the pan from the heat. Cover and let stand for 10 minutes. Fluff with a fork.

Meanwhile, place a steamer basket in a medium pot with 2" of water. Bring to a boil over high heat. Place the potatoes in the steamer basket and steam for 15 minutes, or until tender. Remove the potatoes and place the beans in the steamer basket. Steam for 4 minutes, or until just tender.

Line a serving platter with the lettuce. Mound the couscous in the middle. Surround with the tuna, tomatoes, potatoes, and beans. Scatter the onion over everything.

To make the dressing: In a small bowl, whisk the broth, mustard, vinegar, and oil. Season with the pepper to taste. Drizzle over the salad.

Makes 4 servings

Per serving: 592 calories, 14.5 g fat

Curried Bulgur and Ham Salad

Salad

2½ c water
½ tsp curry powder
½ tsp salt
1 c bulgur
3 oz baked ham (from deli), trimmed of fat and cubed
1 carrot, thinly sliced
2 celery ribs, thinly sliced
1 small red onion, chopped
¼ c currants or raisins
¼ c slivered almonds

Dressing

½ c orange juice
4 tsp lemon juice
4 tsp yellow or honey mustard
  Salt
  Ground black pepper

To make the salad: In a medium saucepan over high heat, bring the water, curry powder, and salt to a boil.

Stir in the bulgur. Reduce the heat to medium and cook for 10 minutes.

Cover and let stand for 10 minutes. Drain off any excess liquid.

Fluff with a fork.

In a large bowl, toss together the bulgur, ham, carrot, celery, onion, currants or raisins, and almonds.

To make the dressing: In a small bowl, whisk the orange juice, lemon juice, and mustard. Season with salt and pepper to taste.

Pour the dressing over the salad and toss to coat thoroughly.

Makes 4 servings

Per serving: 238 calories, 6 g fat

LAZY DAY ANTIPASTO

Many of the country's best restaurants serve artfully prepared antipastos as preludes to elegant meals. But antipastos don't have to be intricate to be delicious, and they work just as well as party snacks and main-meal entrées. Best of all, they're fast to prepare. The trick is to use ready-to-go ingredients from the supermarket.

Line a large tray with whole lettuce leaves. Top the lettuce with olives, marinated artichokes, cherry tomatoes, whole radishes, slices of cheese, and smoked sausage. Add some peeled cooked shrimp, and you're ready to go. To allow the full flavor to come through, antipastos are usually served at room temperature.

Warm Pasta Salad with Chicken

Salad

10 dry-pack sun-dried tomato halves
12 oz bow-tie pasta
2 thin zucchini, thinly sliced
1 package (10 oz) cubed roasted chicken breast
1 bunch watercress, chopped

Dressing

¾ c low-fat buttermilk
1 Tbsp red wine vinegar
1 Tbsp olive oil
½ tsp dried thyme
  Salt
  Ground black pepper

To make the salad: Soak the tomatoes in hot water for 10 minutes, or until soft.

Cook the pasta in a large pot of boiling water for 10 minutes. Add the zucchini and cook for

1 minute longer. Drain and place in a large bowl.

Drain the tomatoes, slice, and add to the bowl with the pasta. Add the chicken and watercress. Toss lightly to combine.

To make the dressing: In a small bowl, whisk the buttermilk, vinegar, oil, and thyme. Season with salt and pepper to taste. Pour over the salad and toss to coat.

Makes 4 servings

Per serving: 430 calories, 6.5 g fat

DRESSED AND READY TO GO

Selecting the proper dressing is the final stage in the quest for the perfect salad. There's a good reason why the vinaigrette has been a favorite for so many years. It's fast to make, and the tartness of the vinegar balances the smoothness of the oil.

Classic Vinaigrette

  2 Tbsp vinegar
  ½ tsp salt
  ¼ tsp ground black pepper
  ½ c olive oil

Mix the vinegar and salt in a small bowl and set aside for a few minutes. Add the pepper and stir in the oil. Adjust the flavor to taste with additional vinegar or salt. Stir or shake well before using.

Variations

Garlic Vinaigrette: Add ½ to 1 tsp minced garlic.
Dijon Mustard Vinaigrette: Add 1½ tsp Dijon mustard.
Curried French Vinaigrette: Add 1 tsp curry powder.
Fruit Salad Vinaigrette: Replace the vinegar with bottled or fresh lemon juice and add ⅓ c honey.

White Beans and Sausage with Greens

  1 package (12 oz) smoked Italian turkey sausage, sliced
  ¼ c balsamic vinegar
  2 Tbsp Dijon mustard
  1 Tbsp olive oil
  2 cans (16 oz each) white kidney beans, rinsed and drained
  2 red bell peppers, finely chopped
  1 large red onion, finely chopped
  ¼ c finely chopped fresh flat leaf parsley or 1½ Tbsp dried
     Ground black pepper (to taste)
  1 bag (10 oz) mixed greens

In a large nonstick skillet over medium heat, cook the sausage for 8 minutes, or until no longer pink.

In a large bowl, whisk together the vinegar and mustard. Whisk in the oil. Stir in the beans, bell peppers, onion, parsley, and black pepper. Add the sausage and toss well.

Place the lettuce on a platter and top with the salad. Serve at room temperature.

Makes 6 servings

Per serving: 279 calories, 4 g fat

Greek Salad with Shrimp

Salad

  1 lb large shrimp, peeled and deveined
  1 tsp Italian Herb Blend (page 15)
     Salt
     Ground black pepper
  1 bag (10 oz) romaine lettuce, torn
  2 tomatoes, cut into wedges
  1 red onion, sliced
  ½ c crumbled feta cheese

WOMEN ASK WHY

Why is olive oil supposed to be good for me when it's 100 percent fat?

Keep in mind that "good" is a relative term. So is "fat." Some fats are much better for you than others, and olive oil is one of them. This doesn't mean that you can gulp olive oil and expect to live to 100. The body needs some fat to function properly, but it certainly doesn't need the amount that most Americans get.

There are two types of fat: saturated and monounsaturated. Most saturated fats are solid at room temperature. Butter is a saturated fat. So is lard. Saturated fat can also be mixed with other fats in liquids. Saturated fat is a problem because it greatly increases the amount of cholesterol in the blood. Worse, it increases a type of cholesterol called low-density lipoprotein, or LDL, the type associated with clogged arteries and heart disease.

A healthier type of fat is monounsaturated fat. Olive oil (along with canola oil) contains a lot of monounsaturated fat. Unlike saturated fat, olive oil actually lowers LDL cholesterol. More important, it does so without lowering levels of high-density lipoprotein (HDL) cholesterol, the type that protects against heart disease.

It's absolutely true that olive oil is 100 percent fat. It contains just as many calories as any other kind of oil. So use it sparingly and in place of other, less healthy fats like butter.

Expert Consulted
Kathleen Zelman, R.D.
Spokeswoman, American
    Dietetic Association
Atlanta

Dressing

- 2 Tbsp lemon juice
- 2 Tbsp water
- 2 tsp Dijon mustard
- 1 tsp olive oil

To make the salad: Place the shrimp in a medium saucepan and add water to cover. Bring to a simmer over medium heat. Turn off the heat and let stand for 1 minute. Drain and place in a large bowl. Add the herb blend. Season with salt and pepper to taste. Toss to mix. Add the lettuce, tomatoes, onion, and cheese. Toss well.

To make the dressing: In a small bowl, whisk together the lemon juice, water, and mustard. Whisk in the oil. Pour over the salad and toss well.

Makes 6 servings

Per serving: 132 calories, 4.5 g fat

Black Bean Citrus Salad

Salad

- 3 navel oranges, peeled, sectioned, and chopped
- 1 can (16 oz) black beans, rinsed and drained
- 1 can (16 oz) red kidney beans, rinsed and drained
- 2 medium cucumbers, peeled and coarsely chopped
- ½ c chopped red onion

Dressing

- 2 Tbsp canola oil
- 2 Tbsp lemon juice
- 1 Tbsp finely chopped fresh cilantro
- ¼ tsp ground black pepper

To make the salad: In a large bowl, combine the oranges, black beans, kidney beans, cucumbers, and onion.

To make the dressing: In a small bowl, whisk together the oil, lemon juice, cilantro, and

pepper. Pour over the salad and toss to mix well. Cover and chill, if desired.

Makes 4 servings
Per serving: 312 calories, 8 g fat

REAL-LIFE SCENARIO

Starvation Isn't the Answer

Almost every week, Betsy and Bill have the same conversation: They're going to eat better and lose a few pounds. Filled with good intentions, they go to the market on Saturday and load up on fish, fruit, and vegetables. For the rest of the weekend they eat fresh, healthy food, and they feel pretty good about things. But by the time Monday or Tuesday rolls around, they're starting to rummage through the freezer for "something real." A day or two after that, the leftover salad (there's a lot of it) goes in the trash, and they head to their favorite restaurant for steak with all the fixings. No matter how hard they try, they just can't convince themselves that healthy cooking is any fun at all. They feel hungry all the time, and they can't imagine how anyone sticks with it. "What's the secret?" they wonder.

Betsy and Bill are suffering from flavor fatigue. People who try to lose weight by eating nothing but fish and vegetables aren't going to be successful because such a limited diet is boring. It's essential that they broaden their horizons by adding pastas, potatoes, and grains to their menu. These are versatile foods that can be cooked hundreds of ways. This alone would make their diets a lot more interesting.

A lot of people think that they have to swear off meats, but there's nothing wrong with having lean beef and pork as long as it's limited to two or three meals a week. Poultry is great, too. They might want to consider stocking some low-fat frozen entrées, like turkey patties or burgers. This will be a big help when their "meat tooth" acts up.

Another concern is that Betsy and Bill may be restricting their calorie intake too much in the early part of the week. This is a terrible way to lose weight. It's not healthy, and people who feel hungry aren't going to stick with any type of diet for very long. This explains their steak-house binges—they feel desperate and more than a little hungry.

It seems as though they're concentrating on the three main meals a day. But there's no reason why they shouldn't be eating between meals. Snacking—as long as the snacks are healthy—is a great way to stay satisfied so that you don't stuff yourself later. At the very least, they should plan on having a snack in the afternoon and another one before they go to bed.

Since Betsy and Bill seem a little confused about the best way to make dietary changes, they might want to talk with a registered dietitian, who will help them work out a more realistic plan. Their current approach is too drastic, and as they've discovered, it's not working.

Expert Consulted
Cindy Moore, R.D.
Director of nutrition therapy
The Cleveland Clinic Foundation

Summer Fruit Salad with Honey-Lime Dressing

Dressing

1 c fat-free yogurt
½ c red raspberries
2–4 Tbsp honey
¼ c lime juice
1 tsp vanilla extract

Fruit Salad

2 peaches or nectarines, sliced
1 c red or black raspberries
1 c pineapple chunks
1 c honeydew chunks
1 c red or green seedless grapes
4 figs, quartered
Red and green leaf lettuce
1 Tbsp shredded fresh mint or 1 tsp dried

To make the dressing: Place the yogurt, raspberries, honey, lime juice, and vanilla extract in a blender. Blend until smooth.

To make the fruit salad: In a large bowl, combine the peaches or nectarines, raspberries, pineapple, honeydew, grapes, and figs. Add the dressing and toss well. Marinate for 30 minutes at room temperature.

Line a serving platter with the lettuce. Top with the salad. Sprinkle with the mint.

Makes 6 servings
Per serving: 143 calories, 0 g fat

Crab Salad with Avocado and Mango

Dressing

¼ c orange juice
3 Tbsp honey
3 Tbsp lime juice
3 Tbsp plain yogurt
¼ tsp celery seeds
¼ tsp poppy seeds

Salad

8 oz lump crabmeat
½ c finely chopped celery
¼ c finely chopped red bell pepper
2 tsp minced scallion
4 tsp lime juice
3–4 tsp mayonnaise
4 red lettuce leaves
6 c mixed greens, torn
1 avocado, peeled and sliced
1 mango, peeled and sliced

To make the dressing: In a small bowl, whisk together the orange juice, honey, lime juice, yogurt, celery seeds, and poppy seeds. Cover and refrigerate for at least 20 minutes to allow flavors to blend.

To make the salad: In a medium bowl, combine the crabmeat, celery, pepper, scallion, lime juice, and mayonnaise.

Line 4 large salad plates with the red lettuce. Divide the mixed greens among the plates. Top with the crab mixture.

Divide the avocado and mango among the plates. Serve drizzled with the dressing.

Makes 4 servings
Per serving: 273 calories, 9 g fat

Key West Crab Salad

Salad

3 c torn spinach
2 c torn leaf lettuce
1 c finely shredded cabbage
2 oranges, peeled and sectioned
1 small red onion, sliced and separated into rings
12 oz cooked crabmeat, broken into chunks

(continued)

Dressing

- ½ tsp grated orange peel
- 3 Tbsp orange juice
- 2 Tbsp balsamic vinegar
- 2 tsp olive or canola oil
- 1 tsp finely chopped fresh tarragon or ¼ tsp dried

To make the salad: In a large bowl, combine the spinach, lettuce, cabbage, oranges, and onion. Add the crabmeat and gently toss until combined; set aside.

To make the dressing: In a small jar with a tight-fitting cover, combine the orange peel, orange juice, vinegar, oil, and tarragon. Cover and shake until blended. Pour over the spinach mixture and gently toss until coated.

Makes 4 servings

Per serving: 181 calories, 4.5 g fat

IMPROV SALADS

Gone are the days when every salad was iceberg lettuce and tomato, maybe with some carrot shavings thrown in. Whether you're using a salad as a side dish or a main meal, produce bins are brimming with much more exciting—and healthier—choices, such as romaine, bibb, and oak leaf lettuces. Arugula is all the rage these days because it adds a tangy taste to milder greens. Equally distinctive are watercress, spinach, and kale. And that's just the beginning.

You don't need a recipe or 11 different herbs and spices to make incredible salads simply and quickly. All you have to do is start adding ingredients, mixing and matching with an eye toward exciting tastes, colors, and shapes. The lettuce is just the beginning. For example:

- ❧ Adding 1 to 2 tablespoons of chopped toasted nuts gives salads a pleasing crunch and nutty flavor.

- ❧ Add green olives for their color and pleasantly pungent flavor. Black olives give a mellower taste.

- ❧ Dried cranberries or chopped dried apricots add a lot of fiber, making salads more filling than a lettuce-only mix. Fresh or dried figs are good, too.

- ❧ Fruit slices work well with almost any mixture of greens.

- ❧ For a blast of vitamin C and an intriguing sprinkle of color, add pomegranate seeds to a leafy salad.

- ❧ Cold meats can be used with almost any kind of salad, as long as the meat—beef, chicken, and pork all work well—is sliced thin and doesn't overwhelm the more delicate ingredients.

- ❧ Adding shrimp or fresh or canned fish such as tuna is another way to edge salads toward main-meal status.

Ultimately, salads can be as varied as the ingredients that you take home from the store. And they don't take a lot of time. Wash the greens and other ingredients when you get them home. Dry them well and store them in a plastic bag in the crisper drawer of the refrigerator. When you're ready to put a salad together, pour some of the leaves into a bowl and start experimenting with other ingredients.

Lots o' Pasta

A mystique has evolved around the proper preparation of pasta. People argue about the types of pots to use, when to add the pasta to the water, and how long to cook it. These make for great arguments, but cooking pasta is hardly rocket science. Boil some water, add the pasta, drain, and dress it up with a simple sauce. It doesn't get quicker or easier than that.

"Pasta is a great base for other foods, so it's a great way to get the kids or your spouse to eat more vegetables," says Katherine B. Goldberg, R.D., a culinary arts specialist at the University of Michigan's M-Fit Health Promotion Program in Ann Arbor and co-author of *The High Fit–Low Fat Vegetarian Cookbook.*

Use the biggest pot you have. It's certainly possible to boil pasta in a small pot, but this slows the cooking time because there isn't enough water for it to roil around in. Larger pots—a good rule of thumb is to use 4 quarts of water for every pound of pasta—give it more room so that it cooks more quickly and evenly.

Save time with fresh. The great thing about dried pasta is that it keeps almost forever

on the shelf, but it usually takes about 10 minutes to cook. You can reduce the cooking time by using fresh, frozen pasta. It cooks to perfection in minutes.

Don't bother with the oil. Many people splash a little cooking oil into the pasta water to prevent the noodles from sticking. It's just an extra step and it isn't necessary. In fact it's a bad idea, says Barbara Pool Fenzl, owner of Les Gourmettes Cooking School in Phoenix. "The oil adds fat, and it prevents the sauce from sticking to the pasta."

Add salt late. Pasta cooked without salt tends to have a slightly flat taste, so you'll want to add a pinch or two to the water. Wait until the water is actually boiling before adding salt. Otherwise, the salty flavor will become too concentrated as the water evaporates during heating.

Add the pasta all at once. Since people tend to cook pasta in pots that are too small, they've gotten into the habit of adding it in batches to prevent sticking. This causes it to cook unevenly. To keep control of the cooking time, it's best to add the pasta all at once and to use a pot that's big enough to allow it.

WOMAN TO WOMAN

She Turned Traditional Italian Meals into Healthy Treasures

Jennifer Bellino of Sands Point, New York, grew up eating her mother's wonderful Italian cooking. Her mother learned to cook from her mother, who was born in Italy and later immigrated to America. But unlike her mother and grandmother, Jennifer, 43, is part of a health-conscious generation. She loved her family's traditional meals, but she wanted to make them healthier. Here's her story.

I've always loved my mother's cooking. We grew up eating these big, elaborate Italian meals. It was all I knew, so when I got married, I started cooking the same meals my mother did.

It's hard nowadays to ignore all the information about fat, salt, and calories, and traditional Italian recipes are loaded with all three. One day when I was at the health food store buying vitamins for my family, I started looking at the cookbooks geared toward healthy cooking. I scanned the shelves for healthy alternatives and began to realize that I could make my dishes healthier just by making a few changes.

One dish I turned around was Chicken Français. Traditionally, this is made by dipping the chicken in batter, then slathering it with a sauce made with lemon and butter. This one was easy to modify. I just replaced the butter with Butter Buds, an all-natural butter substitute with only 5 calories in a teaspoon. Still experimenting, I started using an all-natural instant broth concentrate. It doesn't have any fat and adds a lot of flavor. The final result is more of a gravy than an oily, buttery sauce.

My meatballs have changed, too. Instead of beef, I now use ground turkey. I can't tell the difference, and it's a lot leaner. I add a tablespoon of olive oil for every pound of turkey to give it more body. Then I add a few spoonfuls of tomato sauce for extra flavor.

Many of my favorite dishes have undergone equally simple and healthy alterations. I make lasagna with part-skim cheeses instead of the whole-milk kind. My vodka sauce, which I use on all sorts of recipes, is now made with light cream, not the heavy variety. And when I make escarole and beans, I cut the amount of oil in half and add chicken broth instead.

All of these changes were really easy. I feel much better about my cooking now that it has less fat and salt. Even my mother has borrowed some of my ideas—although she still keeps the skin on the chicken that she throws in her soup. Imagine, my mother imitating me! I couldn't be more flattered.

Drain, but don't rinse it. When your pasta is al dente—tender, but still firm when you bite it—drain it into a colander and quickly toss the warm noodles with your sauce. Letting it sit in a colander will make it sticky, and rinsing it removes the starch, which prevents sauces from clinging well, Fenzl says.

Use sharp cheese. Many traditional pasta dishes earned their fatty reputations from the gobs of butter and rich cheeses with which they were mixed. By choosing sharp, intensely flavored cheeses, you can impart flavor with just a few grated teaspoons, dramatically reducing the fat.

Use canned tomatoes. Don't worry about peeling and seeding your own tomatoes for pasta sauce. Use the canned variety. Better still, hunt out the ones with flavorings already added.

LOW-FAT MEATBALLS IN MINUTES

Low-fat turkey sausage and ground turkey breast turn this full-fat favorite into a low-fat treat. To get the leanest ground turkey available, look for products made only with turkey breast meat. Serve them traditional-style with pasta and tomato sauce, roll them in fresh bread crumbs and bake them for meatball sandwiches, or use them as a quick addition to soups. You can also freeze meal-size servings to thaw overnight or in the microwave for a quick treat.

Turkey Meatballs

1½ slices whole wheat bread, torn into small pieces
4 oz ground turkey breast
4 oz low-fat turkey sausage, casings removed
2 Tbsp minced onion
2 tsp minced garlic
1 tsp Italian Herb Blend (page 15)
   Pinch of ground red pepper
1 egg white, lightly beaten

Place the bread in a food processor or blender and process with on/off turns to make fine crumbs. Crumble the turkey breast and turkey sausage into the food processor. Add the onion, garlic, herb blend, and pepper and process briefly. Add the egg white and process with on/off turns until well-mixed. Shape the mixture into 1" balls.

Coat a Dutch oven or large nonstick skillet with nonstick spray. Place over medium heat and add the meatballs. Cook for 20 minutes, or until the center is no longer pink.

Makes 16
Per serving (4 meatballs): 112 calories, 3 g fat

Penne with Mediterranean Vegetables

8 oz penne
¼ c balsamic vinegar
2 Tbsp minced garlic
1 c finely chopped onion
1 small eggplant, finely chopped
1 small yellow squash, finely chopped
1 red bell pepper, finely chopped
2 c finely chopped tomatoes
¼ c chopped fresh parsley or 1 Tbsp dried
1 Tbsp olive oil
¼ c grated Parmesan cheese
½ tsp salt
1 tsp Italian Herb Blend (page 15)

Cook the pasta according to package directions.

Meanwhile, in a large nonstick skillet over medium-high heat, cook the vinegar and garlic for 3 minutes.

Add the onion, eggplant, squash, and pepper. Cook for 5 minutes.

Add the tomatoes and parsley. Cook, stirring frequently, for 15 minutes.

Stir in the oil, cheese, salt, and herb blend. Cook for 5 minutes, or until the sauce thickens.

Add the sauce mixture to the pasta and toss well.

Makes 4 servings
Per serving: 349 calories, 7 g fat

TWO TOMATO SAUCES IN 15 MINUTES FLAT

When your garden (or the grocery store) is overflowing with ripe, in-season tomatoes, make them into super-fast savory sauces. These recipes are so easy that you can make several batches and freeze the extra.

Quick Tomato Sauce

This sauce offers the summer-fresh flavor that's missing from long-cooking sauces in about the same time it takes to heat the jarred variety.

    1 large onion, chopped
    2 tsp chopped fresh garlic
    2 tsp olive oil
    4 c chopped tomatoes
    ½ c chopped fresh basil
       Salt and pepper

In a large nonstick skillet over medium heat, cook the onion and garlic in the oil for 5 minutes, or until softened.

Stir in the tomatoes and basil. Season with salt and pepper to taste. Increase the heat to medium-high and cook, stirring often, for 10 minutes, or until the tomatoes have softened.

Makes 6 servings
Per ½ cup: 45 calories, 2 g fat

Creamy Tomato Sauce

For a tangy sauce with a smooth, creamy texture, just add a few ingredients to a batch of Quick Tomato Sauce, above.

    3 c Quick Tomato Sauce (recipe above)
    1 red bell pepper, chopped
    1 jalapeño chile pepper, chopped
    1 tsp dried oregano
    1 c low-fat cottage cheese
    ¼ c grated Parmesan cheese

Prepare the Quick Tomato Sauce, adding the bell pepper, chile pepper, and oregano before cooking. When done, transfer the cooked sauce to a food processor (in batches, if necessary). Add the cottage cheese and Parmesan. Blend for 2 minutes until very smooth.

Makes 5 cups
Per ½ cup: 56 calories, 2.5 g fat

Pasta Primavera with Tomato-Basil Sauce

Pasta

     1 c baby carrots
     1 bunch scallions, cut into 1½" pieces
    12 oz asparagus, cut into 1½" pieces
     1 c sugar snap peas
     8 oz penne pasta
     ¼ tsp ground black pepper
     ½ c shredded Romano cheese

Sauce

    1½ Tbsp olive oil
     4 garlic cloves, minced, or 4 tsp prepared minced garlic
     2 c diced tomatoes or 1 can (14½ oz) diced tomatoes
     ¼ c tomato paste
     ¼ c dry red wine or red grape juice
     1 c baby spinach leaves
     ½ c sliced fresh basil

To make the pasta: Bring 2 quarts water to a boil over medium-high heat. Add the carrots and cook for 2 minutes. Add the scallions, asparagus, and peas; cook for 3 minutes. Remove the vegetables and set aside.

Add the pasta to the pot. Cook for 10 minutes, or until just tender. Drain and return to the pot.

To make the sauce: While the pasta is cooking, warm the oil in a large saucepan over medium-high heat. Add the garlic and stir for 1 minute. Stir in the tomatoes (with juice), tomato paste, and wine or grape juice. Cook for 6 minutes. Add the spinach and cook for 1 minute. Stir in the basil and the reserved vegetables. Cook for 1 minute to reheat the vegetables.

Add the sauce, pepper, and ¼ cup of the cheese to the pot with the pasta. Mix well. Sprinkle with the remaining ¼ cup cheese.

Makes 4 servings
Per serving: 410 calories, 1 g fat

Chicken Fingers Parmesan

  8 oz thin spaghetti
  4 boneless, skinless chicken breast halves
  ½ c dry bread crumbs
  ½ c grated Parmesan cheese
  1 tsp dried basil
  1 Tbsp olive oil
  1 can (14½ oz) pasta-style chopped tomatoes
  1 can (6 oz) tomato paste
  ⅓ c water
  ½ c shredded mozzarella cheese

Cook the spaghetti according to package directions.

Meanwhile, cut the chicken into ½" strips. Combine the bread crumbs, Parmesan, and basil in a plastic bag. Place the chicken in the bag and shake to coat.

Heat the oil in a 12" nonstick skillet over medium heat. Place the chicken in the skillet. Raise the heat to high and cook for 4 to 5 minutes, or until the chicken is lightly browned on all sides and no longer pink. Remove from the skillet and set aside.

Add the tomatoes, tomato paste, and water to the skillet. Stir well. Return the chicken to the skillet, covering the pieces with the sauce. Reduce the heat to low and sprinkle with the mozzarella. Cover and simmer for 1 to 2 minutes, or until the cheese melts.

Divide the spaghetti among plates and top with chicken and sauce.

Makes 4 servings
Per serving: 625 calories, 14 g fat

Fettuccine Alfredo

 12 oz fettuccine
  1 c fat-free evaporated milk
  ⅓ c half-and-half
 1½ Tbsp butter
 1½ c grated Parmesan cheese
  2 Tbsp snipped fresh chives

Cook the pasta according to package directions.

In a medium saucepan, heat the milk, half-and-half, and butter over medium heat until the butter is melted and the mixture is hot. Gradually stir in 1¼ cup of the cheese. Cook and stir until the cheese has melted.

Add the pasta. Toss until well coated. Serve sprinkled with the remaining ¼ cup cheese and chives.

Makes 6 servings
Per serving: 400 calories, 13 g fat

WOMEN ASK WHY

Why was spaghetti considered a fattening food 20 years ago, when everyone today says that it's low-fat?

Science is always moving forward, and one year's gospel has a way of becoming the next year's joke. Everyone today knows that the Earth revolves around the sun, for example. But once upon a time, people who believed this were considered heretics.

People were wrong about spaghetti, too. Spaghetti contains complex carbohydrates, better known as starches. A few decades ago, many scientists believed that starches, which tend to be dense, heavy foods, made people dense and heavy. People didn't understand that a gram of fat contains double the amount of calories as a gram of carbohydrate.

They weren't entirely wrong, however. People who ate a lot of spaghetti did sometimes get fat.

But the spaghetti was innocent. It was the toppings that were guilty. Starchy foods like spaghetti and potatoes are fairly bland, and people tend to dress them up with cream sauces, butter, or sour cream, all of which contain tremendous amounts of fat and calories.

It's not really true, incidentally, that pasta is never fattening. It depends what kind you buy. Dried noodles contain mainly flour and water—they're among the leanest foods you can eat. Fresh pasta, however, is made with eggs, which add fat and calories as well as dietary cholesterol.

This doesn't mean that you shouldn't eat fresh pasta. One serving of fresh pasta contains very modest amounts of fat. As long as you don't dress it up with a thick cream sauce loaded with bacon bits, you're going to have a healthy meal, not a heavy one.

Expert Consulted
Diane Quagliani, R.D.
Nutrition consultant
Western Springs, Illinois

Chicken Pesto Pasta

⅓ c reduced-fat pesto sauce
1 c chicken broth
1 package (10 oz) sliced roasted chicken breast
9 oz fettuccine
   Ground black pepper
2 tomatoes, chopped

In a large skillet, combine the pesto sauce and ¾ cup of the broth. Add the chicken and mix well. Cover and cook, stirring occasionally, over medium heat for 5 minutes.

Meanwhile, cook the pasta according to package directions. Drain, place in a large bowl, and toss with the remaining ¼ cup broth. Season with pepper to taste.

Add the chicken mixture and toss to coat. Serve with the tomatoes.

Makes 4 servings
Per serving: 241 calories, 8.5 g fat

Linguine with Mushrooms and Peppers

2 tsp olive oil
1 sweet onion, sliced and separated into rings
1 bay leaf

2 c sliced button mushrooms

2 red, yellow, or green bell peppers, cut into thin strips

1 garlic clove, minced

1½ Tbsp Italian Herb Blend (page 15)

3 Tbsp chopped fresh parsley

⅔ c vegetable broth or defatted chicken broth

8 oz linguine or spaghetti

2 Tbsp grated Parmesan cheese (optional)

Warm the oil in a large nonstick skillet over medium-low heat. Add the onion and bay leaf and cook, stirring occasionally, for 5 minutes.

Add the mushrooms, peppers, and garlic and cook for 4 minutes, or until the mushrooms begin to release their liquid. Add the herb blend, parsley, and broth. Simmer for 5 to 7 minutes, or until the peppers are soft and the broth has reduced slightly.

Meanwhile, in a large pot of boiling water, cook the linguine or spaghetti according to package directions. Drain. Place in a serving bowl and toss with the mushroom mixture. Remove and discard the bay leaf. Sprinkle with the cheese (if using).

Makes 4 servings

Per serving: 327 calories, 4 g fat

Pasta with Red Clam Sauce

8 oz fettuccine or spaghetti

1 can (16 oz) stewed tomatoes

1 can (8 oz) tomato sauce

1 tsp onion powder

1 tsp Italian Herb Blend (page 15)

¼ tsp celery seeds

⅛ tsp ground black pepper

1 large carrot, shredded

2 tsp cornstarch

1 can (6½ oz) chopped clams, rinsed and drained

Cook the pasta according to package directions.

Meanwhile, drain and set aside 2 tablespoons of the juice from the tomatoes. In a medium saucepan, combine the tomatoes, tomato sauce, onion powder, herb blend, celery seeds, and pepper. Bring to a boil over medium-high heat and stir in the carrot. Reduce the heat to low, cover, and simmer for 5 minutes.

In a small bowl, stir together the cornstarch and the reserved 2 tablespoons tomato juice. Stir the cornstarch mixture and clams into the tomato mixture. Cook and stir over medium heat until the mixture thickens and begins to gently boil. Cook and stir for 2 minutes longer. Serve over the pasta.

Makes 4 servings

Per serving: 313 calories, 1.5 g fat

HEALTH BONUS

Beat Cancer with Tomatoes

Tomatoes are red because they contain a huge amount of a pigment called lycopene. A relative of beta-carotene, lycopene is a powerful antioxidant with a similar cancer-fighting punch as its more famous cousin.

Studies have shown that lycopene may inhibit cancers of the colon and prostate gland as well as protect against heart disease. Many healthful substances in foods are damaged during cooking, but lycopene actually becomes more absorbable.

HEALTHY— OR NOT?
Margarine

It was meant to be a healthful alternative to butter, but the development and evolution of margarine proves that better living doesn't always come from chemistry.

It's true that margarine is much lower in saturated fat than butter. That should be good news for people who are worried about cholesterol and yet can't imagine bread without that buttery taste. But it's not that simple. Margarine often contains chemically altered fats called hydrogenated fats. These fats are very stable. They make it possible for margarine to stay solid and fresh when it's kept at room temperature. The problem is that these fats have been shown to dramatically raise cholesterol and may increase the risk of heart disease, says Elizabeth Somer, R.D., author of *Age-Proof Your Body*.

Many nutritionists take a dim view of margarine. They say that it has little nutritional value, it's high in calories, and it can clog your arteries. Why make the switch?

Some margarines, it turns out, are better than others. The harder margarine is at room temperature, the more likely it is to contain artery-clogging hydrogenated fats. Margarines that come in squeeze tubes or tubs, on the other hand, are often made with unhydrogenated vegetable oil and will be better for you. Light margarines are a reasonable choice, too, says Somer.

Taste is another story. Margarines have improved a lot over the years, but unfortunately, they still don't taste like butter.

Asparagus and Orange Linguine

     2 c reduced-fat ricotta cheese
    ¼ c fat-free evaporated milk
    ½ c fat-free plain yogurt
     2 Tbsp grated orange peel
    10 oz linguine
     2 tsp olive oil
     1 lb asparagus, trimmed and cut into 2" pieces
     1 c sliced scallions
    1½ Tbsp grated fresh ginger
     1 orange, peeled and sectioned

In a blender or small food processor, process the ricotta cheese, milk, yogurt, and orange peel until smooth; set aside.

Cook the linguine according to package directions.

Place the oil in a large nonstick skillet and heat over medium-high heat. Add the asparagus, scallions, and ginger. Cook and stir for 4 to 5 minutes, or until the asparagus is crisp-tender. Stir in the ricotta mixture. Cook, stirring occasionally, for 2 to 3 minutes, or until heated through.

Add the linguine and oranges to the skillet. Gently toss until coated.

Makes 4 servings
Per serving: 431 calories, 10.5 g fat

Fusilli Primavera in Spicy Peanut Sauce

    3 Tbsp smooth peanut butter
    3 Tbsp fat-free sour cream
    2 tsp rice vinegar
    1 tsp soy sauce
    ⅛ tsp ground red pepper

10 oz fusilli
2 tsp toasted sesame oil
8 oz snow peas, ends and strings removed
and julienned
1 c scallions, cut into 1" pieces
1 c cherry tomatoes, halved
1 Tbsp sesame seeds, toasted

In a blender or small food processor, process the peanut butter, sour cream, vinegar, soy sauce, and pepper until well-combined. Transfer the mixture to a small bowl and set aside.

Cook the pasta according to package directions.

Meanwhile, add the oil to a large nonstick skillet and heat over medium heat. Add the snow peas, scallions, and tomatoes. Cook and stir for 4 to 5 minutes, or until the vegetables are crisp-tender.

To serve, drain the pasta, reserving 1 tablespoon of the cooking water. Transfer the pasta to a large bowl.

Stir the reserved cooking water into the peanut butter mixture. Add the peanut butter mixture and vegetables to the pasta. Toss until coated. Before serving, sprinkle with the sesame seeds.

Makes 4 servings
Per serving: 417 calories, 11 g fat

Talkin' Turkey and Chicken

Red meat used to be the king of American dinner plates, but it's being challenged by two plucky competitors: chicken and turkey. Partly, this is because women are trying to eat less fat, and poultry without the skin is a lot leaner than many cuts of red meat. Equally important, poultry is so versatile that it is the main ingredient in thousands of recipes. And it's very forgiving: No matter how you use it—stewed, broiled, or stir-fried—it comes up flavorful and tender.

To get the most convenience and enjoy chicken and turkey at their nutritional and tasty best, here are a few things you'll want to do.

Buy and freeze. Chicken is among the least expensive meats in the supermarket. You can save even more money, along with a lot of time, by buying large bags of boneless, skinless breasts that have been flash-frozen, says Sue Snider, Ph.D., food and nutrition specialist at the University of Delaware's department of animal and food sciences in Newark.

They'll keep for at least 6 months in the freezer. You can pull out dinner-size portions when you're ready, then reseal the bag to keep the rest fresh.

Save time with the microwave. You can bring frozen chicken breasts and thighs to cooking temperature in as little as 5 minutes by using the defrost setting on the microwave. Turning the pieces halfway through the heating time and making sure that they aren't stuck together will help them defrost more quickly and evenly.

Get the best of both techniques. Poultry cooked in the microwave will be done in about half the time as poultry cooked in the oven. The trade-off is that you don't get the same crispy skin or attractive browned appearance. This is why many women combine the two techniques: They cook the bird in the microwave until it's almost done, then transfer it to the broiler for quick browning.

Work with small pieces. Poultry meat is dense, which means that it takes a long time for large pieces to cook through. You can shorten the cooking time dramatically by using turkey tenders, slices of chicken breast, or other small

WOMEN ASK WHY

What makes chicken vulnerable to salmonella?

The salmonella bacteria that cause food poisoning thrive in all meats, not just chicken. (They even grow on some fruits and vegetables.) But since chicken is very popular, and we eat so much of it, our risk of encountering the bacteria in chicken is higher than it would be in, say, filet mignon.

In addition, chicken often gets handled a lot before it's cooked. Unlike a roast, which goes straight into the oven, chicken may be cut into pieces or boned. This doesn't make the chicken itself any more dangerous: You're going to cook it, and cooking kills salmonella. But in the process of handling it, you're more likely to get bacteria on your hands and transfer them to something that isn't going to be cooked, like salad greens.

Salmonella is easy to prevent. Probably the best thing to do after handling chicken is to wash your hands with hot soapy water for 20 seconds before handling other foods. A quicker rinse won't do it. Wash the cutting board and knife, too. Dry your hands and the cutting board with paper towels because a dishcloth can hang on to salmonella and pass it on to something else. You may even want to disinfect your faucet and soap bottle after preparing chicken, since you touch them to wash your hands.

Expert Consulted
Edith H. Hogan, R.D.
Spokesperson for the American Dietetic Association
Nutrition consultant
Washington, D.C.

pieces and cooking them in a stir-fry, on the grill, or in a stew. You can also speed things along by using a mallet to pound irregularly shaped pieces of chicken, such as the breast, between two pieces of waxed paper.

Remove the skin after cooking. Most of the fat in poultry is in the skin, and a high percentage of it is saturated fat, says Dr. Snider. Even though you won't want to eat the skin, you will want to leave it on during cooking because it helps the meat retain its natural moisture and flavors. This is especially helpful for breast meat, which tends to get dry and tough during cooking. The sheen of moisture that you see when you peel off the skin after cooking is just that—moisture, not fat.

Slip the seasoning underneath. It doesn't make sense to rub herbs and spices on the skin since you're going to peel it off later. What you can do is use your fingers to slip dried or fresh herbs between the skin and the meat. It's fine to use a knife to make small cuts in the skin so that you can reach underneath.

Eat light meat for low-fat, dark meat for minerals. When you're trying to reduce the amount of fat in your diet, white meat, which comes mainly from the breast, is the best choice because it's very low in fat, with about 1.5 grams in a serving. Dark meat is higher in fat, with about 3.8 grams in a serving, but it contains a lot more minerals such as iron.

Apricot-Glazed Chicken Breasts

1 lb boneless, skinless chicken breast halves

¼ tsp paprika

1 tsp canola oil

2 garlic cloves, minced

(continued)

⅓ c apricot preserves

¼ c orange juice

1 Tbsp minced fresh cilantro

¼ tsp nutmeg

¼ tsp allspice

Rinse the chicken and pat dry with paper towels. Sprinkle the chicken with the paprika.

Spray an unheated large skillet with nonstick spray and heat over medium-high heat. Add the chicken and cook for 4 minutes. Turn the chicken over and cook for 4 to 6 minutes longer, or until a thermometer inserted in the thickest portion registers 160°F and the juices run clear. Transfer to a serving platter and cover to keep warm.

Add the oil to the skillet. Add the garlic. Cook and stir for 30 seconds. Stir in the preserves, orange juice, cilantro, nutmeg, and allspice. Bring to a gentle boil. Remove from the heat and pour over the chicken.

Makes 4 servings

Per serving: 177 calories, 3 g fat

Ginger Chicken

1 package (16 oz) frozen mixed broccoli, carrots, and water chestnuts or a similar combination

12 oz cubed boneless, skinless chicken breast

1 tsp ground ginger

2 c instant rice

¼ c teriyaki sauce

Cook the vegetables according to package directions. Do not drain.

Sprinkle the chicken with the ginger.

Coat a large nonstick skillet with nonstick spray. Add the chicken and cook, turning frequently, over medium heat for 5 minutes, or until the cubes begin to brown.

Meanwhile, cook the rice according to package directions.

Stir the teriyaki sauce into the vegetables. Add the vegetable mixture to the pan with the chicken and stir to mix well. Cook for 2 to 3 minutes longer, or until heated through and the chicken is no longer pink.

Fluff the rice with a fork. Serve the chicken and vegetables over the rice.

Makes 4 servings

Per serving: 358 calories, 2.5 g fat

Tuscan Chicken Legs with Spinach Fettuccine

1 lb skinless chicken legs

1 tsp garlic powder

½ tsp ground black pepper

2 tsp olive oil

1 can (14½ oz) tomatoes, cut up

¼ tsp dried oregano

¼ tsp dried basil

4 c hot cooked spinach fettuccine

Rinse the chicken legs and pat dry with paper towels. Lightly sprinkle with the garlic powder and pepper.

Heat the oil in a large nonstick skillet over medium-high heat. Add the chicken and cook for 2 to 3 minutes, or until lightly browned on all sides.

Stir in the tomatoes (with juice), oregano, and basil. Bring to a boil, then reduce the heat to low. Cover and simmer for 20 minutes, or until a thermometer inserted in the thickest portion of the chicken registers 170°F and the juices run clear.

Serve the chicken over the fettuccine.

Makes 4 servings

Per serving: 321 calories, 6 g fat

WOMAN TO WOMAN

Thanksgiving Day Is a Breeze

Leslie Giering of West Bloomfield, New York, loves Thanksgiving and the food and festivities that go with it. At 70, Leslie has been preparing this holiday feast for so long that she has it down to a science. Even though she cooks everything from scratch for 12 people, she has plenty of time to relax and enjoy the holiday.

I've been making Thanksgiving dinner for 45 years. I love to cook, and I've always preferred making everything from scratch. But it was always such a chore. The only way I've been able to do it all these years is to be super-organized—not just on Thanksgiving Day itself, but in the days and weeks leading up to it.

At least 2 weeks before Thanksgiving, I start by making a complete menu, right down to the cream and sugar. This part isn't a lot of fun, but I've found that it's the only way to be sure that I have everything I need. After I've done the menu, I review all the recipes and make up a grocery list. I ask myself, "What can I keep in the freezer? What can I cut up or make ahead of time?" For example, I'll make a potato casserole days in advance and keep it in the freezer. I do the same thing with a cranberry Jell-O mold. A few days before Thanksgiving, I'll prepare the bread crumbs for the stuffing. Another day, I'll cut up all the celery and onions. By the time it's actually Thanksgiving, I've already prepared just about everything. All I have to do is put it together.

Then I write down every single task that I need to do. Believe it or not, I even jot down a note to set the table—I usually do it 2 days ahead of time. All of this probably sounds a little fussy, but the whole idea is to spread things out over a long period of time. By getting things done early, I'm never frantic at the last minute. And because I do it a little bit at a time, I don't get overwhelmed all at once.

Cooking a 20-pound turkey always takes time, of course. I usually make smoked turkey. I soak it in brine for 24 hours, then smoke it for 3 hours in an electric smoker. After that, it takes about 4 hours to bake.

By doing a little at a time in the days leading up to Thanksgiving, I find that I'm not going crazy in those final hours. With this system, I actually have a lot of free time on Thanksgiving day. When my kids come home with my grandchildren, I'm able to enjoy some quality time with them. That makes all the planning worthwhile.

Chicken Provençal with Garlic Potatoes

1 can (8 oz) sliced mushrooms, drained
6 flat anchovy fillets, rinsed, or 2 Tbsp anchovy paste (optional)
2 c light marinara sauce
1 package (10 oz) sliced roasted chicken breast
12 pitted black olives
4 tsp olive oil
2 cans (15 oz each) sliced white potatoes, drained
2 tsp minced garlic
   Ground black pepper

Place the mushrooms and anchovies or anchovy paste (if using) in a large saucepan. Stir, breaking up the anchovies, over medium heat for 1 minute. Add the marinara sauce, chicken, and olives. Cook for 5 minutes, stirring once. Cover and set aside.

Warm the oil in a large nonstick skillet over high heat. Add the potatoes. Cook, turning often, for 5 minutes, or until browned. Stir in the garlic and cook for 1 minute. Season with pepper to taste. Serve topped with the chicken mixture.

Makes 4 servings
Per serving: 194 calories, 8.5 g fat

Thai Chicken Kabobs

2 c quick-cooking rice
12 oz roasted chicken breast, cut into 1" cubes
2 green bell peppers, cut into 1" pieces
12 cherry tomatoes
¼ c Thai peanut sauce, plus additional sauce for dipping

Preheat the broiler.

Cook the rice according to package directions.

Meanwhile, thread the chicken, peppers, and tomatoes onto skewers. Place in a large baking dish and brush with ¼ cup of the peanut sauce.

Broil for 2 minutes per side. Serve the kabobs over the rice with additional sauce for dipping.

Makes 4 servings
Per serving: 204 calories, 3.5 g fat

THANKFUL FOR LEFTOVERS

Thanksgiving dinner is hardly a 30-minute meal (unless you're talking eating time), but you can use those leftovers to your timesaving advantage for many, many meals. Here are some flavorful ideas.

- Baked turkey tetrazzini with mushrooms and peas in a cream sauce over linguini
- Turkey stir-fry with vegetables, dark sesame oil, and toasted almonds
- Turkey quesadilla with pepper cheese, green peppers, and chopped tomatoes on a flour tortilla
- Turkey chili with canned Mexican-style tomatoes, kidney beans, and corn
- Turkey noodle soup with chopped celery, canned tomatoes, and leftover vegetables such as carrots or peas
- Turkey pasta salad with broccoli, mushrooms, rotini pasta, and Parmesan cheese
- Turkey rice salad with diced turkey, wild rice, smoked ham, chopped apples, and sliced red bell peppers
- Turkey chef salad with crumbled blue cheese, sliced tomato, and hard-cooked egg
- Fruity turkey salad with sliced onion, chopped apples, grapes, raisins, and pecans
- Turkey melt sandwich with sliced breast meat, sliced smoked Cheddar, and cranberry sauce on an open-face onion bagel
- Turkey salad pita with shredded turkey, sliced tomato, shredded lettuce, shredded low-fat cheese, and dressing
- Turkey club sandwich with bacon, lettuce, and tomato on whole grain bread
- Warm turkey baguette with mozzarella, sautéed spinach, and balsamic vinaigrette
- Turkey barbecue with bottled barbecue sauce on a kaiser roll

Chicken and Waffles

8 small frozen whole grain waffles
1 Tbsp olive oil
6 oz sliced mushrooms
1 c sliced onion
1 can (10½ oz) cream of mushroom soup
1 package (10 oz) sliced roasted chicken breast
1 tsp dried tarragon

Heat the waffles in a toaster or oven.

Heat the oil in a large nonstick skillet over medium-high heat. Add the mushrooms and onion and cook, stirring, for 5 minutes, or until the onion is soft and the mushrooms release their liquid. Add the soup, chicken, and tarragon. Warm through. Serve over the waffles.

Makes 4 servings
Per serving: 377 calories, 10 g fat

Chicken and Grape Salad in Pitas

½ c low-fat lemon yogurt
1 Tbsp fat-free mayonnaise
1 tsp minced fresh rosemary or ¼ tsp crushed dried rosemary
2 c cubed cooked chicken breast
½ c halved green grapes
4 whole wheat pitas (6" in diameter)
4 lettuce leaves

In a medium bowl, stir together the yogurt, mayonnaise, and rosemary. Fold in the chicken and grapes.

To serve, cut the top from each pita. Line each pita with a lettuce leaf and spoon in about ¾ cup of the chicken mixture.

Makes 4 servings
Per serving: 306 calories, 7 g fat

EASY ROASTER: RELAX AND WATCH IT COOK

Roast chicken has a reputation for being time-consuming to prepare, but unless you're making a lot of side dishes, the bird itself is a breeze. Apart from occasional basting, you're free to do something else. Talk about a time-saver!

This chicken-and-vegetable dinner requires about 20 minutes of hands-on time from start to finish.

Season it first. Before putting the bird in the oven, rub it well with herbs, pepper, or a little salt.

Bend the wings. Bending the wings back behind the body lifts the back slightly off the baking dish. This allows for better heat circulation.

Drain the oil. To prevent the chicken from soaking in its own fat, use a roasting pan with a rack.

Heat it fast. To brown the bird and lock in the juices, put it in a preheated 400°F oven. After 20 to 30 minutes, reduce the heat to 325°.

Check for doneness. Before putting the bird in the oven, insert a meat thermometer in the thickest part of the thigh muscle. Cook until the temperature reaches 180°F, but plan on approximately 15 minutes of cooking time for each pound of chicken. A 5-pound roaster generally takes 1 to 1½ hours to bake.

Baste it often. Roasting is a dry process. Basting every 15 to 30 minutes will add flavor and help prevent the meat from drying. Small birds require more frequent basting than large ones.

Add vegetables toward the end. During the last 45 minutes of cooking time, add vegetables to the rack. Large pieces of carrot and potato work well. So do onion halves and heads of garlic. If you time it right, the meat and the vegetables will all be done at the same time.

REAL-LIFE SCENARIO

She's Too Clean for Comfort

Mary Belle learned the hard way that potato salad and bacteria are a terrible mix. Ten years ago, she got a nasty case of food poisoning, and she took the lesson to heart—some might say to extremes. She threw away her old cutting board and bought two new ones—one for vegetables, the other for meats. She doesn't use sponges, only paper towels. She never puts warm leftovers in the refrigerator because she's afraid the heat will cause other food to spoil, so she lets them cool on the counter first. Leftovers make her nervous, so she throws them away after 2 days. She even washes chicken with soap and water before cooking it. Lately, she has learned that rare beef can harbor unsavory organisms, so she insists on cooking it well-done. For her husband, Carl, this is the last straw. He likes his beef rare, and he's tired of seeing a trash can full of used paper towels. Mary Belle, he says, has gone too far. Has she?

Yes, giving a chicken a Saturday night bath is certainly going a little too far. But Mary Belle has some right ideas. Having two cutting boards is a good idea. So is keeping meats separate from ready-to-eat foods like breads and vegetables. It will help prevent the cross-contamination that occurs when bacteria in meat, which is destroyed during cooking, crosses over to foods that are eaten raw or only lightly cooked.

Sorry, Carl, but she's also right to be concerned about beef as well as chicken. *All* meats can harbor salmonella, a bacteria that causes food poisoning. The only way to kill salmonella and other bacteria is to get the meat good and hot. This doesn't mean that it has to be well-done, however. For roasts and steaks, cooking until the internal temperature is 145°F—that's medium-rare—is enough to kill bacteria. For a whole chicken, the internal temperature has to be higher—at least 180°F—because the muscle tissue is tighter.

Mary Belle's wrong, however, in letting leftovers cool on the counter. Food is much more likely to be contaminated at room temperature when it's left out for more than 2 hours, so it's best to get it in the refrigerator quickly. Once it's in there, it's safe from most bacteria. And it's good to throw out old leftovers, of course; she's just jumping the gun by 2 days. Most cooked foods can be kept safely for up to 3 to 4 days. Plain cooked rice will keep for up to a week.

Mary Belle may be going through a lot of paper towels, but again, this isn't such a bad thing because sponges and cloth dish towels are more likely to harbor bacteria. She could get the same protection—at much less cost—by using a sponge and rinsing it in a weak bleach solution or running it through the dishwasher. When it looks worn or gets smelly, it should be thrown away.

Expert Consulted
Bettye Nowlin, R.D.
Spokesperson for the American Dietetic Association
Los Angeles

Fast Chicken Curry

½ c fat-free plain yogurt

½ c fat-free mayonnaise

3 Tbsp finely chopped onion

1 tsp ground ginger

1 tsp curry powder

1 lb boneless, skinless chicken breasts, cut into ½"-wide strips

1 tsp paprika

½ tsp ground black pepper

2 c hot cooked rice

In a small bowl, stir together the yogurt, mayonnaise, onion, ginger, and curry powder; set aside.

Place the chicken in a medium bowl. Combine the paprika and pepper in a cup. Sprinkle over the chicken and toss until coated.

Coat a large nonstick skillet with nonstick spray and place over medium-high heat. Add the chicken. Cook and stir for 3 to 4 minutes, or until the chicken is no longer pink.

Stir in the yogurt mixture. Cook and stir for 2 minutes. Serve over the rice.

Makes 4 servings

Per serving: 281 calories, 2.5 g

Sesame Turkey Cutlets

2 Tbsp hoisin sauce

2 Tbsp water

1 lb turkey breast cutlets

Ground black pepper

1 Tbsp sesame seeds

In a small bowl, stir together the hoisin sauce and water; set aside.

Rinse the turkey and pat dry with paper towels. Sprinkle each cutlet with the pepper.

Coat a large nonstick skillet with nonstick spray and warm over medium-high heat. Add the turkey and cook for 1 minute. Turn the cutlets and cook for 2 to 3 minutes longer, or until no longer pink.

Place the sesame seeds in a small nonstick skillet. Cook, shaking the pan often, over medium heat for 2 to 3 minutes, or until golden and fragrant.

Pour the hoisin sauce mixture over the turkey and cook until the mixture comes to a boil. Sprinkle with the sesame seeds.

Makes 4 servings

Per serving: 142 calories, 2 g fat

GREAT GAME BIRDS

If you're yearning for an alternative to chicken and turkey, roasted game birds are a delicious and healthy option. Most supermarkets stock frozen ducks and geese all year long. Despite the thick layers of fat that keep these birds warm in the water, the meat itself is on the lean side once the skin is removed.

Another tasty choice is Cornish hens. These small hybrid chickens weigh up to 2½ pounds, and the meat is tender and delicate.

Here's a look at how game meats score in fat and calories compared with chicken and turkey.

Poultry (3 oz cooked boneless meat)	Calories	Fat (g)
Chicken breast, broiler-type	142	3.1
Cornish hen	115	3.3
Duck, breast	132	2
Duck, leg	163	5
Goose	202	10.8
Turkey, dark meat	159	6.1
Turkey, white meat	151	5

Compared with the traditional hot dog, turkey dogs are almost healthy. They generally have less fat and fewer calories. But don't let the word "turkey" make a turkey out of you.

"They're better than regular hot dogs, but they're still quite high in fat," says Connie Diekman, R.D., a nutrition consultant in St. Louis and a spokeswoman for the American Dietetic Association. An average turkey dog may contain almost 8 grams of fat and about 102 calories, she explains. That's less than a regular old baseball park frank, which has 12.8 grams of fat and 142 calories, but it's still a lot.

In addition, turkey dogs may contain as much salt as their all-beef counterparts, says Sheah Rarback, R.D., assistant professor in the department of pediatrics at the University of Miami School of Medicine and a spokeswoman for the American Dietetic Association. One turkey hot dog with cheese, for example, has about 4,815 milligrams of sodium, more than 20 percent of the recommended daily amount.

This isn't to say that turkey dogs are a bad choice, but only if they're an occasional treat, says Diekman. Since the amounts of fat and salt will vary widely among brands, take a moment to read the label before putting the turkey dogs in your shopping cart.

Turkey and Sausage Jambalaya

    2 tsp canola oil
    1 c chopped scallions
    1 large celery rib, sliced
    1 small coarsely chopped red or green bell
       pepper
    ⅓ c chopped fresh parsley
    1 lb boneless, skinless turkey breasts, cut
       into ¾" cubes
    2 c chicken broth
 1¼ c quick-cooking white rice
    ½ c chopped low-fat smoked turkey sausage
    ¼ tsp ground red pepper
    ⅛ tsp ground black pepper
    ½ tsp Poultry Seasoning (page 15)
    1 can (16 oz) chopped tomatoes

Warm the oil in a large nonstick skillet over medium heat. Add the scallions, celery, bell pepper, and parsley. Cook, stirring, for 3 minutes, or until the scallions are tender.

Add the turkey and cook, stirring, for 4 minutes. Stir in the broth, rice, sausage, red pepper, black pepper, and poultry seasoning. Reduce the heat to medium-low and gently simmer, stirring occasionally, for 3 minutes.

Stir in the tomatoes (with juice) and cook until the mixture comes to a simmer. Turn off the heat, cover, and let stand for 5 minutes. Stir well before serving.

Makes 6 servings
Per serving: 231 calories, 3.5 g fat

Turkey Piccata

    1 lb turkey breast tenderloins, cut
       crosswise into ¾"-thick strips
       Ground black pepper
    1 tsp olive oil
    1 large garlic clove, minced, or ¾ tsp
       minced prepared garlic
    1 Tbsp lemon juice
    4 tsp capers, rinsed and drained

Lightly sprinkle the turkey with the pepper, as desired.

Heat the oil in a large nonstick skillet over medium heat. Add the turkey and garlic and cook for 2 minutes. Turn the strips over and cook for 1 to 2 minutes longer, or until the turkey is no longer pink.

Remove the skillet from the heat and drizzle the lemon juice over the turkey. Sprinkle with the capers. Serve immediately.

Makes 4 servings
Per serving: 143 calories, 3 g fat

Turkey Divan with Peaches

  2 turkey breast tenderloins (about 1 lb total)
  1 package (16 oz) frozen cut broccoli
  ½ c fat-free sour cream
  2 Tbsp fat-free mayonnaise
  1 tsp Everyday Spice Blend (page 15)
  1 can (16 oz) peach halves, drained
  2 Tbsp grated Parmesan cheese

Preheat the broiler.

Bring about 1" of water to a boil in a large skillet. Carefully add the turkey and simmer, covered, for 15 to 20 minutes, or until the pieces are no longer pink. Remove from the water and set aside.

Cook the broccoli according to package directions.

Meanwhile, in a small bowl, stir together the sour cream, mayonnaise, and spice blend.

Spray a shallow baking pan with nonstick spray. Add the turkey, then arrange the broccoli and peach halves around the tenderloins. Spoon the sour-cream mixture on top and sprinkle with the cheese.

Broil for 5 to 6 minutes, or until the sour-cream mixture is puffy and lightly browned.

Makes 4 servings
Per serving: 253 calories, 3 g fat

Turkey Hash

  8 oz ground turkey
  1 c chopped onion
  2 c frozen hash brown potatoes, thawed
  ¼ c grated Parmesan cheese
  1 Tbsp Poultry Seasoning (page 15)
  ½ tsp ground black pepper

In a medium nonstick skillet, cook the turkey and onion, stirring occasionally, over medium heat for 5 minutes, or until the turkey is no longer pink and the onion is tender.

Add the potatoes. Cook and stir the mixture for 2 to 3 minutes, or until the potatoes are tender. Stir in the cheese, poultry seasoning, and pepper.

Makes 4 servings
Per serving: 174 calories, 3 g fat

Fresh and Divine Seafood

Unless you grew up cooking seafood, there's something a little daunting about opening the refrigerator and seeing a whole fish, in all its scaly, finny glory, staring back at you. It's not that fish is any harder to cook than poultry or meat. In fact, it's easier. But people who aren't used to cooking it assume that it's going to be a chore, and a strong-smelling chore at that.

Here's something that isn't a fish story: Fish is perfect for women who are short on time, says Doris Hicks, a seafood specialist with the University of Delaware's Sea Grant Marine Advisory Service in Lewes. The delicate flavors of fresh fish require nothing more complicated than brushing on a little lemon, garlic, and olive oil. And because the flesh is so soft and tender, most fish dishes can be cooked and ready for the table in 15 minutes or less.

Buy it boned and filleted. Whole fish are easy to cook as long as they've been scaled and cleaned, but fish fillets are even faster. Flounder fillets, for example, need only 6 to 8 minutes under the broiler.

Trust your nose. Since fish is usually prepared simply, freshness is essential. Smelling fish is the best way to gauge whether it's truly fresh. "Buy what looks the best and smells good," Hicks says. It should have a fresh, slightly briny scent. If it smells unmistakably and pungently fishy, it's older than it should be, and you're not going to get the best taste or texture.

Stock up on frozen fish. If you don't have the luxury of buying fresh fish, you'll probably want to buy frozen fish fillets. Supermarkets often sell large bags of fillets at very reasonable prices. It cooks up just as moist and tender as fresh.

Cook fresh fish right away. Given its perishable nature, fresh fish should be eaten within 24 to 48 hours after you buy it. It won't be harmful after that, but it will have given up the firm texture and delicate flavors that make fish so attractive in the first place. It's okay to freeze fish once you get it home, but only if it hasn't been frozen before. Check the label to see if it says "previously frozen," or ask the merchant to be sure.

She Loves Fish, He Hates It

Mary Ellen Harvey of Loch Arbour, New Jersey, absolutely loves fish, bluefish especially. Her husband, on the other hand, is a meat-and-potatoes kind of guy. Patrick will eat the occasional flounder, shrimp, or lobster, but on the whole, he'd just as soon avoid anything that tastes "too fishy." Here's how Mary Ellen, 38, restored family harmony and even got her husband to join in.

Growing up on the shores of New Jersey, I always had an affinity for fish of any kind, even anchovies. My dad would catch bluefish, and he and I would eat them while my mother and sister stayed clear.

As I got older, I was happy to learn that the fish I always loved is among the healthiest foods you can eat. I wanted to share this with my husband, Patrick, but he was impossible to convince. He simply hates fish. I have a hard time understanding this, I admit. I love the fishy taste of bluefish. My friends know this, and they always share their catches with me. It drives Patrick crazy when he opens the freezer and sees that it's jammed with bluefish.

I tried just about everything to turn him around. Simple recipes, recipes with exotic ingredients, and recipes with lots of butter, lemon, and garlic. He always refused to eat it. This was starting to cause some friction because every time I made bluefish for supper, I had to make something else for Patrick. I talked to my mother-in-law and told her what was going on. Knowing his finicky tastebuds, she had a great suggestion.

She recommended that I really dress the fish up to disguise that fishy flavor. So I put it in foil and surrounded it with lots of tomatoes, onions, and garlic, plus some salt and pepper. I cooked it on the grill for about 15 minutes and served it with rice.

The mound of vegetables and all the seasonings helped take the edge off the fishy smell and taste, so much so that Patrick ate it, not just that first time but afterward as well. I won't say that he loves it; he doesn't. In fact, the deal is that I can't make it more than once a week. But he has gotten to the point where he doesn't complain, and that works for me. I don't have to cook an extra meal, and I'm still able to enjoy my favorite dish. The fact that we're not fighting about it anymore is a great bonus.

Poach for convenience. Fish cooks so quickly that most techniques—sautéing, grilling, and steaming, for example—work well. Poaching is one of the easiest methods, especially if you are cooking a whole fish. Even if you cook it a little too long, the moist, steamy heat will ensure that the fish is moist and tender. Fish that has been poached is also great as a leftover because it holds moisture and stays tender.

Reduce the fishy smell. One reason why people don't cook fish more often is because they dislike the penetrating smell as it cooks. You can subdue odors by adding a small amount of an acidic ingredient, such as lemon juice or flavored vinegar, during cooking.

Follow the 10-minute rule. Whether you're baking, broiling, steaming, poaching, or grilling whole fish, plan on cooking it 10 minutes for every inch of thickness, turning it halfway through the cooking time. If the fish is being cooked in foil or in a sauce, add 5 minutes to the total time. Fillets may take less time.

Roast Salmon with Ginger and Garlic

4 salmon steaks (8 oz each and 1" thick)
1 tsp oil
1 tsp minced ginger
2 tsp minced garlic

FRIED FISH—THE HEALTHY WAY

If you love the taste of fried fish but want to avoid the fat and fuss, try this easy fish coating. The secret is cereal flakes and a small amount of butter or oil. The mixture gives fish a nice crumbly coating, with one-fourth the fat of a traditional breaded fried fish fillet.

Crispy Fish Fillets

1 c unsweetened cereal flakes, such as Wheaties or Special K
2 Tbsp all-purpose flour
1 Tbsp crab-boil seasoning, such as Old Bay
4 flounder, trout, or tilapia fillets
1 Tbsp butter or oil

Pour the cereal into a plastic bag and crush with a rolling pin into fine crumbs. Add the flour and crab-boil seasoning. Shake to mix well. Place a fish fillet in the bag, close, and shake gently to coat with the crumbs. Shake off the excess. Repeat with the remaining 3 fillets.

Heat the butter or oil in a 12" nonstick skillet over medium heat. Place the fillets in the skillet. Raise the heat to medium-high. Cook for 4 to 5 minutes, or until the fish is golden brown. Turn and brown on the other side.

Preheat oven to 500°F. Coat the broiler rack with nonstick spray.

Place the salmon on the rack and drizzle with the oil. Sprinkle with ginger and garlic, patting the steaks lightly and evenly over the surface. Bake for 9 to 13 minutes, or until the fish is opaque.

Makes 4 servings
Per serving: 317 calories, 15 g fat

Crab Cakes

8 oz lump or backfin crabmeat, flaked
1 c fresh white or whole wheat bread crumbs
1 Tbsp finely chopped onion
1 Tbsp finely chopped celery
1 Tbsp finely chopped red bell pepper
1 Tbsp finely chopped fresh parsley
1 egg, lightly beaten
1 egg white, lightly beaten
2 tsp Worcestershire sauce
1 tsp lemon juice
½ tsp hot-pepper sauce
⅛ tsp ground black pepper
2 tsp canola oil

In a medium bowl, combine the crabmeat, bread crumbs, onion, celery, bell pepper, parsley, egg, egg white, Worcestershire sauce, lemon juice, hot-pepper sauce, and black pepper. If time permits, cover and chill to make handling easier.

Shape the crab mixture into 4 cakes.

Warm the oil in a large nonstick skillet over medium-high heat. Add the crab cakes and cook for 5 to 7 minutes per side, or until golden.

Makes 4 servings
Per serving: 87 calories, 4.5 g fat

HEALTHY— OR NOT?
Shrimp

Shrimp has a bad reputation because it's one of the few types of seafood with a substantial amount of cholesterol. Four large shrimp, for example, have 43 milligrams of cholesterol, 14 percent of the maximum recommended daily amount. One big shrimp dinner could blow a woman's cholesterol budget for the entire day.

Researchers have found, however, that most of the cholesterol in shrimp and other foods is broken down in the liver. In fact, dietary cholesterol doesn't play a big role in raising cholesterol in the blood. What does raise blood cholesterol is saturated fat, and shrimp has virtually no saturated fat, says Sheah Rarback, R.D., assistant professor in the department of pediatrics at the University of Miami School of Medicine and a spokeswoman for the American Dietetic Association.

Shrimp does contain fat, only it's a special kind of fat. Along with other types of shellfish, shrimp contains omega-3 fatty acids, which have been shown to reduce the risk of heart disease. In fact, people who eat a lot of seafood tend to have lower cholesterol and blood pressure levels than even vegetarians who don't eat shellfish. There's some evidence that omega-3's may reduce the risk of breast cancer and gallstones as well.

Apart from their omega-3's, shrimp also contain nutrients such as vitamin B_{12}, which are difficult to get from other food sources. So you really can't go wrong by eating more shrimp, as long as you don't eat it breaded and deep-fried or swimming in a sea of butter.

Blackened Catfish

1 c quick-cooking white rice
2 c water
1 tomato, finely chopped
¼ c minced scallions
¼ tsp salt
Pinch of dried thyme
4 catfish fillets (4 oz each and ½" thick)
2 Tbsp Cajun Spice Rub (page 83)

In a medium saucepan, combine the rice, water, tomato, scallions, salt, and thyme. Bring to a boil over medium-high heat. Cover, reduce the heat to low, and cook for 10 minutes, or until the rice is tender and the liquid is absorbed.

Meanwhile, heat a large cast-iron skillet over high heat for 8 minutes, or until a drop of water sizzles on the surface.

Coat the catfish with nonstick spray. Rub in the spice rub, coating each piece well. Place the catfish in the skillet and cook for 2 minutes per side, or until the fish flakes easily. Serve over the rice.

Makes 4 servings
Per serving: 236 calories, 7.5 g fat

Roasted Swordfish with Herbed Crust

4 swordfish steaks (5 oz each)
1 Tbsp lemon juice
⅓ c unseasoned bread crumbs
1½ tsp Italian Herb Blend (page 15)
1 Tbsp minced fresh parsley or 1 tsp dried
½ tsp salt
½ tsp ground black pepper

Heat the oven to 400°F. Coat a large nonstick baking dish with nonstick spray.

(continued)

Sprinkle the swordfish with the lemon juice and set aside for 10 minutes.

In a shallow bowl, combine the bread crumbs, herb blend, parsley, salt, and pepper. Dip the swordfish into the bread crumb mixture and press gently to coat both sides.

Place the swordfish in a single layer in the prepared baking dish. Generously coat the surface of the fish with nonstick spray. Bake for 20 to 25 minutes, or until the swordfish is opaque.

Makes 4 servings

Per serving: 210 calories, 6.5 g fat

Poached Sole with Italian Vegetables

- 1 c chicken broth
- 1 tomato, peeled and chopped
- 1 small green bell pepper, cut into thin strips
- 1 small onion, sliced
- 1 c sliced mushrooms
- 1 garlic clove, minced
- ⅛ tsp ground black pepper
- 4 skinless sole fillets (about 4 oz each and ¼"–½" thick)
- 2 Tbsp grated Parmesan cheese

In a large skillet, combine the broth, tomato, bell pepper, onion, mushrooms, garlic, and black pepper. Cover and bring to a boil over medium-high heat. Carefully add the sole. Reduce the heat to low, cover, and gently simmer for 3 to 6 minutes, or until the fish flakes easily and is opaque.

Using a slotted spatula or spoon, transfer the sole to a serving platter. Spoon the vegetable mixture over the sole. Sprinkle with the cheese.

Makes 4 servings

Per serving: 156 calories, 3 g fat

HEALTHY— OR NOT?
Sushi

Sushi has become increasingly popular, but a lot of women are still reluctant to eat raw fish, not necessarily because of the taste but because of concerns about safety. As with raw meats, raw fish may contain harmful bacteria and parasites. The resulting digestive discomfort can make the flu seem like a holiday.

Don't let worries about health keep you out of sushi bars, says Sheah Rarback, R.D., assistant professor in the department of pediatrics at the University of Miami School of Medicine and a spokeswoman for the American Dietetic Association. Food poisoning from sushi is extremely rare, she explains. As long as fish is bought fresh, kept cold, and prepared in a clean environment, it's no more likely to cause illness than the steak or seafood that you cook at home.

In fact, sushi may be even safer than home-cooked fish, says Rarback. Sushi chefs spend years learning about proper food hygiene, and they know the importance of handling fish carefully. In addition, the fish that are served in sushi bars, such as bluefin tuna, swordfish, and flounder, rarely harbor parasites.

There is one caveat, however. Busy sushi bars sell fish almost as fast as they can slice it, which means that it's always fresh. Smaller, out-of-the-way restaurants may wind up keeping fish for several days. This increases the risk of contamination. "Go to a clean sushi bar that does a lot of business," Rarback says. "That way, you'll know you're getting fresh fish."

FRESH FISH TOPPINGS

Poached or steamed fish cooks in minutes, making it one of the fastest meals you can make. To add additional flavors without sacrificing speed, try these fish toppings. They're ready in minutes, and they give fish depth and complexity that you can't get with lemon alone.

Creamy Horseradish Sauce

¼ c reduced-fat sour cream
1½ tsp drained prepared horseradish
1 tsp Dijon mustard

In a small bowl, combine the sour cream, horseradish, and mustard.

Makes ¼ cup
Per 1 teaspoon: 22 calories, 1.5 g fat

Dill Sauce

¼ c low-fat cottage cheese
¼ c fat-free plain yogurt
2 tsp Dijon mustard
1 tsp lemon juice
1 tsp minced scallions
⅛ tsp soy sauce (optional)
1 Tbsp finely chopped fresh dill or
   ½ teaspoon dried

Using a blender or food processor, puree the cottage cheese, yogurt, mustard, lemon juice, scallions, and soy sauce (if using) until smooth. Transfer to a small bowl and stir in the dill. Cover and refrigerate. Serve at room temperature.

Makes ½ cup
Per 1 tablespoon: 21 calories, 0.5 g fat

Tartar Salsa

⅓ c mild thick-and-chunky salsa
⅓ c fat-free mayonnaise
1 Tbsp lemon juice

In a small bowl, combine the salsa, mayonnaise, and lemon juice. Mix well.

Makes ⅔ cup
Per 2 tablespoons: 26 calories, 0 g fat

Baked Cod with Crumb Topping

¼ c fine bread crumbs
2 Tbsp grated Parmesan cheese
1 Tbsp cornmeal
1 tsp olive oil
½ tsp Italian Herb Blend (page 15)
⅛ tsp garlic powder
⅛ tsp ground black pepper
4 skinless cod fillets (about 4 oz each and ½" thick)
1 egg white, lightly beaten

Preheat the oven to 450°F.

In a small shallow bowl, stir together the bread crumbs, cheese, cornmeal, oil, herb blend, garlic powder, and pepper; set aside.

Coat the rack of a broiler pan with nonstick spray. Place the cod on the rack, folding under any thin edges of the fillets. Brush with the egg white, then spoon the crumb mixture evenly on top.

Bake for 10 to 12 minutes, or until the fish flakes easily and is opaque.

Makes 4 servings
Per serving: 164 calories, 4 g fat

PERFECT POACHING WITH COURT BOUILLON

Poaching captures the real flavor of seafood because it doesn't mask its subtle tastes. Poaching means cooking food in barely simmering liquid.

The usual rule is to simmer food for 15 minutes for every inch of thickness. You can poach in plain water, but many chefs prefer to use a classic poaching broth like the one in this recipe.

Court Bouillon

2 large carrots, sliced
1 large onion, sliced
1 tsp coriander seeds
4 fresh parsley sprigs
1 bay leaf
1 fresh thyme sprig (optional)
3 Tbsp vinegar (any type other than balsamic)
4 c water
1 c white wine
   Salt
   Ground black pepper

In a large saucepan, combine the carrots, onion, coriander seeds, parsley, bay leaf, and thyme (if using). Stir in the vinegar, water, and wine. Bring to a boil over high heat. Season to taste with salt and pepper. Boil for 10 minutes. Remove and discard the bay leaf, thyme, and parsley sprigs.

Use immediately, or cover and store in the refrigerator for up to 3 days or in airtight containers in the freezer for up to 6 months.

When using, bring to a good simmer before adding fish. Use enough to just cover the fish in the pan.

Makes 5 cups
Per cup: 61 calories, 0.5 g fat

Broiled Barbecued Sea Bass

1 can (8 oz) tomato sauce
3 Tbsp canned diced green chile peppers or jalapeño chile peppers
2 Tbsp fat-free Italian salad dressing
1 Tbsp finely chopped onion
1 Tbsp honey
2 tsp Worcestershire sauce
4 sea bass steaks (4 oz each and 1" thick)

Preheat the broiler.

In a small bowl, stir together the tomato sauce, peppers, salad dressing, onion, honey, and Worcestershire sauce. Transfer 1 cup of the mixture to a small saucepan and set aside until just before serving.

Coat the rack of a broiler pan with nonstick spray. Place the bass on the rack. Broil for 4 minutes. Turn the bass over and generously brush with some of the sauce in the bowl. Broil, brushing occasionally with the remaining sauce, for 6 to 8 minutes longer, or until the fish flakes easily.

Just before serving, bring the sauce in the saucepan just to a boil over medium-high heat. Serve the sauce with the bass.

Makes 4 servings
Per serving: 191 calories, 5.5 g fat

Herbed Scallops with Tomatoes

12 oz sea scallops
1 Tbsp reduced-calorie margarine
1 tsp Poultry Seasoning (page 15)
1 large onion, cut into thin wedges
2 large tomatoes, cut into thin wedges
1 Tbsp lemon juice

Pat the scallops dry with paper towels. Cut any large scallops into 1" pieces.

Melt the margarine in a large skillet over medium-high heat. Add the poultry seasoning. Blend, stirring constantly.

Add the scallops and onion. Cook and stir for 3 minutes, or until the scallops are opaque. (If the scallops release water during cooking, use a slotted spoon to remove the scallops and onion. Cook the liquid over medium heat until most of it has evaporated. Then return the scallops and onion to the skillet.)

Add the tomatoes and lemon juice. Cook, stirring occasionally, for 1 minute, or until the tomatoes are heated through.

Makes 4 servings
Per serving: 118 calories, 2.5 g fat

HEALTH BONUS

More Fat, Better Tuna

The next time you're buying canned, water-packed white tuna, take a moment to read the label. Those with the most fat—the usual range is 0.5 to 5 grams a serving—will provide the largest amount of heart-healthy omega-3 fatty acids.

Meat Treats

With the exception of roasts, most cuts of beef and pork cook quickly—as fast, in many cases, as a side dish of vegetables. They freeze well, so they're always on hand and ready. And because they're so full of flavor, you don't have to spend time creating extravagant sauces or otherwise dressing them up.

Of course, there is that pesky issue of fat. Women have adjusted by reducing serving sizes and sometimes using meat as an ingredient rather than an entrée in its own right, says Sue Snider, Ph.D., food and nutrition specialist at the University of Delaware's department of animal and food sciences in Newark.

To get the best tastes from meats in the shortest possible time, here are some easy tips that you may want to try.

Slice thin, cook fast. You can't cook large cuts of meat quickly—even the average steak may take 8 to 10 minutes per side. But you can substantially reduce cooking time by slicing meat thin and grilling, stir-frying, or sautéing it, Dr. Snider says. As long as the pan is hot when you start, beef and pork slices will cook in as little as 3 minutes. At that point, they can be eaten alone or added to stir-fries, soups, or stews.

Make an instant marinade. Traditional marinades usually require soaking meats in a liquid for several hours or overnight to tenderize and add flavor. When meat is cut thin, however, it will tenderize in as little as 20 to 30 minutes. You can make a quick marinade by combining an acidic ingredient such as vinegar or lemon juice with a little oil and spices.

Braise for convenience. Cooking on the grill or stove top is fast, but you have to watch the meat constantly. An alternative is braising. With this technique, pot roasts or other large cuts of meat are slowly simmered in a flavorful liquid. Braising takes an hour or more, but it's hands-off cooking. Once the meat is browned and covered with liquid, you can forget about it until it's done.

Slow cookers, or Crock-Pots, incidentally, are just a modern type of braising. Slow-cooking is slow, but it requires even less attention than conventional braising, says Dr. Snider. Many women load their slow cookers in the morning

WOMAN TO WOMAN

She Turned Comfort Foods into Healthy Foods

Susan Weiner, R.D., chief dietitian of the Hain Food Group in Long Island, New York, is the first to admit that she hasn't always practiced what she taught. Even though Susan has worked as a nutritionist since the 1980s, at one time, she rarely took the time to apply what she knew about nutrition to her own cooking. Then her father-in-law died of a heart attack and her father had a stroke. Susan had a wake-up call. Here's her story.

Even though I'm a registered dietitian, cooking was never a priority in my life. I've always had such a hectic work schedule, and I have two boys to raise. To be honest, we ate a lot more take-out food than home-cooked meals. Even when I did cook, I used traditional recipes. I didn't think about fat. My lasagna was more meat and cheese than noodles. I don't even want to think about what it was doing to my health.

Then my father-in-law died of a heart attack. He was only 62. A couple of years later, my father, who was the picture of good health, had a serious stroke. Both of these incidents made me sit up and take notice. I decided that healthy cooking had to be a priority.

I didn't want to give up our favorite foods, and my family didn't want to give them up either. And yet, I knew they were loaded with fat and calories. So I started thinking: Maybe there was some way to keep the comfort foods but somehow incorporate them into a healthier style of eating.

I started reading cookbooks with recipe makeovers. I quit using ground beef and started using ground chicken in meat loaf. Once I'd added the sauce and spices, I couldn't tell the difference. I even created my own spinach and turkey meat loaf, and it tasted great. I knew I was on to something.

One experiment led to another. For lasagna, I started substituting tofu for ground beef. And instead of just using lasagna noodles to line the pan, I started adding strips of zucchini.

Now, I have a whole repertoire of healthy substitutes. In place of ground beef, I'll use either ground turkey or chicken, or sometimes textured vegetable protein. Instead of eggs, I use mashed tofu. Instead of high-fat cheese and milk, I substitute soy.

None of these changes added to the time that I spent in the kitchen. In some ways, in fact, I'm saving time. I always make sure that there are plenty of ingredients in the pantry and freezer, and I've gotten in the habit of doubling recipes. That way, there are always leftovers, which I freeze for ready-to-eat meals later in the week. I've also started doing a lot of cooking on Sundays. I have more time then, so I can make a few different things to keep us going during the week.

Ever since I started making these changes, I keep coming up with ways to do things faster and more efficiently. More important, we're still eating the same foods that we've always loved. All that has changed is what goes into them. We're eating healthier than we ever did before, and looking back, I'm surprised that I ever did it any other way.

with meats and other ingredients, then leave for the day. When they come home, the house is filled with good smells, and a completed meal is ready to go.

Save time with hams. Depending on how they're trimmed, fresh hams can be high in fat, but preserved, precooked hams are often quite lean. And because they're already cooked (be

WOMEN ASK WHY

Why is comfort food so com-forting—and so fattening?

Everyone has different foods that they feel are special. There's no such thing as a universal comfort food. But all comfort foods do have something in common. They're generally foods that remind us of our childhoods.

Maybe it's the aroma and taste of pot roast, or cookies and milk in the afternoon, or a big piece of warm apple pie crested with a melting dome of vanilla ice cream. These foods once gave us the feeling that we were home, safe, and cared for. As adults, we unconsciously try to re-capture that warm glow by turning to foods that we associate with simpler, less stressful times.

Unfortunately, most of our comfort foods have their origins in a time when we knew a lot less about nutrition than we know today. It wasn't so long ago, in fact, that official food guides recommended very high fat diets. We've since learned that our bodies actually need more whole grains, fruits, and vegetables and less fat. But our emotions don't see it this way, so we continue to seek solace in high-fat foods.

We do have the unique opportunity to change the future, however. Just as we look back to our childhoods and our childhood foods, our children will someday look back to theirs. Their warmest memories may be of low-fat carrot cake on a special day, or a baked pear on a cold winter's night. Many years hence, when they're adults and looking for comfort of their own, they'll find themselves turning to the foods that they remember best. And their choices may be a lot healthier than ours have been.

Expert Consulted
Sue Snider, Ph.D.
Food and nutrition specialist
Department of animal and food
*   sciences*
University of Delaware
Newark

sure that it says "fully cooked" on the label), all you have to do is heat them in the oven or microwave until they're warmed through.

Buy it whole, cut it small. It's convenient to use prepackaged stew meats, but the pieces generally haven't been well-trimmed. You can get almost the same convenience by buying larger cuts, cutting them into pieces, and freezing them in meal-size packages. Doing this once a month or so means that you'll always have meat in the freezer that's ready to go.

Here's a shortcut for trimming fat or cutting meat into chunks: Do it when the meat is par-tially frozen. The firm meat won't slide around, and as long as your knife is sharp, you'll be done in a few minutes.

Beef and Noodle Paprikash

    8 oz extra-lean ground beef
    1 large onion, chopped
    1 small celery rib, chopped
    1 small apple, chopped
 1⅔ c sliced mushrooms
    2 c defatted beef broth
  ½ tsp dried thyme

¼ tsp caraway seeds

2 c medium egg noodles

1 Tbsp paprika

3 Tbsp tomato paste

2 Tbsp fat-free plain yogurt

Coat a large nonstick skillet with nonstick spray. Crumble the beef into the pan. Add the onion, celery, apple, and mushrooms. Cook, breaking up the mixture with a wooden spoon, over medium-high heat for 4 to 5 minutes, or until the meat is lightly browned.

Stir in the broth, thyme, caraway seeds, and noodles. Bring to a boil.

Reduce the heat to medium-low, cover, and simmer for 5 to 8 minutes, or until the noodles are just tender.

Stir in the paprika and tomato paste. Cover and simmer for 5 minutes.

Remove from the heat and stir in the yogurt.

Makes 4 servings
Per serving: 275 calories, 8 g fat

Corned Beef Hash

2 c finely chopped cooked reduced-fat corned beef

1 can (15 oz) potatoes, drained and chopped

1 small onion, finely chopped

1 teaspoon Everyday Spice Blend (page 15)

In a large bowl, combine the corned beef, potatoes, onion, and spice blend. Mix well.

Coat a large nonstick skillet with nonstick spray and place over medium heat until hot. Spread the mixture evenly in the pan, pressing firmly with a spatula. Cook, stirring or turning frequently, for 10 to 15 minutes, or until browned.

Makes 4 servings
Per serving: 130 calories, 2.5 g fat

HEALTHY— OR NOT?

Liver

It's one of those foods that everyone loves to hate. Chefs love the texture and intense flavors of liver, but they're never sure if anyone will order it. Dietitians appreciate liver's nutritional payload but not its massive amounts of cholesterol. And children, well, they just hate it.

First, cholesterol: Liver contains more cholesterol than just about any other food. Three ounces of beef liver, for example, contain 331 milligrams of cholesterol. Chicken liver is even worse, with 536 milligrams in a serving. To put this in perspective, an egg, which is hardly a cholesterol lightweight, has just 212 milligrams of cholesterol.

These astronomical numbers aren't as bad as they seem because the cholesterol you get in foods generally isn't as harmful as the cholesterol your body makes. Still, if your cholesterol is running high—say, more than 200 milligrams per deciliter of blood—liver isn't going to be the best choice.

On the plus side, liver is packed with nutrients, especially iron. A serving of beef liver has 6 milligrams of iron, more than twice the amount in other cuts of beef. This is why liver is often recommended for people with iron deficiency anemia. Liver is also very high in vitamin B_{12}, and it's loaded with vitamin A— 30,300 international units (IU) in a serving, far in excess of the Daily Value of 5,000 IU.

The bottom line is this: If you enjoy the taste of liver and your cholesterol is in a healthy range, having it a few times a month isn't going to be a problem.

Skillet Beef and Rice

　1　tsp olive oil
　1　large onion, coarsely chopped
1¼　lb extra-lean ground beef
　2　tsp minced garlic
　1　tsp Italian Herb Blend (page 15)
　8　oz sliced mushrooms
　1　green bell pepper, coarsely chopped
　2　tsp Worcestershire sauce
　1　can (14½ oz) beef broth
　1　can (10¾ oz) reduced-fat cream of mushroom soup
2½　c instant rice
　　Salt
　½　cup finely shredded sharp Cheddar cheese

Warm the oil in a deep nonstick skillet over medium heat. Add the onion. Then add the beef and raise the heat to high. Add the garlic, herb blend, and mushrooms. Cook, turning and breaking up the meat from time to time.

Add the pepper and Worcestershire sauce. Cook, stirring frequently, for 5 to 6 minutes, or until the meat is crumbled and browned. Stir in the broth, soup, and rice. Cover and bring to a boil. Cook, stirring occasionally, for 5 minutes, or until the rice absorbs most of the liquid.

Season to taste with salt and sprinkle with the cheese. Cover and cook for 1 to 2 minutes, or until the cheese melts.

Makes 6 servings
Per serving: 320 calories, 8 g fat

Variations

French Beef and Rice: Add 2 tablespoons chopped fresh tarragon or 2 teaspoons dried fines herbes (a blend of tarragon, parsley, chives, and chervil, available at grocery and cooking stores).
Indian Beef and Rice: Stir in 2 teaspoons mild or hot curry powder and 2 tablespoons chopped fresh coriander.
Mexican Beef and Rice: Mix in 1 tablespoon chili powder.

Bangers and Beans

　1　can (16 oz) baked beans
　1　package (14 oz) low-fat kielbasa
　4　slices whole wheat bread
　　Yellow mustard
　　Prepared horseradish

Place the beans in a small saucepan and bring to a simmer over medium heat.

Preheat the broiler. Halve the kielbasa lengthwise, then quarter it crosswise. Place, cut side up, on the broiler pan and broil for 5 minutes, or until browned.

Lightly toast the bread. Top with the beans and kielbasa. Serve with mustard and horseradish.

Makes 4 servings
Per serving: 273 calories, 6 g fat

Pork Cutlets with Apple Slices

　1　tsp grated lemon peel
　1　tsp fresh thyme or ¼ tsp dried
　1　garlic clove, minced
10　oz pork tenderloin, trimmed of all visible fat and cut into 8 equal slices
　1　tsp olive oil
2–3　tart baking apples (such as Granny Smith or Jonathan), cut into ½" wedges
　2　Tbsp lemon juice

On a plate, combine the lemon peel, thyme, and garlic. Lightly rub the pork with the herb mixture.

Warm the oil in a large nonstick skillet over medium heat. Add the pork and cook for 3 minutes per side to brown.

Push the pork to one side of the pan. Add the apples and 1 tablespoon of the lemon juice.

Cook, turning the apples as they brown, for 5 minutes.

Rearrange the pork so that the slices are in a single layer under the apples. Cover and cook for 5 minutes, or until the apples are tender and the pork is tender and no longer pink.

Transfer to a platter. Add the remaining 1 tablespoon lemon juice to the pan and scrape up any browned bits. Drizzle the juices over the pork and apples.

Makes 4 servings
Per serving: 133 calories, 3.5 g fat

Cranberry-Glazed Pork Chops

      4 pork loin chops (about 4 oz each), trimmed of all visible fat
    ¼ tsp ground black pepper
    2 tsp cornstarch
    ¾ c apple-cranberry juice
    ½ c dried cranberries
    I Tbsp minced fresh tarragon or ½ tsp dried
    I Tbsp minced fresh parsley or I tsp dried
    I tsp honey
    2 c hot cooked brown rice

Sprinkle both sides of the chops with the pepper; set aside.

Coat a large nonstick skillet with nonstick spray and place over medium heat. Add the chops and cook for 3 minutes. Turn the chops and cook for 2 to 3 minutes longer, or until no longer pink. Transfer to a plate.

In a small bowl, stir the cornstarch into the apple-cranberry juice until dissolved. Add the juice mixture to the skillet, stirring and scraping to loosen any browned bits from the bottom. Stir in the cranberries, tarragon, parsley, and honey. Cook and stir until slightly thickened.

Add the chops to the skillet. Spoon the sauce over the chops. Cook for 1 to 2 minutes longer, or until heated through. Serve with the rice.

Makes 4 servings
Per serving: 296 calories, 6 g fat

MARBLE GARBLE

Think you're better off spending more for a marbled cut of meat? If you don't mind spending the money and you're not worried about fat, then go for the marbling. Otherwise, don't.

"Marbling" refers to the small flecks of fat that are tucked away within a muscle, says Terry Dockerty, director of research information for the National Cattlemen's Beef Association in Chicago. Beef cuts with more marbling are usually labeled "prime" or "choice." Although many of today's health-conscious consumers have concerns about fat, more heavily marbled beef cuts continue to be perennial favorites.

Cuts of beef with less marbling, such as those labeled "select," aren't fat-free, but most of the fat rims the edges and is easily trimmed away. These meats are fine for stews and stir-fries, but they're not so good on the grill because they don't have enough fat to stay tender in a dry-heat environment.

When you're in the mood for steak, especially for grilling, you want to go with the "choice" grade. "The difference between choice and select isn't that great," Dockerty says. "For a 3-ounce portion, we're talking about a difference of 18 calories and about 2 grams of fat. You'll make a greater impact by trimming the outside fat than by going from choice to select."

Sloppy Burger Sandwiches

½ c boiling water

½ c bulgur

¾ c canned pinto or pink beans, rinsed and drained

½ c finely chopped onion

8 oz lean ground beef

⅔ c barbecue sauce, heated

6 whole grain hamburger buns

Onion slices

Lettuce leaves

Tomato slices

Fat-free blue cheese dressing

In a medium bowl, pour the water over the bulgur; let stand for 10 minutes. Drain well.

In a large bowl, mash the beans with a fork. Mix in the chopped onion and bulgur. Add the beef and mix well.

Coat a large nonstick skillet with nonstick spray. Add the beef mixture and cook, stirring occasionally, over high heat for 8 to 10 minutes, or until browned.

Spoon a little barbecue sauce over each bun bottom. Stir the remaining barbecue sauce into the beef mixture. Divide among the buns. Top with onion slices, lettuce, and tomato slices. Generously spread the dressing on the inside of the bun tops.

Makes 6 servings
Per serving: 251 calories, 2.5 g fat

Savory Beef Rolls

8 oz extra-lean ground sirloin

8 oz ground turkey breast

½ c dry bread crumbs

¼ c fat-free egg substitute

3 Tbsp finely chopped fresh cilantro or fresh parsley

3 Tbsp finely chopped fresh mint or 1 Tbsp dried

1 Tbsp ground cumin

1 Tbsp lemon juice

1 tsp ground ginger

1 Tbsp olive oil

In a large bowl, combine the sirloin, turkey, bread crumbs, egg substitute, cilantro or parsley, mint, cumin, lemon juice, and ginger. Work lightly with your hands until well-mixed. Form the mixture into small logs about 4" × ½".

Warm 1½ teaspoons of the oil in a large non-stick skillet over medium heat. Add half of the beef logs. Cook, turning occasionally, for 6 to 8 minutes, or until browned on all sides and no longer pink. Transfer to a platter and keep warm. Repeat with the remaining 1½ teaspoons oil and beef logs.

Makes 6 servings
Per serving: 194 calories, 10 g fat

Lamb Curry with Rice

1 medium eggplant, thinly sliced

1 onion, finely chopped

1 tsp minced garlic

1 c chicken broth

1 lb lean lamb (such as loin or shoulder), trimmed of fat and cut into ½" cubes

1 can (14 oz) whole tomatoes, chopped

1 Tbsp curry powder

1 tsp ground black pepper

½ tsp ground coriander

2 c hot cooked rice

½ c fat-free plain yogurt

¼ c finely chopped fresh cilantro

In a large nonstick skillet over medium-high heat, cook the eggplant, onion, garlic, and ⅓

PORK: IS IT REALLY WHITE MEAT?

Some years back, when the media began reporting about the health risks of fatty red meats, pork producers devised an ingenious advertising campaign. They started referring to pork as "the other white meat." Their message was that pork can be just as healthy as chicken, the "original" white meat.

Advertising gimmick or truth? Actually, a little of both, says Audrey Maretzki, Ph.D., professor of food science and nutrition at Pennsylvania State University in University Park. It's true that some cuts of pork are respectably low in fat. A 3-ounce serving of pork tenderloin, for example, has 4.1 grams of fat, which is not much more than a skinless chicken breast, with 3 grams of fat.

Well-trimmed pork chops and hams are also fairly lean. A cured ham, on the other hand, has 9 grams of fat per serving, and 3 ounces of pork backribs have 25 grams of fat. To put this in perspective, a serving of lean top loin steak has only about 6.6 grams of fat.

There's no reason not to eat pork, says Dr. Maretzki. It's high in thiamin, iron, and other nutrients. When you buy one of the leaner cuts and trim excess fat from the edges, you'll have a perfectly healthy meal as long as you don't go whole-hog on the portions. But that can be said of any meat, beef and chicken included.

---

cup of the broth for 5 minutes. Add the lamb, tomatoes (with juice), curry powder, pepper, coriander, and the remaining ⅔ cup broth. Bring to a boil.

Reduce the heat to medium. Cook, stirring occasionally, for 25 minutes, or until the lamb is no longer pink. Serve over the rice, topped with yogurt and cilantro.

Makes 4 servings
Per serving: 358 calories, 7 g fat

Vegetarian Specialties

Many women would like to cook more vegetarian meals. What they don't want is to spend even more time in the kitchen. Meat, after all, is a forgiving ingredient. It has strong flavors, so you don't have to worry too much about seasonings. And it's filling, which means that it's possible to make an entire meal of broiled chicken, maybe throwing together a salad as an afterthought. With vegetarian cooking, just about everything needs to be seasoned. Then there are all those vegetables to be washed and chopped. It sure can seem like a lot of bother.

It's true that preparing a vegetarian entrée might take more time than, say, frying a hamburger. But it's faster than roasting a chicken or defrosting and grilling a steak. Vegetables cook very quickly, especially when you use frozen or canned ingredients, says Leslie Moskowitz, R.D., a nutritionist with the Coventry Family Practice medical group in Phillipsburg, New Jersey. And the payoff—getting less saturated fat and more dietary fiber and important nutrients—makes learning a few vegetarian shortcuts well worth your time.

Quick-cook beans. Beans provide virtually all the nutrients that you'd get from meat, plus they're loaded with fiber. Dried beans, however, are very slow to cook. You can dramatically speed the cooking time by using a pressure cooker, which will cook beans in as little as an hour—three to four times faster than simmering them in an open pot. Canned beans, of course, come already cooked and just need to be heated.

Cook grains and beans in advance. Many vegetarian recipes call for grains and beans, either as part of the entrée or as side dishes. Since they keep well in the refrigerator and freezer, you can save a lot of time by cooking a big batch and storing meal-size portions in airtight containers.

Buy prepared vegetables. It doesn't take all that long to cut up an onion or strip the strings from peas, but it is one extra step. An easy shortcut is to load up on precut, prewashed vegetables at the supermarket. They'll keep for a week or more in the crisper drawer in the refrigerator, and they'll be ready whenever you are.

REAL-LIFE SCENARIO

Her Vegetarian Cooking Needs Some Help

Allyson, a health-conscious executive at a radio station, wants to instill good eating habits in her family, so she decided to cook vegetarian meals 3 nights a week. She knows, though, that the only way to get her kids to eat meatless meals is to cook things they truly like. Pasta was an instant hit. So were eggplant parmigiana, vegetable casseroles (with cheese), and pizza (with lots of cheese). The kids also developed a taste for baked potatoes—piled with broccoli and Cheddar cheese. Even though Allyson keeps seeing cheese-based recipes in her vegetarian cookbooks, she worries about the amount of fat and calories that she's putting on the table. She feels as though all her good intentions have gone totally awry. Have they?

Allyson is making the same mistake that a lot of new vegetarians make. She's assuming that the only way to get protein without meat is to eat a lot of cheese. That's simply not true. Whole grains and beans are good sources of protein; the cheese isn't necessary.

Not that cheese is a bad thing. It contains a lot of calcium, which she and her family need. And there are dozens of low-fat cheeses in supermarkets and specialty stores. They provide the same nutrients as whole cheese, with a lot fewer calories. Low-fat milk is another way to get calcium, and these days, it tastes virtually the same as whole milk. Most kids won't know the difference.

The fact that her family is clamoring for cheese-filled recipes suggests that she needs to spice up her cooking. Meats add a lot of flavor to foods, and when you stop using them, you have to compensate somehow. She could be serving things like meatless chili or tacos made with beans, lettuce, tomatoes, and a little shredded cheese (which goes a long way). Her kids will like these foods just as much as pizza.

If she finds that her family is truly missing meat, she may want to look into using soy-based substitutes. These used to taste pretty bad, but food producers have come a long way in improving the flavor and texture of foods such as soy burgers, which can be grilled in the same way as meat burgers.

It's good that the kids are eating pasta. It's healthy and it's very easy to dress up, with mushrooms, tomatoes, and broccoli, for example. Or, she could make vegetable lasagna, replacing full-fat cheese with low-fat cottage cheese or low-fat or nonfat ricotta.

Finally, Allyson needs to think beyond traditional meals a little bit. For example, she'd be very popular serving French toast at supper, maybe with a little fresh fruit. It tastes like dessert, but it's very nutritious. The more creative she gets, the more her children are going to look forward to vegetarian nights and the more likely they'll be to eat healthy foods when they're older.

Expert Consulted
Althea Zanecosky, R.D.
Spokesperson for the American Dietetic Association
Nutrition education specialist
Philadelphia

WOMAN TO WOMAN

She Became a Vegetarian to Save Her Son

Mary Purcell of Syracuse, New York, turned to vegetarian cooking after her son developed allergies. But the 40-year-old wife and mother knew that it wouldn't be easy changing the eating habits of her meat-eating family. So she tried a few tricks and got great results.

Like most of us, I grew up eating hamburgers, hot dogs, meat loaf, and other hearty meat dishes. I always thought that dinner had to revolve around meat—usually red meat.

Then, a few years ago, my then-7-year-old son developed allergies. I read that, in addition to dust and pollen, his allergies could be aggravated by red meat—more specifically, by the hormones, antibiotics, and pesticides that are given to livestock. I also read that eating too much red meat can compromise the immune system, making allergies worse.

Well, I never liked the idea of slaughtering animals anyway, and I didn't want to take chances with my son's health, so I started to read up on vegetarian diets and began trying some recipes.

I never told my family what I was up to. Like me, they were used to having meat, and I didn't want to cause a stir. So I made changes slowly. At first, I just reduced the amount of meat that I was using. Then, I began preparing meatless meals, not all the time, but pretty often. No one seemed to notice, so I kept at it. The more I experimented with vegetarian recipes, the more I realized how expendable meat really is. I made tomato sauces without hamburger, for example. For chili, I added oatmeal or bulgur wheat. I even made milkshakes with silken tofu.

I noticed the difference right away. Personally, I began to feel better. I noticed that I wasn't getting colds as often as I used to, and it became easier to maintain my weight. What's more important, my son's allergies began to clear up. I can't say for sure that it was because he was eating less meat. Maybe he just outgrew his allergies. But I suspect that the diet that was making me feel so much better had to be doing the same thing for him.

Cooking vegetarian has other advantages I hadn't thought about. For one thing, it's fast, and that counts a lot. I can steam or sauté vegetables in a few minutes. Grains and beans keep well, so it's easy to make quick meals out of leftovers.

Another bonus is that I'm saving money. Our weekly food bills have dropped $50.

I'm the only one in the family who has turned totally vegetarian. My son, like his father, still has red meat occasionally. But his allergies haven't come back. So, in a way, I'm grateful that this happened. We're all eating a lot healthier than we were before, and in the long run, that has to be good.

Take advantage of steam. Steam is hotter than boiling water, which is why steaming is an ideal way to cook vegetables quickly. Microwaving is even faster. Despite the technology, cooking vegetables in the microwave is really the same as steaming them, only faster.

Sauté with water. Vegetarian recipes often call for vegetables to be sautéed as a prelude to further cooking. You'll need some oil, or at least nonstick spray, to help them brown. You can reduce the oil to a smidgen by adding a tablespoon of water when the vegetables are about halfway

HEALTHY— OR NOT?
Milk

Despite an advertising campaign that has painted milk mustaches on the country's top athletes and celebrities, milk isn't always the wholesome food that it's made out to be. Quite simply, if you don't watch the type of milk you drink, you can end up with a glass that's loaded with fat: One glass of whole milk has 9 grams.

With this downside, why drink milk? Here's the trade-off: Milk is loaded with calcium, and it's one of the best food sources. One glass of whole milk has 290 milligrams of calcium, almost a third of the Daily Value of 1,000 milligrams. Since it's nearly impossible to get this much calcium from other food, doctors usually recommend drinking milk. It's especially important for women, who need large amounts of calcium to prevent the bone-thinning disease osteoporosis.

As it turns out, you can get all the benefits of milk without the problems by switching to fat-free, or skim, milk, says Elizabeth Somer, R.D., author of *Age-Proof Your Body*. "When they take the fat out, only the calories go down," she says. In fact, less fat means that there is more room for beneficial nutrients. Fat-free milk offers even more bone-building calcium than whole milk does, with 302 milligrams per serving.

Fat-free milk, incidentally, isn't the thin, gray watery stuff that it used to be. Many manufacturers, wise to the fact that people want good flavor without the fat, now offer richer-tasting versions.

done. This prevents sticking and helps them soften.

Add instant flavors. When you aren't in the mood to get creative with herbs and spices, you can season foods quickly at the table by splashing them with hot sauces or herbal vinegars.

Watch for hidden fat. People who are new to vegetarian cooking often make the mistake of replacing meat with regular cheese or by using lots of vegetables—fried. That three-cheese macaroni and fried zucchini may be meatless, but it isn't fatless. "At that point, you might as well go ahead and have hamburgers," says Marie Oser, author of *Soy of Cooking*.

To get the full benefits of vegetarian cooking, keep fat to a minimum by baking rather than frying, for example, or by using reduced-fat cheeses and milk. "Reduced-fat cheeses tasted pretty rubbery when they first came out, but they've gotten much better," says Deborah Slawson, R.D., Ph.D., nutrition coordinator of the Prevention Center at the University of Memphis.

Stuffed Red Tomatoes

½ c orzo or other small pasta
3 red tomatoes
1 Tbsp finely chopped fresh basil or 1 tsp dried
1 Tbsp finely chopped fresh parsley or 1 tsp dried
1 Tbsp chopped onion
2 Tbsp balsamic vinegar
1 Tbsp olive oil
1 tsp minced garlic
  Salt
  Ground black pepper
3 Tbsp shredded Parmesan cheese

Cook the pasta according to package directions. Drain.

Remove the stems from the tomatoes and halve crosswise. Remove the pulp and seeds, leaving the shells; set the shells aside. Measure ½ cup pulp and chop finely; place in a medium bowl. Stir in the basil, parsley, onion, vinegar, oil, and garlic. Season with salt and pepper to taste. Add the pasta and cheese; mix well.

Divide the pasta mixture among the tomato halves. Serve at room temperature.

Makes 6 servings

Per serving: 108 calories, 4 g fat

Spinach and Mushroom Frittata

½ c chopped onion
4 oz mushrooms, sliced
5 oz frozen chopped spinach, thawed and squeezed dry
4 eggs
6 egg whites
2 tsp water
1 tsp dried thyme
1 tsp dried oregano or marjoram
½ tsp salt
Pinch of ground black pepper

TOFU: VERSATILE AND HEALTHY

Although tofu has long been a staple in Asian cooking, here in America it has been seen more as a health food joke than as the truly versatile food that it is. Tofu's bad reputation is due mainly to the fact that, for a long time, most folks didn't know how to cook it, says Wendy Esko, a macrobiotic cooking instructor at the Kushi Institute in Becket, Massachusetts. It was often served overcooked, rubbery, and devoid of flavor.

Fortunately, most people have gotten over that and see tofu for what it really is—an extremely healthy food that can please almost any palate.

Tofu is made from soybeans, which contain compounds that may lower the risk of breast, endometrial, and colon cancers and also help prevent osteoporosis and strokes. Tofu also has the distinct ability to conform to the tastes of the ingredients with which it is served. So if the taste is off, it's more the fault of the cook, not the food.

Tofu is simple to incorporate into many recipes and can easily be used as a substitute for poultry and meat, says Esko. Many cooks use tofu as a substitute for meat in lasagna and other baked casseroles. It can also be used instead of, or to augment, the eggs in egg salad.

There are several varieties of tofu. The firm and extra-firm varieties are used for grilling and stir-frying as well as for meat substitutes. Soft tofu is often used for desserts such as cheesecake. Silken tofu, which has a soft, creamy texture, is often used for salad dressings and smooth sauces.

Esko has developed dozens of quick, healthy, and good-tasting ways to use tofu.

- Mix it with vinegar, dill, and scallions, then run it through the blender to make an extra-healthy salad dressing. You can also use this dressing to replace mayonnaise on sandwiches.

- Cut it into thin slices and pan-fry it in a small amount of olive or sesame oil. Then season it with soy sauce and maple syrup, and add a little water. You can then add these aromatic slices to salads or stir-fries.

- Marinate cubes of tofu in low-sodium soy sauce and a little rice wine vinegar, then crumble it into a salad as a substitute for feta cheese.

- Replace the ricotta cheese in lasagna with an equal amount of crumbled tofu.

Preheat the broiler.

Coat a large ovenproof nonstick skillet with nonstick spray. Warm over medium heat until hot. Add the onion and mushrooms. Cook, stirring occasionally, for 4 minutes, or until the mushrooms begin to release their liquid.

Add the spinach to the skillet and cook, stirring frequently, for 5 minutes, or until most of the liquid has evaporated.

Meanwhile, in a medium bowl, beat together the eggs, egg whites, water, thyme, oregano or marjoram, salt, and pepper. Add to the skillet and swirl to evenly distribute. Cook for 5 minutes, gently lifting the egg mixture from the sides of the skillet with a spatula as it becomes set. Cook until the eggs are set on the bottom but still moist on the top. Remove from the heat.

Wrap the handle of the skillet with 2 layers of heavy foil. Broil for 1 minute, or until the top is golden.

Use a spatula to loosen the frittata and slide it onto a serving plate. Cut into wedges and serve.

Makes 4 servings
Per serving: 123 calories, 5.5 g fat

Vegetarian Paella

    2 tsp canola oil
    8 oz firm tofu, drained and cubed
    1 large red bell pepper, cut into strips
    1 onion, chopped
    1 teaspoon minced garlic
2½ c crushed canned tomatoes
    1 package (10 ounces) frozen artichoke hearts, thawed
1½ cups frozen corn
    1 c frozen peas
1½ c chicken broth
    ½ tsp dried thyme
    ⅛ tsp ground saffron
    1 c couscous

Heat the oil in a paella pan or large skillet over medium heat. Add the tofu, pepper, onion, and garlic. Cook, stirring, for 4 to 5 minutes, or until the tofu is golden.

Stir in the tomatoes (with juice), artichokes, corn, and peas. Bring to a boil over high heat, then reduce the heat to low. Simmer for 5 to 7 minutes, or until the vegetables are tender and the liquid thickens slightly.

Add the broth, thyme, and saffron. Bring to a boil, then stir in the couscous. Remove the pan from the heat. Cover and let stand for 10 minutes. Fluff the couscous with a fork before serving.

Makes 4 servings
Per serving: 444 calories, 9 g fat

Tofu Layered with Three Cheeses

    ¼ c plus 2 Tbsp tomato sauce
    1 large egg white, lightly beaten
    1 c fat-free ricotta cheese
    ¼ c grated Parmesan cheese
    ¼ tsp ground nutmeg
    ¼ tsp ground black pepper
10 oz firm tofu, drained
    1 large tomato, cut into 8 slices
    ½ c loosely packed chopped fresh basil
    1 c shredded light mozzarella cheese

Preheat the oven to 350°F.

Spread ¼ cup of the tomato sauce in the bottom of an 8" × 8" baking dish; set aside.

In a medium bowl, stir together the egg white, ricotta, Parmesan, nutmeg, pepper, and the remaining 2 tablespoons tomato sauce; set aside.

Squeeze the tofu between layers of paper towels. Repeat until the towels no longer get very wet, then cut into 8 slices. Place 4 of the slices in the baking dish. On top of the tofu, layer half of each in the following order: the ricotta mixture, tomato slices, basil, and mozzarella. Repeat layering with the remaining tofu, ricotta mixture, tomatoes, basil, and mozzarella.

Bake 15 to 20 minutes, or until bubbly and the cheese is melted. Let stand for 5 minutes before cutting.

Makes 4 servings
Per serving: 264 calories, 13.5 g fat

Quick-Fry with Tofu and Vegetables

    2   c instant white or brown rice
    1   lb firm tofu, drained
    2   Tbsp soy sauce plus additional for seasoning
 1½   tsp peanut or canola oil
    2   Tbsp minced fresh ginger
    1   Tbsp minced garlic
   ½   tsp crushed red-pepper flakes
    6   oz mushrooms, sliced
    1   large red bell pepper, cut into thin strips
    6   scallions, cut into 1½" diagonal slices
    1   lb bok choy, coarsely chopped
    1   can (15 ounces) baby corn, drained
 1½   tsp toasted sesame oil

Cook the rice according to package directions.

Meanwhile, set the tofu between 2 plates and place a heavy pot on top. Set aside for 10 minutes to release excess water. Cut into ½" cubes and place in a container with a tight-fitting lid. Add the 2 tablespoons soy sauce and marinate, shaking occasionally, for 10 minutes.

Warm a wok or large nonstick skillet over medium-high heat. Add the peanut or canola oil and swirl to coat the pan. Add the ginger

HEALTH BONUS
Eggs Are Good for the Eyes

Egg yolks contain two compounds, lutein and zeaxanthin, that are members of the carotenoid family. People who get a lot of these compounds have lower rates of macular degeneration, a serious disease of the retina that's the leading cause of blindness in people over age 65.

The fat that's in egg yolks actually helps the body absorb these compounds. You'll get the protective benefits by eating four eggs a week.

and garlic. Stir-fry for 10 seconds. Add the red-pepper flakes, mushrooms, and bell pepper. Stir-fry for 2 to 3 minutes, or until the mushrooms release their liquid and the liquid has evaporated.

Stir in the scallions, bok choy, tofu, and tofu marinade. Cover and cook for 1 to 2 minutes, or until the bok choy is crisp-tender.

Stir in the corn, sesame oil, and additional soy sauce to taste. Serve over the rice.

Makes 4 servings
Per serving: 444 calories, 15.5 g fat

Red, White, and Green Pizza

    1   jar (7 oz) roasted red peppers
   ¼   c loosely packed fresh basil leaves
    1   Tbsp balsamic vinegar
    1   large prebaked pizza shell (such as Boboli)
    2   tsp olive oil
    2   Italian frying peppers, cut into strips
    1   green bell pepper, cut into strips
    1   red bell pepper, cut into strips

1 c rinsed and drained canned white beans

1 c thawed frozen chopped spinach, squeezed to remove excess moisture

1 c shredded reduced-fat mozzarella cheese

Preheat the oven to 425°F.

In a blender or food processor, combine the roasted peppers (with liquid), basil, and vinegar until smooth.

Place the pizza shell on a large baking sheet or pizza stone. Spread with the roasted pepper mixture; set aside.

Heat the oil in a large nonstick skillet over medium heat. Add the Italian peppers, green pepper, and red pepper. Cook and stir for 4 to 5 minutes, or until the peppers are tender.

To assemble the pizza, sprinkle the peppers, beans, spinach, and cheese on top of the pizza shell. Bake for 15 to 20 minutes, or until the cheese is melted and the crust is golden.

Makes 4 servings

Per serving: 452 calories, 10.5 g fat

HEALTH BONUS
Broccoli Fights Cancer

Want to add an easy cancer-fighting boost to your meals? Eat more broccoli. One study found that people who consume ½ cup of broccoli—that's about one stalk—a week are less likely to get cancer of the colon and rectum than people who eat none.

---

the lime juice, cumin, and hot-pepper sauce; set aside at room temperature for at least 1 hour.

Meanwhile, cook the pasta according to package directions. Drain.

Place the pasta in a large serving bowl. Add the salsa mixture and toss to mix well. Serve chilled or at room temperature.

Makes 4 servings

Per serving: 492 calories, 10 g fat

Wagon Wheels with Mexican Salsa

1 tomato, chopped

1 medium avocado, finely chopped

1 can (19 oz) black beans, rinsed and drained

½ c thawed frozen corn

2 Tbsp chopped fresh cilantro

1 Tbsp chopped canned chile pepper

Juice of 1 lime

1 tsp ground cumin

4–5 drops hot-pepper sauce

12 oz wagon wheel pasta

In a large bowl, combine the tomato, avocado, beans, corn, cilantro, and chile pepper. Stir in

---

Stuffed Spaghetti Squash

2 small spaghetti squash, halved lengthwise

1 Tbsp olive oil

1 large red bell pepper, chopped

1 c fresh or frozen peas

3 scallions, chopped

2 garlic cloves, minced

1 tsp dried oregano

1 tsp dried mint

1½ c tomato juice

1 c couscous

4 oz crumbled feta cheese

Place the squash halves, cut side down, on a microwaveable plate. Microwave on high power for 10 to 12 minutes, or until the squash is easily pierced with a fork. Cool until easy to handle. Spoon out and discard the seeds. With a fork, separate the flesh into strands and place in a large bowl. Reserve the squash shells.

Preheat the oven to 350°F.

In a large nonstick skillet over medium heat, warm the oil. Add the pepper, peas, scallions, garlic, oregano, and mint. Cook, stirring occasionally, for 5 minutes, or until the vegetables are tender.

Stir in the tomato juice and bring to a boil.

Stir in the couscous. Cover, remove from the heat, and let stand for 5 minutes, or until the couscous is soft. Fluff with a fork.

Add the couscous mixture and the cheese to the bowl with the squash. Toss to mix well. Divide among the reserved squash shells. Cover each shell with foil, place in a large baking dish, and bake for 15 to 20 minutes, or until heated through.

Makes 4 servings
Per serving: 369 calories, 10.5 g fat

Great Grills

The fantasy about grilling: A summer evening, happy friends and neighbors gathered in the yard, and aromatic odors wafting through the neighborhood.

The reality about grilling: A frustrating hour getting the coals started, unexpected bursts of flame, and a meal of charred, leathery meat, followed by another hour scraping granite-hard deposits from the grate.

Is it any wonder that many families grill only on the Fourth of July?

It's unfortunate that grilling has come to be seen as such an arduous process. It shouldn't be. Grilling can be just as fast as cooking indoors, and it's a super way to add rich, complex flavors to meats, vegetables, and even fruit, says Katherine B. Goldberg, R.D., culinary arts specialist at the University of Michigan's M-Fit Health Promotion Program in Ann Arbor and co-author of *The High Fit–Low Fat Vegetarian Cookbook.*

Start with a hot grate. You can virtually eliminate the knuckle-bruising ritual of cleaning the grate by just leaving the grill on high for 10 minutes after you have finished cooking and then scrubbing it with a stiff brush. You can reduce sticking even more by lightly spraying the cold rack with nonstick spray or by pouring a little cooking oil on a paper towel and rubbing it on the grate before adding heat.

Take the chill off poultry. Before grilling chicken or turkey, let it stand, covered, at room temperature for 15 minutes. Taking away the chill helps it cook more quickly and evenly.

Pre-cook poultry. Unless poultry is sliced very thin, it always cooks slowly on the grill. The long cooking time means that it often winds up charred on the outside even when it's raw inside. You can prevent this by poaching, baking, or microwaving poultry until it's about 50 percent done, then moving it to the grill for final cooking.

Slice tough vegetables. Most vegetables cook quickly on the grill, but potatoes, turnips, winter squash, and other dense vegetables are too tough for fast cooking. Cutting them into 1/2-inch slices and microwaving them for a few minutes will help them grill completely and evenly.

REAL-LIFE SCENARIO

She's Better Off Eating at Home

Nancy, determined to knock off the 15 pounds that she has put on over the years, wants to eat fish and salads, but her husband, John, is an adamant meat lover. Since they both work at well-paying jobs and Nancy hates to cook, they figured that the solution was simple enough: They'd just eat out a lot. What a great idea! Nancy loved the choices—mahimahi, salmon, paella, lobster, seafood gumbo, turbot. Dieting never seemed so good. Or so Nancy thought, until she started seeing the scale go up instead of down. John, meanwhile, is enjoying feeding his made-for-meat appetite, but he'd much rather be doing it at home, where he loves to grill. Pork tenderloin, flank steaks, and barbecued chicken are his specialties. He wants Nancy to get off the fish kick and get back to real food. Besides, they're spending too much money. Nancy, meanwhile, is just plain befuddled as to why her weight-loss plan isn't working.

It's no wonder Nancy isn't losing weight. Restaurant portions are notoriously large. That alone would explain the weight gain. Add to this the calories from all those sauces, drinks, and desserts, and it would be amazing if she *didn't* gain weight. If Nancy is serious about losing weight, she not only has to watch what she eats but also how much. Calories are calories, even when they come from healthier foods.

John's situation isn't any better. He's probably putting on a few pounds himself. Their plan, while well-intentioned, isn't doing either of them any good. They need to make a change, and the sooner they do it, the happier—and thinner—they're going to be.

The fact that John considers himself a grill master may be the solution for both of them. John is already grilling flank steak. This is good because flank steak is one of the leanest cuts, so Nancy should feel free to indulge. Chicken is good, too, as long as the skin is removed. Maybe it's time he started grilling some fish. A full-flavored fish such as salmon is absolutely wonderful grilled, and it cooks more quickly than meat or poultry. And why not grill vegetables? Slices of onion, chunks of squash, and even mushrooms stand up well to grilling, and they take on deep, smoky tastes that are impossible to get any other way.

Anyone who's trying to lose weight needs to cut down on her restaurant dining. Cooking at home makes it possible to control the ingredients as well as the portions. John and Nancy aren't going to be sacrificing taste in the slightest. They may discover that they've never eaten so well.

Expert Consulted
Connie M. Weaver, Ph.D.
Department head and professor
Department of food and
    nutrition
Purdue University
West Lafayette, Indiana

Slice and marinate. As with poultry, steaks and other thick cuts of meat take a long time to grill. This isn't a problem for heavily marbled meats because the fat keeps them moist. Lean meats, however, tend to get dry and tough before they're done. You'll get more tenderness and shorten the cooking time by cutting lean meats into slices and marinating them. "Marinating imparts flavor and moisture, just as fat does," says Goldberg.

Rub It the Right Way

One of the easiest ways to increase the flavor of meat while cutting back on fat is to slather the surface with spices or herbs. Spread these rub mixtures into the entire exposed surface of meat, poultry, or fish before grilling to create a zesty-flavored crust. Rubs can be put on dry, though adding a teaspoon of water or broth will help spread them more evenly. They're also tasty on baked or roasted potatoes and other vegetables.

Expect to use about a tablespoon of herbs per serving of meat. Just mix the ingredients together and store in an airtight container in a cool, dark place. They'll keep indefinitely.

Pepper Blend Rub

2 Tbsp ground black pepper
2 Tbsp paprika
¼ c chili powder
1 Tbsp crushed red pepper
¼ tsp garlic powder

Makes about ½ cup

Basic Barbecue Dry Rub

2 Tbsp paprika
2 Tbsp brown sugar
1 Tbsp garlic powder
1 Tbsp chili powder
1 Tbsp ground cumin
1 Tbsp ground black pepper
1 tsp dry mustard

Makes about ½ cup

Cajun Spice Rub

3 Tbsp paprika
3 tsp garlic powder
3 tsp onion powder
1½ tsp dried thyme
1½ tsp dried oregano
½ tsp ground black pepper
¼ tsp ground red pepper

Makes about ½ cup

When you're pressed for time, basting is as good as marinating because you don't have to plan ahead, Goldberg adds. Basting liquids are brushed onto meats and vegetables while they're cooking, she explains.

Recipes for marinades and basting liquids often will call for a lot of oil. You don't need it. Follow the recipe, but you can replace the oil with chicken or beef broth or with vegetable juice.

You can also add citrus juice or lemon zest. These ingredients will give food a tangy flavor. Don't add salt to basting liquids because it will draw moisture out of food, making it dry and tough.

Pepper-Marinated Flank Steak

2 tsp dried thyme
1 Tbsp minced garlic
½ tsp ground black pepper
1 Tbsp olive oil
1 lb flank steak, trimmed of all visible fat
1 lb sweet potatoes, peeled
4 small yellow squash, halved lengthwise

Preheat the grill.

In a cup, mix the thyme, garlic, and pepper with 1 teaspoon of the oil.

(continued)

Rub three-quarters of the mixture over the steak. Cover and refrigerate for at least 15 minutes to marinate. (Or marinate the night before and leave in the refrigerator overnight.)

CREATE YOUR OWN SUPER SALSAS

It's the new queen of condiments, and it's all you need to turn something simply cooked into something special. Salsa is now so popular that it's rivaling ketchup as America's favorite condiment. It's low-fat and full of nutritious ingredients. And it's your key to elevating fast, after-work dinners into something special.

If you haven't perused the salsa aisle lately, you'll be surprised at all the new brands and varieties that have cropped up. Verde, tomatillo, chipotle, mango, black bean, habanero, raspberry, and others share shelf space with more familiar types.

Most salsas are very low in fat, so you can generously spoon them over grilled chicken breasts and other lean foods. Many also contain nutrients such as vitamins C and A, iron, and fiber, so they earn their place on the table.

You can turn store-bought salsa into your own creations. Simply stir in . . .

- Chopped orange, mango, papaya, or pineapple
- Chunks of avocado and chopped cooked egg white
- Drained canned hominy
- Minced cilantro, parsley, garlic, onions, scallions, shallots, or hot peppers
- Drained canned black beans and thawed white corn kernels
- Mustard relish
- Toasted ground cumin, fennel, caraway, or anise

Add the remaining 2 teaspoons oil to the remaining herb mixture.

Cut the sweet potatoes in half lengthwise. Then cut each half lengthwise to make 4 long spears from each potato. Brush the sweet potatoes and squash halves with some of the herb mixture.

Place the sweet potatoes on the grill. Ten minutes later, add the squash. Cook both vegetables for 10 minutes, turning them frequently to grill evenly.

Place the steak on the grill. Cook for 6 minutes per side, or until a thermometer inserted in the center registers 160°F for medium.

Makes 4 servings
Per serving: 359 calories, 18 g fat

Warm Steak Salad

    1 beef top round steak (12 oz), cut ¾"
       thick and trimmed of all visible fat
    2 c spinach cut into ½"-wide shreds
 1½ c bite-size broccoli florets
   ¼ c rice vinegar
    2 Tbsp beef broth or water
    2 Tbsp soy sauce
    1 tsp honey
   ½ tsp grated fresh ginger
    1 garlic clove, minced

Cook the meat on a hot grill for 6 to 8 minutes per side, or until a thermometer inserted in the center registers 160°F for medium. Place the meat on a cutting board and slice on the diagonal into strips.

Arrange the spinach in a mixing bowl. Add the beef strips and broccoli.

In a small bowl, stir together the vinegar, broth or water, soy sauce, honey, ginger, and garlic. Pour over the steak and vegetables. Toss until coated. Arrange on a platter and serve.

Makes 4 servings
Per serving: 145 calories, 4 g fat

PERFECT GRILLED VEGETABLES

Grilling vegetables is not an exact science. Many variables come into play, from grill temperature to the size of the vegetables. Here are some guidelines for a few typically grilled vegetables.

Vegetable	Time per Side (min)	Grilling Instructions	Comments
Bell peppers (halved, stem and seeds removed)	3–5	Start skin side down; turn when grid marks appear	Don't overcook; cut side may take only 1 minute
Carrots (whole)	3–5	Cook covered	Brown; then wrap tightly in foil to complete
Corn (whole cobs, husks and silks removed)	5–7	Brown lightly on all sides	Serve whole, or cut kernels from the cobs
Eggplant (small: halve lengthwise; large: slice crosswise)	3–5	Turn when marks appear and it softens	Don't overcook
Mushrooms (whole, stems removed)	2–4	Top side down; turn when marks appear	Large mushrooms work best
Onions (halved)	5–7	Start cut side down; turn when fully browned	Best choice: medium yellow or red onions
Potatoes (halved lengthwise)	2	Cook cut side down until marks appear	Move to the edge; cover to complete; cut side may take up to 2 minutes longer
Sweet potatoes (halved lengthwise)	6–8	Cook cut side down until marks appear	Move to the edge; cover to complete
Zucchini or yellow squash (halved lengthwise)	3–5	Cook cut side down; turn when marks appear	Don't overcook

Zesty Barbecued Chicken Breasts

¼ c chili sauce

2 Tbsp ketchup

1 Tbsp honey

1 Tbsp red wine vinegar

1 tsp ground ginger

1 tsp Dijon mustard

¾ tsp ground black pepper

¾ tsp garlic powder

¼ tsp ground red pepper

4 boneless, skinless chicken breast halves

Coat a grill rack with nonstick spray. Preheat the grill.

In a small saucepan, combine the chili sauce, ketchup, honey, vinegar, ginger, mustard, black pepper, garlic powder, and red pepper. Bring to a boil over medium heat. Remove from the heat and set aside.

Place the chicken on the grill and brush with some of the sauce. Turn and brush on the other side with the remaining sauce. Grill the chicken for 5 minutes.

Turn and grill the chicken for 5 to 10 minutes longer, or until a thermometer inserted in the thickest portion registers 160°F and the juices run clear.

Makes 4 servings
Per serving: 180 calories, 3.5 g fat

BETTER BURGERS: HEALTH IN A BUN

Building a better burger means rethinking what goes into the mix and replacing fattier meats with healthy, low-fat ingredients. To get started, you'll need the leanest ground beef or ground poultry or a mixture of both. Add meaty sautéed chopped mushrooms and pungent seasonings. Then grill the burger so that excess fat drains away.

You can build upon the basic recipe by adding tasty cooked grains, such as bulgur, or vegetables, like shredded or chopped zucchini and red bell peppers. You can even add reduced-fat silken tofu.

When your burger is ready, slip it into a whole grain bun and pile it high with fresh lettuce, tomatoes, and flavorful fat-free toppings like salsa and mustard. You'll end up with a fast, stick-to-your-ribs meal that is actually good for you.

Mushroom-Onion Burgers

¼ c minced onion

½ c finely chopped mushrooms

1 tsp dried parsley or thyme

1 Tbsp Worcestershire sauce

¼ tsp hot-pepper sauce

12 oz extra-lean ground beef or ground poultry breast

Coat an unheated grill rack with nonstick spray. Light the grill and carefully place the rack on it.

Meanwhile, coat a medium nonstick skillet with nonstick spray and warm over medium heat. Add the onion and mushrooms. Cook, stirring frequently, for 4 to 5 minutes, or until the mushrooms are lightly browned. Place in a medium bowl and allow to cool.

When the vegetables are cool, stir in the parsley or thyme, Worcestershire sauce, and hot-pepper sauce. Add the meat and mix quickly with your hands to combine. Shape into 4 burgers, ¾" thick.

Place the burgers on the rack and grill for 5 to 6 minutes per side, or until browned and no longer pink.

GRILLING
WITHOUT THE RISKS

Today's healthy grilling styles are a big improvement over the high-fat carnivorous feeds of yesteryear, but researchers still worry about the health risks linked to the grill.

When meat is grilled, it produces two compounds—heterocyclic aromatic amines and polycyclic aromatic hydrocarbons—that may increase the risk of cancer. So far, no studies involving humans have confirmed this. Even so, in a 1999 update of its cancer prevention guidelines, the American Cancer Society warns that grilling meats at high temperatures could potentially be a problem.

Don't disassemble the Weber just yet. The risk of cancer from grilling, assuming that there even is one, won't be very large to begin with, especially because most people grill only a few times a week, at most. But it's still worth taking a few precautions to reduce your exposure to these compounds.

- Charcoal cooks at lower temperatures than propane grills, making it less likely to produce harmful compounds.

- One study found that marinating chicken breasts before grilling reduced some suspected cancer-causing compounds. When medallions of chicken breast were marinated in olive oil, brown sugar, and spices before grilling, they contained 90 percent less heterocyclic amines than nonmarinated meat that had been grilled the same way.

- Pre-cooking meat in the microwave reduces grilling time and, with it, the release of hydrocarbons.

- Using lean meats and trimming away fat before grilling reduces smoke, which has been found to be the major source of polycyclic hydrocarbons.

- Moving the grilling rack farther away from the heat will reduce levels of suspected carcinogens.

Jamaican Pork

½ c water
5–6 thin slices fresh ginger
2 dried chile peppers, crumbled
½ onion, chopped
¼ c white wine vinegar
1 Tbsp hot-pepper sauce
1 tsp dried thyme
½ tsp ground allspice
½ tsp ground black pepper
1¼ lb pork, cut into 1" cubes

In a blender, combine the water, ginger, chile peppers, onion, vinegar, pepper sauce, thyme, allspice, and black pepper. Puree until fairly smooth.

Pour the marinade into a large bowl. Add the pork and stir to coat well. Cover and refrigerate overnight.

Coat a grill rack or broiler pan with nonstick spray. Preheat the grill or broiler.

Thread the pork onto skewers, reserving the marinade.

Transfer the marinade to a saucepan, and bring to a boil over medium-high heat. Reduce the heat to low and keep warm.

Grill or broil the pork for 5 minutes per side, or until no longer pink. Brush the marinade on the pork before turning and again a minute or so before it is finished.

Makes 4 servings
Per serving: 178 calories, 3.6 g fat

Grilled Tuna Steaks with Chive and Dill Sauce

⅔ c chicken broth
1 Tbsp finely chopped fresh chives or 1 tsp dried
1 Tbsp finely chopped fresh dill or 1 tsp dried
1 tsp coarse-grain mustard
1 Tbsp olive oil
4 tuna steaks (about 5 oz each)

Preheat the grill.
In a large nonstick skillet over high heat, combine the broth, chives, dill, and mustard. Bring to a boil, whisking frequently. Continue to boil and whisk for 3 minutes, or until the sauce has been reduced to about half its volume.

To keep the skillet warm, transfer it to the side of the grill rack.

Rub the oil over the surface of each steak. Grill for 4 to 5 minutes per side, or until the fish is just opaque.

Remove the tuna from the grill, then drizzle the sauce equally over the steaks. Serve warm.

Makes 4 servings
Per serving: 184 calories, 5 g fat

WOMEN ASK WHY

Why do so many men avoid the kitchen, but turn into super chefs at the barbecue grill?

Scientists haven't been able to find a barbecue gene in the male of the species, so it's probably safe to assume that the phenomenon of men donning aprons at the grill and nowhere else is a cultural one. For whatever reason, men in our society are expected to cook over glowing charcoal or flaming propane burners, and they're happy to oblige. It doesn't hurt that anyone can learn to grill hot dogs and flip burgers without spending 2 years at a culinary academy.

Actually, grilling has become more sophisticated lately, and men are keeping up with the trends. Those frankfurters and burgers are being replaced with breasts of chicken basted in marinades. Vegetables like zucchini, eggplant, peppers, onions, and portobello mushrooms are sizzling side by side with the steaks. Dinners are getting more flavorful and men are getting more skilled.

More than a few women have wondered when men are going to take their grill skills indoors. It's starting to happen already. As men gain confidence, more and more of them have begun taking over the kitchen—where, it just so happens, grills have become standard equipment on some of the newer stoves.

Experts Consulted
Mary Ellen Camire, Ph.D.
Associate professor
Department of food science
*   and human nutrition*
University of Maine
Orono

Grilled Sea Scallop Kabobs

    2 Tbsp barbecue sauce
    1 Tbsp lemon juice
    2 tsp olive oil
    1 tsp Worcestershire sauce
    2 garlic cloves, minced
    1 lb sea scallops

In a medium bowl, combine the barbecue sauce, lemon juice, oil, Worcestershire sauce, and garlic. Add the scallops and stir to coat. Cover and marinate in the refrigerator for 35 to 40 minutes.

Thread the scallops onto 4 long metal skewers, piercing them through the sides so that the round parts face outward and leaving some space between them. Discard any leftover marinade.

Coat the grill rack with nonstick spray. Preheat the grill.

Place the kabobs on the rack and grill about 5" from the heat for 3 to 5 minutes per side, or until the scallops are opaque.

Makes 4 servings
Per serving: 112 calories, 2.5 g fat

Teriyaki Swordfish Kabobs

    1 lb swordfish steaks (1" thick)
    1 tsp sesame seeds
    1 can (15¼ oz) pineapple chunks in juice
    2 Tbsp soy sauce
    2 tsp canola oil
    ½ tsp ground ginger
    1 small red bell pepper, cut into 1" pieces

Cut the swordfish into ¾" pieces. Remove and discard the skin and bones. Place the swordfish in a large resealable plastic bag; set aside.

Place the sesame seeds in a dry nonstick

skillet over medium heat. Toast the seeds, shaking the skillet often, for 3 to 5 minutes, or until fragrant.

In a strainer over a small bowl, drain the pineapple and set aside. Transfer ⅓ cup of the juice to another small bowl. To the ⅓ cup juice, add the soy sauce, oil, sesame seeds, and ginger. Pour over the swordfish in the bag. Seal the bag and marinate in the refrigerator for 30 to 45 minutes, turning the bag occasionally.

Coat a grill rack or broiler pan with nonstick spray. Preheat the grill or broiler. Drain the swordfish well and discard the marinade.

Thread the swordfish, pineapple, and pepper onto skewers, leaving a small space between the pieces. Place the kabobs on the prepared rack or pan. Cook for 2 to 3 minutes, turn, and cook for 2 to 3 minutes longer, or until the fish is opaque.

Makes 4 servings
Per serving: 248 calories, 7.5 g fat

Freestyle Stir-Fries

The computer ate your business proposal. The car blew a tire on the way home. And in a half-hour, 15 Girl Scouts will be practicing knots in your living room. This is when a wok is truly a working woman's wonder tool.

Few meals are quicker on the stove than stir-fries. And because high heats cook so rapidly, sear in flavors, and lock in moisture, few meals are more nutritious, says Sue Snider, Ph.D., food and nutrition specialist at the University of Delaware's department of animal and food sciences in Newark. Despite its Asian heritage, there's nothing exotic about stir-fry cooking. At its most basic, it involves nothing more than adding vegetables and meats to a cooking utensil with a large enough surface area to allow you to move food from one hot area to the next for faster cooking. Woks are great because their high sides give you more room to maneuver. Large cast-iron skillets work nearly as well.

The great thing about stir-fries is that they're pure improvisation—you can mix and match almost everything with great results. Here are a few ways to make them even better.

Add very little oil. Since woks cook so quickly and at such high heats, it takes very little oil—as little as a teaspoon in some cases—to prevent food from sticking, says Dr. Snider. It's best to add the oil when the wok or skillet is already hot. Adding oil too early causes it to break down, reducing its lubricating qualities.

Cut the ingredients small. Wok cookery is designed to heat foods through very quickly. This only works, however, if the ingredients are cut into small enough pieces. The tougher a food is, the smaller the pieces should be. Broccoli, for example, is very dense and should be cut into small pieces. Summer squash, on the other hand, is largely water and even large pieces will be done in a few minutes.

Play with ingredients. Fresh vegetables are perfect for stir-fries, but so are canned beans and pre-shredded carrots. You can reduce your slicing-and-dicing time by using whole vegetables that cook quickly, such as snow peas and button mushrooms, says Jackie Newgent, R.D., a nutrition and culinary consultant in New York City and spokesperson for the American Di-

WOMAN TO WOMAN

Marriage Brought Her Back to Traditional Cooking

As a child of Chinese immigrants, Yu Ying-Hsin of Albany, New York, grew up eating stir-fries and other traditional Chinese foods. She figured that everyone else did, too. But as happens with many second-generation Americans, she soon adopted American habits, and pizza quickly became her favorite food. As the years went by, she found herself eating less and less of her parents' native cuisine. Things changed when Yu, who's now 36, met a man whose knowledge of Chinese food was limited to chicken chow mein. She figured that it would be fun to teach him a thing or two about real Chinese cooking.

When I first met my husband in 1993, he was living on peanut butter sandwiches, pizza, and cereal. Jeff's idea of a gourmet dinner was a can of black beans poured on top of a plate of instant white rice. I have to admit that my diet wasn't much better. I did like to make soups, pasta, and stir-fries, but it just wasn't worth the time and effort to cook for one person. I generally ate out a lot.

Once we got together, Jeff and I started eating more Chinese food. He really liked it. He went wild over my mother's stir-fries, homemade dumplings, and sweet-and-sour pork. He liked her cooking so much that he joked that the reason he stuck with me was to eat more of my mother's cooking.

I was inspired by Jeff's obvious enjoyment of traditional Chinese meals. I realized that I now had an eager audience, and that it was a perfect opportunity to hone my cooking skills. I wasn't an experienced cook, so I started slowly, making simple stir-fries with ingredients such as broccoli, carrots, and mushrooms. Gradually, I began to incorporate different meats or tofu, and I experimented with more exotic vegetables, like black mushrooms and bamboo shoots. The great thing about stir-fries is that you can combine a lot of different tastes and textures, and it's almost impossible to go wrong. I always experiment—my stir-fries are different every time.

After a while, I got more adventurous. These days, I'm always making hot-and-sour soups and egg rolls. I even got my mom's recipe for dumplings. They're time-consuming to make, but they're incredibly good.

Jeff is crazy about my cooking. He doesn't cook much himself, but sometimes he tries a few recipes. Stir-fries are still our favorites. All you have to do is chop some ingredients, toss them with a little oil, and throw everything into the pan—in the proper order, of course, because some ingredients cook more quickly than others. It's the easiest style of cooking there is. I still love pizza, but I'm grateful that I took the time to learn more about Chinese cuisine. The meals are lighter, and eating healthier foods has encouraged us to do other healthy things. Jeff and I now take more walks together, and we both belong to a gym. Now that we're not kids anymore, we want all the good health we can get.

etetic Association. You can even add fruits to stir-fries. One-inch chunks of canned pineapple or slices of mandarin orange cook almost instantly and add a delicate sweetness to the recipe.

Create visual interest. Completed stir-fries sometimes look flat with all the ingredients jumbled together. You can create visual sparks by varying shapes and colors, says Dr. Snider. Julienned red peppers, for example, will help set off

the pan cools, the food needs to be moved to a hotter spot, usually in a matter of seconds. This perpetual hopscotch from hot spot to hot spot is what makes it possible for stir-fries to be completed in as little as 5 minutes.

Add flavored liquids. A fast way to boost the flavor of stir-fries is to pour in a little beef, chicken, or vegetable broth. White grape juice or unsweetened pineapple juice will add complexity to the flavors with just a hint of sweetness.

All in the Timing

Meats and vegetables all cook at different rates. The most challenging part of preparing a stir-fry, apart from deciding what seasonings to use, is to ensure that the ingredients are all done at the same time. It's important to add slow-cooking vegetables early in the cooking process and fast-cooking ingredients later. (Thinly sliced meat cooks very quickly. It's usually browned in the wok, set aside, then returned to the wok when the vegetables are almost done.)

Slow-Cooking Vegetables	Fast-Cooking Vegetables
Broccoli	Baby corn
Carrots	Bean sprouts
Cauliflower	Endive
Celery	Mushrooms
Fennel	Peppers
Kale	Snap peas
Onions	Snow peas
Parsnips	Spinach
Potatoes	Summer squash
Winter squash	Zucchini

a bed of caramelized onions, and bright green beans will accent stir-fried pork.

Keep things moving. As the name suggests, stir-frying requires that the ingredients stay in nearly constant motion. As soon as one area of

Rapid Wraps

Wraps are all the rage in restaurants these days, but they're hardly new.

What's a burrito, after all, but a mixture of meat, beans, and salsa, all wrapped in a flour or corn wrap called a tortilla?

"The beauty of wraps is that they're about as quick and easy as you can get," says Gwyneth Doland of Jane Butel's Southwestern Cooking School in Albuquerque, New Mexico. "Anything can be a wrap. Whatever interesting stuff you have left over from dinner can go into a creative wrap the next day."

It's easy enough to make the wrap that holds the filling from scratch, but this just adds more time. Buy them ready-made, Doland suggests. You'll get the convenience of fast food with a lot more flavor.

Here are a few more of Doland's recommendations for fast and easy wrap sandwiches.

Use flour tortillas. These make the best wraps because they're thin and flexible enough to wrap easily and strong enough so that the ingredients won't leak out.

Corn tortillas are more nutritious and have a bit more flavor, but they're less flexible and harder to work with. Rice wraps, available at Asian markets, also work well, although they tend to fall apart when they're wrapped around moist ingredients.

Start with a warm wrap. Cold tortillas are too stiff to wrap well. It's best to use them at room temperature. Warming them for 10 seconds in the microwave makes them more flexible.

Cut ingredients the long way. It's not impossible to wrap chunks of meat or vegetables, but the resulting wrap will be lumpy, and the spiky edges of the ingredients will tend to tear through the sides. Wraps work best when ingredients are cut the long way, using strips of grilled chicken or turkey, for example, or julienned vegetables such as green bell peppers, squash, or carrots.

Fold it well and don't overload it. Wraps using dry ingredients are the easiest to eat because they don't leak. When you're adding sauces or the meat is juicy, you'll need to fold the wrap carefully.

WOMAN TO WOMAN

She Taught Her Kids to Run the Kitchen

Nursing is rarely a cushy, 9-to-5 profession, and Lydia Janning was hitting her limit. At 42, the Columbus, Ohio, resident was on her feet all day, working long, stress-filled hours. Then there was her second job—raising three children. Everything was under control until Lydia also enrolled in a master's program to become a nurse practitioner. She knew she had to get some extra help. So she organized the most convenient, inexpensive kitchen crew she could find: her three kids.

I have always believed that children, as part of a family, should be required to do their fair share of chores. I know that some mothers let their kids sit and watch TV all day while they cook their meals, do their laundry, and clean their rooms. Not me. I work way too hard for that.

My kids have helped me in the kitchen ever since they were old enough to stand on chairs. When I bake, I always recruit one of the kids to put the dough on the baking sheets. For holiday baking, we've even set up assembly lines. Each person in line is responsible for one part of the decorating.

As my life got more hectic, I started giving them more and more responsibility. At first, I had them doing small things, like grating cheese or cutting tomatoes. Now that they're older—my daughters are 14 and 12, and my son is 10—I expect them to take over some of the big jobs, too, like actually making our supper.

My husband is a schoolteacher, and he gets home earlier than I do, so he usually gets them started.

Sometimes I call from work and leave a message telling them what to do. They're pretty good about following through.

They understand that it's up to them to get dinner started. I'll help out if I get home in time. If not, all I really have to do is help them clean up.

The meals are not anything fancy, but that is fine with me. We'll have things like burritos, spaghetti with meat sauce, or grilled cheese sandwiches.

The kids don't seem to mind. Actually, they enjoy the fact that they get to cook what they like, not just what I like. I feel good knowing that they're becoming more self-sufficient. And I certainly feel good knowing that one job, at least, isn't on my shoulders.

Put the ingredients in a single or double line running most of the length of the wrap, stopping about ½ inch before the edges. Fold the left and right edges toward the middle, then roll the wrap upward from the bottom, slightly pressing the ingredients downward into the pocket as it forms.

Wrap up a meal. Since the idea of wraps is to save time, it makes sense to pack in all the key ingredients that you need for a complete meal. A nutritionally complete wrap might include a strip of fruit (mango and papaya are great choices), protein in the form of meat or beans, and a splash of salsa.

Celebrate with festive wraps. Flour tortillas are perfect when you want a fast meal, but sometimes you will want something more colorful.

Specialty food stores sell tortillas in all the colors of the rainbow. You can mix and match colors—bright green spinach tortillas next to tortillas made with sun-dried tomatoes, for example—for a brilliant effect. For dessert, you can even buy fruit-flavored tortillas to wrap around frozen yogurt.

Bean Burritos

½ c canned low-fat refried beans
1 tsp ground cumin
1 tsp minced garlic
½ c green or red salsa plus additional for topping
1 c cooked rice
2 Tbsp chopped fresh cilantro
4 flour tortillas (8" diameter)
1 large tomato, chopped
¼ c reduced-fat shredded Cheddar cheese
1 c shredded romaine or lettuce mix
1 small red onion, sliced
½ avocado, sliced
  Fat-free sour cream
  Cilantro leaves

In a medium microwaveable bowl, mix the beans, cumin, garlic, and ¼ cup of the salsa. Microwave on high power for 45 seconds, or until warm.

In another medium microwaveable bowl, mix the rice, cilantro, and the remaining ¼ cup of salsa. Microwave on high power for 45 seconds, or until warm.

Wrap the tortillas in damp paper towels. Microwave on high power for 30 to 60 seconds, or until soft. Spread some of the bean mixture down the center of each tortilla. Top with tomato, some of the rice mixture, cheese, let-

tuce, and onion. Roll to enclose the filling. Serve topped with avocado slices, sour cream, additional salsa, and cilantro.

Makes 4 servings
Per serving: 276 calories, 8 g fat

Pork and Cabbage Roll-Ups

2 c shredded cooked pork
¼ c orange juice
⅓ c hoisin sauce
4 flour tortillas (8" diameter)
2 c shredded green cabbage

Place the pork, orange juice, and hoisin sauce in a medium saucepan. Cook over medium heat for 5 to 6 minutes, or until the pork absorbs most of the sauce.

Wrap the tortillas in damp paper towels. Microwave on high power for 30 to 60 seconds, or until soft.

Divide the pork mixture among the tortillas. Top with the cabbage. Roll to enclose the filling.

Makes 4 servings
Per serving: 350 calories, 13.5 g fat

Beefy Tortilla Stack

6 oz cooked roast beef, cut into bite-size pieces
¼ tsp ground cumin
1 jar (16 oz) garden-style salsa
6 corn tortillas (6" diameter)
6 Tbsp fat-free sour cream
1 can (15½ oz) black beans, rinsed and drained
½ c canned sliced jalapeño chile peppers

2 Tbsp chopped fresh cilantro (optional)
1 c shredded Monterey Jack cheese

Preheat the oven to 350°F.

In a small bowl, toss together the beef and cumin.

Spread 2 tablespoons salsa in the bottom of a 1½-quart round baking dish. Top with 1 tortilla and one-sixth each of the sour cream, beans, beef, peppers, cilantro (if using), and cheese. Repeat layering, starting each layer with salsa and ending with cheese, until all the ingredients are used. After adding each tortilla, press down slightly on the stack to keep it level.

Bake for 15 to 20 minutes, or until the cheese is melted and the salsa is bubbling.

Makes 4 servings
Per serving: 415 calories, 15 g fat

Thai Tuna Wraps

1 tuna steak (16 oz)
¼ c bottled peanut dipping sauce
8 scallions
2 Tbsp plain low-fat yogurt
2 Tbsp light mayonnaise
2 Tbsp chopped fresh mint
¼ tsp red-pepper flakes
4 whole wheat tortillas (10" diameter)
2 c mixed greens
1 cucumber, peeled, seeded, and cut into thin strips
1 red bell pepper, sliced
1 lime, quartered

Preheat the grill or broiler.

Cut the tuna into 4 lengthwise slices. Place in a bowl and add the peanut sauce. Toss gently to coat. Let stand for 5 minutes. Transfer the tuna to the grill rack or broiler pan. Cook for 4 to 5 minutes per side for

medium doneness, brushing with the peanut sauce. Cut the tuna into small pieces. Discard any remaining peanut sauce.

Lightly coat the scallions with nonstick spray and grill or broil for 3 minutes per side. (Do not spray the scallions once they're on the grill or broiler.)

In a small bowl, stir together the yogurt, mayonnaise, mint, and pepper flakes. Spread about 2 tablespoons onto each tortilla. Top with the greens, tuna, scallions, cucumber, and bell pepper. Squeeze the juice from 1 lime quarter over each tortilla. Roll tightly.

Makes 4 servings
Per serving: 309 calories, 7.5 g fat

Asparagus Quesadillas

Filling
1 lb asparagus spears
1 tsp olive oil
1 large red onion, finely chopped
2 Tbsp minced garlic
1 tsp Mexican Spice Mix (page 15)
6 cherry tomatoes, quartered

Quesadillas
6 flour tortillas (8" diameter)
2 oz low-fat Monterey Jack cheese, shredded
1 Tbsp olive oil
1 c green or red salsa, warmed
6 cherry tomatoes, halved or quartered
¼ c chopped fresh cilantro (optional)

To make the filling: Trim the tough woody ends from the asparagus. Cut the spears into 2" pieces. Place a steamer basket in a medium pot with 2" of water. Bring to a boil over high heat. Place the asparagus in the steamer basket and steam for 5 minutes, or until tender.

(continued)

Warm the oil in a large nonstick skillet over medium heat. Add the onion. Cook, stirring occasionally, for 3 to 4 minutes, or until soft. Add the garlic and spice mix. Stir for 1 minute.

Add the asparagus and tomatoes. Cook, stirring, for 3 to 4 minutes. Transfer to a large bowl.

To make the quesadillas: Divide the filling among the tortillas, positioning it on half of each. Sprinkle with the cheese. Fold in half.

Clean the skillet. Brush with ½ teaspoon of the oil and warm over medium-high heat. Add 1 tortilla and cook for 2 to 3 minutes per side, or until golden; press with a spatula to flatten slightly. Repeat to use all of the oil and tortillas.

To serve, cut each quesadilla in half and top with salsa, tomatoes, and cilantro (if using).

Makes 6
Per serving: 188 calories, 7.8 g fat

Spinach-Cheese Quesadillas

    1 small onion, finely chopped
    1 c fresh spinach, finely chopped
       Pinch of nutmeg
    3 Tbsp shredded reduced-fat Cheddar
       cheese
    3 Tbsp shredded reduced-fat Monterey
       Jack cheese
    ½ tsp chili powder
       Pinch of ground red pepper (optional)
    2 large flour tortillas (12" diameter)
       Salsa for dipping

Generously coat a large nonstick skillet with nonstick spray and warm over medium heat. Add the onion and cook, stirring occasionally,

for 6 minutes, or until lightly browned. Add the spinach and nutmeg. Cook for 1 to 2 minutes, or until the spinach is just wilted and heated through. Transfer the mixture to a medium bowl and set aside.

Meanwhile, in a small bowl, stir together the Cheddar, Monterey Jack, chili powder, and red pepper (if using). Set aside.

Return the skillet to medium-low heat and place 1 tortilla in the skillet. Spread half of the cheese mixture over the surface of the tortilla.

Spread the spinach mixture evenly over the cheese. Sprinkle with the remaining half of the cheese mixture and top with the second tortilla. Using a spatula, gently press the quesadilla to combine the layers.

Cook for 4 minutes per side, or until lightly browned and the cheese is melted. Cool slightly and cut into 8 wedges. Serve warm with salsa for dipping.

Makes 8 servings
Per serving: 49 calories, 1.5 g fat

Meatless Sloppy Joes

    1 lb firm tofu, frozen, drained, and thawed
  1½ tsp canola oil
    ⅔ c chopped onion
    ⅔ c chopped green bell pepper
    ⅓ c thinly sliced celery
    1 can (16 oz) tomato sauce
    4 tsp cider vinegar
  2½ tsp prepared mustard
    ¾ tsp Worcestershire sauce
    1 tsp sugar
       Salt
       Ground black pepper
    4 whole wheat or multigrain buns

Set the tofu between 2 plates and place a heavy pot on top. Set aside for 10 minutes to release excess water. Pat dry. Coarsely mash or crumble with a fork.

Warm the oil in a medium nonstick skillet over medium heat. Add the tofu, onion, bell pepper, and celery. Cook, stirring occasionally, for 8 minutes, or until the tofu is well-browned and the vegetables are tender.

Stir in the tomato sauce, vinegar, mustard, Worcestershire sauce, and sugar. Cook, stirring frequently, for 5 minutes. Season to taste with salt and black pepper.

Mound equal amounts of the mixture onto the buns.

Makes 4 servings

Per serving: 344 calories, 13 g fat

Super Sides

If you find yourself in France or any of the Mediterranean countries having a home-cooked meal, the first thing you'll notice is that the table will be groaning under the weight of salads, grains, vegetables, and other side dishes. The meat, assuming there is one, will be off to the side somewhere, acting as a supporting player to the "main" dishes.

In this country, of course, it's the reverse. The meat is the main event, and vegetables and salads are lucky to come along for the ride. The reason we don't take advantage of side dishes more often, apart from old habits, is the perception that they're time-consuming to prepare. But they're not. In most cases, you can create delicious, low-fat side dishes in less time than it takes to cook a steak.

Open some cans. This is probably the least-known fact about successful chefs: They use a lot of canned foods—not straight from the can to your plate, necessarily, but as a timesaving foundation for their favorite recipes. Canned vegetables can have the same amount of nutrients (in some cases, more) than fresh. And when they're part of a recipe, their taste and textures are virtually indistinguishable.

"A lot of people have the idea that fruits and vegetables in the diet need to be fresh for good nutrition, but that's just not true," says Sue Snider, Ph.D., food and nutrition specialist at the University of Delaware's department of animal and food sciences in Newark. And you can't beat the speed of opening a can. Take canned beans. They're every bit as healthy as beans cooked from scratch, and you can have them on the table in minutes, whereas dried beans take hours to cook.

Keep them frozen and ready. Supermarkets have an enormous variety of frozen vegetables, by themselves and in interesting combinations. You can have an excellent side dish in the time that it takes to heat it in the microwave.

Make whole grains quickly. Brown rice and other whole grains are much more nutritious than white rice, but they're slow to cook. You can speed things up by using a pressure cooker. Brown rice cooked in a pressure cooker is done in about 15 minutes. That's faster than white rice cooked on the stove top. In addition, many whole grains are now available in quick-cooking versions.

ONE POT OF RICE, FIVE DELICIOUS DISHES

Rice is a busy woman's friend. It's a breeze to make, it keeps for up to a week in the refrigerator, and it can be used for main courses, side dishes, and even desserts.

Two cups of rice and 4 cups of water make about 5 cups of cooked rice. So cook up a big batch all at once and try some of the following recipes. Or experiment on your own, adding interesting leftovers or some of your favorite flavors to dress up the taste of this standard fare.

Cuban Black Beans and Rice

In a large nonstick skillet over medium-high heat, stir together 1 can (14 oz) black beans (drained), 1/2 cup minced onion, 1 tablespoon minced garlic, 1 teaspoon olive oil, and 1/2 teaspoon ground cumin for 5 minutes. Add 3 cups cooked rice. Season with salt and pepper. Cover and heat through. Top with 1 cup salsa.

Makes 4 servings
Per serving: 287 calories, 2.5 g fat

Rice and Broccoli Salad

In a large bowl, mix together 2 cups cooked rice, 1 cup frozen broccoli florets (steamed), 1/4 cup chopped red bell peppers, and 1 teaspoon toasted chopped walnuts. Sprinkle with 2 tablespoons olive oil, 1/4 teaspoon salt, and balsamic vinegar or lemon juice to taste. Toss well.

Makes 4 servings
Per serving: 225 calories, 7.5 g fat

Herbed Rice

In a large nonstick skillet, stir together 1/3 cup minced onion, 1/3 cup minced celery, 1/3 cup raisins, 1/4 cup chicken broth, and 1 teaspoon olive oil. Cook over medium-high heat for 3 minutes. Stir in 2 cups cooked rice, 1 cup bread crumbs, and 1 teaspoon Poultry Seasoning (page 15).

Makes 4 servings
Per serving: 285 calories, 3 g fat

Quick Pilaf

In a large nonstick skillet over medium-high heat, stir together 1 cup frozen mixed vegetables, 1 tablespoon chopped almonds, and 1 teaspoon minced garlic for 5 minutes. Add 3 cups cooked rice, 1/4 cup chicken broth, and 2 tablespoons chopped fresh parsley. Stir for 5 minutes, or until the liquid has evaporated and the rice is golden brown. Season with salt and pepper to taste.

Makes 4 servings
Per serving: 214 calories, 2 g fat

Rice-Raisin Pudding

In a large bowl, mix 1 1/2 cups cooked rice, 1 cup chopped apples, 3/4 cup fat-free milk, 1/2 cup raisins, 1/2 cup brown sugar, 2 beaten eggs, and 1 teaspoon vanilla extract. Transfer to a 1 1/2-quart casserole. Bake at 325°F for 1 hour, or until firm and golden brown.

Makes 6 servings
Per serving: 219 calories, 2 g fat

WOMEN ASK WHY

Why does cooking cabbage have such a strong odor?

The smell that wafts through the house when cabbage is on the boil is nothing more than sulfur. Cabbage and other so-called cole vegetables, such as broccoli and Brussels sprouts, are rich in sulfur, which is released during cooking.

Cabbage contains other redolent compounds as well. Vegetables with dark colors and strong, distinctive flavors tend to be richest in phytochemicals—naturally occurring plant compounds that have been linked to reduced risks for heart disease, cancer, and other conditions. These and other compounds may contribute somewhat to the strong smell of cooking cabbage, although the strong sulfur scent will pretty much overwhelm everything else.

People who like cabbage usually don't object to its strong smell. One way to take the edge off, however, is to boil a sprig or two of mint in a separate pan. This will help mask the sulfur smell until the cooking is done.

Expert Consulted
*Connie Diekman, R.D.
Nutrition consultant
Spokesperson for the American Dietetic Association
St. Louis*

Enjoy quick potatoes. Along with other so-called winter vegetables, such as turnips and butternut squash, potatoes are enormously versatile and easy to prepare. They're long-lasting, so you can stock up in advance. Even cooked, they'll keep for several days in the refrigerator. And in the age of the microwave, they don't take a lot of time to cook—usually 4 to 5 minutes.

Put pasta on the side. Though typically a main dish, pasta also works as a side dish. It cooks quickly and has a neutral flavor that won't overwhelm the main meal. It doesn't even need sauce. For example, boil some pasta (any shape), then toss it in a bowl with ½ cup chicken broth and some chopped garlic sautéed in olive oil. Apart from time to boil the pasta, it's ready to go in just a few minutes.

Make fruit part of the meal. Restaurants often serve fruit after meals as a kind of refreshing mouthwash. But chefs have begun serving fresh fruits with meals. Lightly grilled pineapple or mango slices, for example, make an excellent side dish. They cook in 3 to 4 minutes, and they add a lot of nutrients and some delectable sweetness to the meal, says Dr. Snider. Fruit salsas are also a popular way of adding taste and color to fish and poultry dishes.

Potato Pancakes

2 c shredded potatoes
6 egg whites, lightly beaten
1½ Tbsp all-purpose flour
⅛ tsp ground black pepper
1 Tbsp grated onion
  Fat-free sour cream or apple sauce (optional)

Squeeze excess moisture from the potatoes. Transfer to a large bowl. Stir in the egg whites. Stir in the flour, pepper, and onion.

Lightly coat a large skillet or griddle with nonstick spray. Place over medium heat. Drop the batter by ⅓ cups onto the pan and cook for 5 minutes on each side, or until lightly browned and crisp. Serve immediately. Top with a dollop of fat-free sour cream or apple sauce, if desired.

Makes 6 servings
Per serving: 61 calories, 0 g fat

HEALTHY— OR NOT?
Baked Potato

Potatoes come into this world as nearly perfect food. They're loaded with vitamin C, potassium, fiber, and complex carbohydrates, and that's just the flesh. The peel contains a bonus—an anti-cancer compound called chlorogenic acid, which has been shown to absorb one of the carcinogens found in smoked foods.

But the healthiest foods won't stay healthy very long when they're slathered with butter, sour cream, and bacon bits. A baked potato with lots of butter and sour cream (forget the bacon bits) has more than 10 grams of fat. That's nearly double the fat that you'd get in a lean T-bone steak. And a baked potato with all the trimmings has 243 calories, almost 100 more calories than the T-bone.

So the answer to the question, "Are baked potatoes healthy?" depends on whether you're talking about nature's original potato or the new "improved" potato.

Nutritionists admit that it's hard to resist the urge to gussy up a baked potato. They do tend to be starchy and a little dry. Elizabeth Somer, R.D., author of *Age-Proof Your Body*, recommends topping baked potatoes with steamed broccoli or salsa. Hot sauce is good, too. These will add much-needed moisture and flavor without the fat that you get from butter and sour cream.

Another way to enjoy potatoes without high-fat fixings is to inspect them at the grocery store. Potatoes with a greenish tinge have been overexposed to light and will have a slightly bitter taste that needs concealment. Those with the normal brown skins are more palatable and don't need as much help.

Corn and Spinach Fritters

- 1 package (10 oz) frozen chopped spinach
- 1 c frozen or canned corn
- ¼ c finely shredded carrot
- ¼ c shredded reduced-fat mozzarella cheese
- 2 egg whites
- 1 Tbsp cornstarch
- ¼ tsp minced garlic (optional)
- 2 tsp olive oil

Thaw the spinach, drain, and squeeze dry. Use half and reserve the rest for another use.

Transfer the spinach to a medium bowl. Add the corn, carrot, cheese, egg whites, cornstarch, and garlic, if using. Stir well to combine.

Heat a large cast-iron or nonstick skillet over medium-high heat. Add the oil. Use a tablespoon to measure out well-rounded scoops of the batter and form them into patties (they'll be a bit loose). As they're formed, place the patties in the skillet and flatten them gently with a spatula.

Cook the fritters for 3 minutes per side, or until lightly browned. Serve warm.

Makes 4 servings
Per serving: 93 calories, 4 g fat

Brussels Sprouts with Dill

- 1 lb small Brussels sprouts
- 2–3 tsp butter
- 2 Tbsp minced fresh dill or 1 tsp dried
- 2 Tbsp snipped fresh chives

Remove any discolored or wilted leaves from the Brussels sprouts and neatly trim the bottoms. Cut an X about ⅜" deep into the stem end to promote even cooking. Place a steamer basket in a medium pot with 2" of water. Bring to a boil over high heat. Place the Brussels sprouts in the basket and steam for 5 minutes, or just until tender when pierced with a sharp knife; do not overcook.

Melt the butter in a large nonstick skillet over medium heat and stir for 2 minutes, or until it starts to brown lightly. Add the Brussels sprouts, dill, and chives. Toss and stir for 2 minutes.

Makes 4 servings

Per serving: 62 calories, 2.5 g fat

Speedy Spanish Rice

    1 can (14½ oz) vegetable or chicken broth
    ½ c salsa
    1½ c instant rice

In a medium saucepan, combine the broth and salsa. Bring to a boil. Add the rice, cover, and simmer for 5 minutes.

Makes 6 servings

Per serving: 212 calories, 0 g fat

Roasted Vegetable Medley

    1½ lb small red potatoes, quartered
    12 oz fresh or canned green beans, cut into 1" pieces
    2 red bell peppers, thinly sliced
    1 red onion, thinly sliced crosswise and separated into rings
    ½ c chicken broth
    2 garlic cloves
    2 Tbsp red wine vinegar
    1½ Tbsp olive oil
    1 tsp crushed dried rosemary

HEALTH BONUS

Berries and Spinach: The New Brain Foods

Want to remember your bank card PIN or where you left your car at the mall? Try blueberries and spinach.

Research has shown that elderly rats given daily supplements containing blueberry or spinach extracts showed reversals in memory decline. The extracts were the equivalent of eating 1 cup of blueberries or 2 cups of raw spinach a day. Animals given the extracts performed better on memory tests than those that didn't get the supplements. Researchers believe that the improvements were related to the abundant antioxidants, especially flavonoids, in spinach and blueberries. Flavonoids reduce inflammation, which may impair brain tissue as we age.

    ¼ tsp ground black pepper
    8 kalamata olives, pitted and sliced
    1–2 Tbsp lemon juice

Preheat the oven to 425°F. Coat a 13" × 9" baking dish with nonstick spray. Add the potatoes, beans, bell peppers, onion, broth, and garlic. Mix well. Roast, stirring every 10 minutes, for 20 to 30 minutes, or until the vegetables are tender.

Remove the garlic and mash in the bottom of a small bowl. Whisk in the vinegar, oil, rosemary, and black pepper.

Place the vegetables in a large bowl. Add the dressing and olives. Toss to mix well. Sprinkle with the lemon juice just before serving. Serve warm or chilled.

Makes 4 servings

Per serving: 274 calories, 7 g fat

REAL-LIFE SCENARIO

Is Convenience Worth the Cost?

Stephanie has never been much for cooking, so when she shops for the family groceries, she spends most of her time in the canned and frozen food aisles. These are the foods that she ate growing up, and she feels comfortable preparing them for her family. She likes the convenience of frozen dinners—complete meals that include a meat, vegetable, and starch. She also purchases a lot of frozen and canned vegetables. She has tried using more fresh produce, but she has never heard of most of the stuff in the produce department, and she wouldn't have the slightest idea how to cook it. Her sister-in-law, Kara, is always scolding Stephanie for buying processed foods that she says are loaded with harmful food dyes as well as too much salt and sugar. Besides, she says, all of the nutrients have been processed right out of them. Stephanie isn't convinced, but sometimes she wonders if Kara knows something that she doesn't.

As long as she can afford it, Stephanie isn't doing her family a disservice. Anyone who takes the time to read nutrition labels will find that many frozen meals are perfectly good choices, as long as they're truly low-fat, which is less than 3 grams of fat per serving. And because the portion sizes are fairly small, they'll help keep her family trim.

Frozen foods are not nutritionally inferior to fresh. In fact, what we call fresh has often been shipped long distances, losing nutrients along the way. Many fruits and vegetables are picked before they're fully ripe. It's the only way they can survive long storage and shipping times. But foods that are picked early haven't had time to develop their full nutritional potential. Frozen foods, on the other hand, are most likely to be picked when they're ripe and processed soon afterward. They have at least as much nutrients as fresh, even more in some cases.

The issue isn't quite as clear-cut with canned vegetables. While canned corn, peas, and beans are okay nutritionally, they may have lost some of their vitamin C during processing.

Nutrition isn't the only issue, of course. Frozen and canned foods are incredibly convenient. People who normally won't take the time to prepare fresh foods are still able to eat nutritionally balanced meals by using canned and frozen foods. So Stephanie's approach isn't a bad one, as long as she's reading labels to make sure that what she's buying is as healthy as it can be.

The one disadvantage is that all of this convenience doesn't come cheap. Stephanie is probably spending two to three times more money buying frozen meals than she would making meals from scratch. If Kara is truly concerned about Stephanie's diet, she could do her a real favor by buying her a good vegetable cookbook. Supermarkets stock a huge variety of produce, and no one knows how to prepare it all. Once Stephanie discovers how easy and fast it is to prepare most vegetables, she may find that she isn't as willing to spend the extra money getting canned or frozen.

Expert consulted
Lynn Brown, R.D., Ph.D.
Associate professor of food science
Pennsylvania State University
University Park

Crunchy Cabbage Slaw

3 c thinly sliced red cabbage
2½ c thinly sliced green cabbage
1 large carrot, julienned
3 scallions, julienned
¼ c lemon juice
¼ c light or fat-free mayonnaise
1 garlic clove, minced
1½ tsp grated fresh ginger
2 Tbsp snipped fresh chives

In a large bowl, combine the red cabbage, green cabbage, carrot, and scallions.

In a small bowl, whisk together the lemon juice, mayonnaise, garlic, and ginger. Pour over the cabbage mixture and toss well to combine. Sprinkle with the chives.

Makes 6 servings
Per serving: 52 calories, 3 g fat

Maple-Glazed Carrots with Radishes

⅔ c apple cider
2 Tbsp maple syrup
2 Tbsp apple cider vinegar
2 tsp Dijon mustard
½ tsp dried thyme
10 oz baby carrots, trimmed
10 oz icicle radishes, trimmed and halved

In a large skillet, combine the cider, maple syrup, vinegar, mustard, and thyme. Bring to a boil over medium-high heat.

Add the carrots. Cover and cook over medium heat for 5 minutes. Add the radishes. Cover and cook for 20 to 25 minutes, or until the vegetables are just tender.

Remove the lid and raise the heat to medium-high. Cook, stirring often, for 5 minutes, or until the liquid is reduced to a glaze.

Makes 4 servings
Per serving: 87 calories, 0 g fat

Stuffed Tomatoes

1 c fresh whole wheat bread crumbs
1 c grated fresh Parmesan cheese
⅓ c chopped fresh basil
2 Tbsp chopped fresh parsley
¼ tsp ground black pepper
4 tsp extra-virgin olive oil
6 medium tomatoes
4 c hot cooked white rice

In a medium bowl, combine the bread crumbs, cheese, basil, parsley, and pepper. Mix well. Add the oil and stir until well-combined.

Slice the tomatoes in half crosswise and squeeze gently to remove the seeds. Place 2 tablespoons of the bread-crumb stuffing into each tomato half, mounding slightly. Place on a broiler pan or a nonstick baking sheet coated with nonstick spray. Broil for 1 to 2 minutes, or until lightly browned. Serve with the rice.

Makes 6 servings
Per serving: 248 calories, 7 g fat

Zucchini Marinara

1 small onion, thinly sliced
2 tomatoes, seeded and chopped
1 garlic clove, minced
1 tsp dried parsley
1 tsp dried basil
½ tsp minced fresh marjoram or
   ¼ teaspoon dried
⅛ tsp cracked black pepper

HEALTH BONUS
Eat Nuts to Lower Cholesterol

Health-conscious people always think twice before eating nuts because they're extremely high in fat and calories. A third of a cup—a very small handful—of walnuts, for example, contains around 253 calories and 24 grams of fat. That's almost half the amount of fat that you should get in a whole day.

Most nuts contain mainly monounsaturated and polyunsaturated fats, however. These are the fats that actually help lower cholesterol. Research has shown, in fact, that people who eat nuts four or five times a week have a much lower risk for heart disease than people who abstain from the crunchy treats. Nuts also contain large amounts of vitamin E, magnesium, and copper.

Still, there are those calories to contend with. To get the benefits of nuts without putting on weight, nutritionists advise having no more than 2 tablespoons, or ½ ounce, at a time.

1½ cups zucchini sliced ¼" thick on the diagonal
2 Tbsp shredded reduced-fat mozzarella cheese (optional)

Coat a large nonstick skillet with nonstick spray and warm over medium heat. Add the onion and cook, stirring occasionally, for 4 minutes. Stir in the tomatoes, garlic, parsley, basil, marjoram, and pepper. Cook, stirring occasionally, for 2 minutes, or until heated through.

Stir in the zucchini. Cover and cook, stirring occasionally, for 5 minutes, or until the zucchini is crisp-tender.

Transfer the mixture to a serving dish. Sprinkle with the cheese, if using.

Makes 4 servings
Per serving: 29 calories, 0.5 g fat

Oven Fries

1 Tbsp extra-virgin olive oil
1 tsp chopped fresh thyme or rosemary
¼ tsp ground black pepper
3 large baking potatoes

Preheat the oven to 475°F.

In a large bowl, combine the oil, thyme or rosemary, and pepper.

Cut each potato lengthwise to make several ½"-thick wedges. Add to the oil mixture and toss to coat.

Coat a nonstick jelly-roll pan with nonstick spray. Place the potatoes in a single layer on the prepared pan. Bake, turning occasionally, for 15 to 20 minutes, or until the potatoes are lightly browned and tender.

Makes 4 servings
Per serving: 196 calories, 4 g fat

Did You Say Dessert?

Women don't have the leisure time that their mothers did for creating complicated cakes, tortes, and pies.

But this doesn't mean saying *sayonara* to desserts, or resorting to overly rich (and under-flavored) supermarket baked goods. Some of the best desserts are the simplest—and the fastest, says Katherine B. Goldberg, R.D., a culinary arts specialist at the University of Michigan's M-Fit Health Promotion Program in Ann Arbor and co-author of *The High Fit–Low Fat Vegetarian Cookbook*.

Once you know a few tricks, you can have healthy, full-flavored desserts almost instantly—in many cases, without turning on the oven. And because you choose the ingredients, there won't be any high-fat surprises to push up the scale later.

Combine fresh and frozen fruits. Dessert is all about sweetness, and the fructose and sorbitol in fruits make them very sweet. You can make a delicious fruit dessert just by combining slices of peach, blueberries, and kiwifruit and topping them with some light whipped cream.

Depending on the fruits you use, the juices will combine in refreshing and unexpected ways, says Deborah Beall, R.D., manager of the California Department of Health Services' "Five a Day" program in Sacramento.

You can save even more time by adding frozen fruits, such as berries. They require no preparation, and the flavors are intensely concentrated, Beall explains.

Cook in the sweetness. Thanks to the microwave, you don't have to spend hours in the kitchen to enjoy the taste of baked fruit desserts. Here's a quick recipe that everyone loves: Core a few apples, fill the inside with brown sugar and a little ground cinnamon, and microwave, uncovered, for 3 to 5 minutes.

Heating apples mellows their natural tartness, and the wonderful aroma will linger in the kitchen for hours.

Pears, with their softer flesh, don't hold up as well to microwaving as apples do. But poaching is almost as fast. All you have to do is add apple cider or red wine to a cup of water, mix in some sugar, vanilla extract, and lemon rind if you have

Tantalizing Toppings

When you hear the words *fruit sauce*, the first thing that comes to mind is probably the pale, thin, watery applesauce that comes in a jar. Yet homemade fruit sauces and toppings can be incredibly rich, adding texture and robust flavors to low-fat shortcake, angel food cake, and ice cream. You can make toppings from almost every fruit under the sun.

Raspberry Dessert Sauce

- 1 package (10 ounces) frozen raspberries in syrup, thawed
- 1 tsp lemon juice
- ¼ tsp almond extract
- ½ tsp unflavored gelatin

Press the raspberries through a fine sieve into a small saucepan. Discard the seeds.

Add the lemon juice, almond extract, and gelatin to the pan. Set the mixture aside for 5 minutes, or until the gelatin is softened.

Cook, stirring constantly, over medium heat until the gelatin is dissolved and the mixture is hot. Remove from the heat and cool slightly.

Refrigerate any leftover sauce in an airtight container.

Makes 2 cups
Per ¼ cup: 38 calories, 0.5 g fat

Creamy Strawberry Sauce

- ⅓ c white grape juice
- 1 Tbsp honey
- 2 c strawberries, hulled
- ½ c fat-free vanilla yogurt

In a food processor or blender, combine the grape juice, honey, and 1 cup of the strawberries. Process until smooth. Slice the remaining 1 cup strawberries. Gently fold into the sauce along with the yogurt.

Refrigerate any leftover sauce in an airtight container.

Makes 2 cups
Per ¼ cup: 33 calories, 0.5 g fat

Peach and Blueberry Sauce

- 1 Tbsp cornstarch
- 1 c orange juice
- 3 Tbsp maple syrup
- ½ tsp ground cinnamon
- ⅛ tsp ground nutmeg
- ¼ tsp almond extract
- 2 c peeled and sliced peaches
- ¼ c blueberries

In a medium saucepan, dissolve the cornstarch in a small amount of the orange juice.

Stir in the maple syrup, cinnamon, nutmeg, and the remaining orange juice. Bring to a boil over medium heat, stirring constantly. Cook and stir for 2 minutes, or until the sauce thickens. Stir in the almond extract, peaches, and blueberries.

Refrigerate any leftover sauce in an airtight container.

Makes 2½ cups
Per ¼ cup: 46 calories, 0.5 g fat

it, and simmer halved and cored pears until they're tender.

Make your own sorbet. Making ice cream and sorbet at home used to be a chore because you needed a heavy-duty mixer and big, messy sacks of rock salt and ice. Now you can get fairly inexpensive ice-cream makers that consist of nothing more than a metal insert that gets supercold in the freezer. If you use soft fruits like berries, sweetened with a little chilled sugar syrup, you can make a sorbet with almost no preparation time.

Puree the fruit, add the sweetener, and pour the mix into the container and put it into the freezer. Forget about it for a few hours, until you're ready to scoop some out.

Save time on crusts. The messiest, most time-consuming part of making pies is preparing the crusts. Store-bought crusts are often too high in fat to take seriously. You can substitute a ready-made dough called phyllo, which comes in paper-thin frozen sheets. It's low in fat and can be formed into a crust in a few minutes. Spray phyllo dough with a butter-flavored cooking spray between layers to create an even flakier crust.

Freeze ahead. If you enjoy making your own crusts, you can save a lot of time by doubling or tripling the recipe and freezing leftover dough. When it's rolled into rounds, stacked between sheets of waxed paper, and sealed in a plastic bag, it will keep for sev-

---

WOMEN ASK WHY

Why do bananas turn black in the refrigerator?

First of all, don't judge a banana by its color. The darkening of the peel that occurs at cold temperatures doesn't affect the taste at all.

It looks ugly, but you're eating the fruit, not the peel.

Banana peels contain enzymes that normally turn the skin yellow. Cold temperatures kill these enzymes, causing refrigerated bananas to turn black or brown. The fruit inside will be just as nutritious as it was before.

It will have the same texture and taste. And it will stay fresh for up to a week no matter how ugly the peel gets.

There's usually no reason to put fresh bananas in the refrigerator. When you bring them home from the store, allow them to ripen nat-

urally at room temperature. The exception is when bananas are ripening faster than you can eat them.

Putting them in the refrigerator will quickly stop the ripening and keep them from getting mushy.

Conversely, you may have green bananas that aren't ripening fast enough. You can speed the process by putting them in a paper bag and twisting the top shut.

As with many fruits, bananas release ethylene gas. When they're bathed in this gas for a day or two, they'll quickly turn their customary yellow color.

Expert Consulted
Cindy Moore, R.D.
Director of nutrition therapy
Cleveland Clinic Foundation
Spokesperson for the
*   American Dietetic*
*   Association*

WOMEN ASK WHY

Why is it so easy to eat dessert on a full stomach?

Habit, habit, habit! Many women crave sweets at the ends of meals, when their taste sensations are still on a roll. You've enjoyed a meal, and your tastebuds want to keep going.

Our craving for sweets is largely a holdover from our younger years. Children learn early that if they're good and finish their Brussels sprouts, they'll get something sweet and fatty when they're done—and for children, sweet and fatty is hard to resist.

This goes for adults, too.

It wouldn't seem to make much sense to keep eating when you are already full, but the force of an irresistible craving has a way of winning out.

Another factor that comes into play is the fact that there's a delay between the time when your stomach is satisfied and when your brain gets the message. This is why many people who order dessert can't finish it. They felt like they were still hungry right after the meal, but by the time dessert arrived, their brains had finally gotten the "stuffed" signal.

There's nothing wrong with giving in to your inner child and capping a nice dinner with dessert. But if you're watching calories, try splitting a dessert with your dining partner or waiting 10 minutes or so after dinner before ordering dessert.

You may discover that you don't want it as much as you thought you did.

Expert Consulted
Althea Zanecosky, R.D.
Spokesperson for the American
*   Dietetic Association*
Nutrition education specialist
Philadelphia

---

eral months. Move the dough from the freezer to the refrigerator 24 hours before using it.

Bake with fat substitutes. The desserts that women love are usually crammed with butter, chocolate, and other high-fat ingredients. You can get nearly the same flavors and textures with a variety of fat substitutes, Goldberg says. For example:

➤ Replace each tablespoon of vegetable oil with a tablespoon of applesauce.

➤ Replace up to half the butter, oil, or lard in a recipe with applesauce, mashed banana, canned pumpkin, or a homemade fruit puree, made by combining 8 ounces prunes with ⅓ cup water in a food processor and blending until smooth. These substitutes work well in muffins, cakes, or quick breads, but they don't work as well for pie crusts, which require more fat to retain their flaky texture.

➤ Replace 1 ounce of semisweet chocolate with 4 tablespoons cocoa powder mixed with 2 tablespoons sugar and 6 tablespoons fat-free evaporated milk. Heat the mixture until it dissolves.

➤ Substitute low-fat or nonfat plain yogurt for regular sour cream.

➤ Use fat-free evaporated milk in place of heavy cream in custards and puddings.

➤ Toast nuts to bring out their flavor, and you'll need to use only half as much.

Key Lime Pie

3 egg yolks
1 can (14 oz) fat-free sweetened
  condensed milk
½ c plus 2 Tbsp bottled Key lime juice
1 Tbsp grated lime peel (optional)
½ c sugar
1 prepared 9" graham cracker pie crust
  Reduced-fat whipped topping (optional)

Preheat the oven to 375°F.

Place the yolks in a large mixing bowl. Add the milk and beat with an electric mixer on medium speed until smooth. Add the lime juice and peel. Gradually add the sugar and mix until incorporated.

Pour into the pie crust and bake for 15 minutes, or until a wooden pick inserted in the center comes out clean. Cool for at least 1 hour. Add the whipped topping (if using).

Makes 8 servings
Per serving: 191 calories, 9 g fat

Banana-Raspberry Rice Pudding

1 package instant banana pudding mix
2 c fat-free milk
½ tsp vanilla extract
2 c cooked brown rice
2 bananas, thinly sliced
2 c fresh or frozen raspberries
  Fat-free whipped topping (optional)

In a medium bowl, combine the pudding mix, milk, and vanilla extract. Whisk well. Fold in the rice and bananas. Spoon into 8 dessert dishes. Chill for 2 hours.

To serve, top with the raspberries (they're great crushed) and a dollop of whipped topping (if using).

Makes 8 servings
Per 1 cup: 320 calories, 2 g fat

Italian Biscotti Parfaits

2 tsp instant espresso powder
½ c boiling water
8 fat-free chocolate chip biscotti, crushed
2⅔ c fat-free vanilla frozen yogurt
4 tsp grated semisweet chocolate

In a small bowl, dissolve the espresso powder in the water. Set aside to cool.

Divide one-third of the biscotti crumbs among 4 parfait glasses. In each glass, layer ⅓ cup of the frozen yogurt, 1 tablespoon of the espresso, and ½ teaspoon of the chocolate. Repeat. Top with the remaining biscotti crumbs. Serve immediately or freeze for up to 1 hour.

Makes 4 servings
Per serving: 186 calories, 1.5 g fat

10-Minute Brownies

1 box low-fat brownie mix (without nuts
  or chocolate chips)
⅔ c water

Preheat the oven to 350°F. Lightly coat two 13" × 9" jelly-roll pans with nonstick spray.

In a medium bowl, combine the brownie mix and water until no dry lumps remain. Divide the batter equally between the prepared pans and spread evenly.

Bake for 10 minutes, or until there's no shine to the batter and the edges slightly pull away from the sides of the pans.

Cool and cut into squares.

Makes about 24

Per serving: 98 calories, 2 g fat

Chocolate Mousse

⅓ c sugar

3 Tbsp unsweetened cocoa powder

3 Tbsp cornstarch

2 c fat-free milk

1 tsp vanilla extract

½ container (8 oz size) frozen light whipped topping, thawed

In a medium saucepan, whisk together the sugar, cocoa, and cornstarch. Whisk in the milk. Whisk over medium heat for 5 minutes, or until the mixture thickens and almost comes to a boil. Stir in the vanilla extract. Place the pan in a bowl of ice water and cool.

Fold in the whipped topping. Divide among 6 dessert dishes. Chill for at least 1 hour before serving.

Makes 6 servings

Per ½ cup: 134 calories, 2.5 g fat

HEALTHY—OR NOT?

Frozen Yogurt

Once myths get started, the truth has a hard time getting out. Frozen yogurt is a case in point. It sure sounds like it's healthy. Yogurt is known for its calcium and its rich supplies of live-culture bacteria, organisms that aid digestion, help prevent yeast infections, and possibly strengthen the immune system. Everyone assumes that frozen yogurt has the same benefits.

As it turns out, however, yogurt by another name isn't quite as sweet. It has virtually none of the live cultures that make regular yogurt so healthy, says Kristine Napier, R.D., a nutrition consultant in Mayfield Village, Ohio. It does have quite a bit of calcium—106 milligrams in a ½-cup serving—but that's not nearly as much as you'd get in a glass of fat-free milk. And the fact that it tastes so good means that people tend to eat a lot of it, along with all the fat that it may contain.

Even though frozen yogurt has a reputation for being healthier than ice cream, it contains nearly as many calories, depending on the kind that you buy. A ½-cup serving of regular ice cream, for example, has about 133 calories and 7 grams of fat. An equal serving of regular frozen yogurt? About 115 to 180 calories and between 4 and 12 grams of fat.

"It's perceived to be healthier, but there's really no difference," Napier says. "You can buy fat-free and reduced-fat frozen yogurts, which have less fat, but you can also buy ice cream that's just as low in fat." And both ice cream and frozen yogurt contain a lot of sugar.

The bottom line is this: As treats go, frozen yogurt isn't bad as long as you buy a reduced-fat or fat-free variety. It does provide calcium and other nutrients. It's better for you than, say, a chocolate bar. "If you like frozen yogurt, go for it, but keep in mind that it's still a treat," Napier says.

WOMAN TO WOMAN
Fruit Is Her New Love

Amy Fong, 35, admits that she has always had a sweet tooth. Brownies, cookies, pies—as long as desserts were sweet and rich, she had a hard time saying no. That wasn't a problem when she was young. But as she got older, she had to start watching her weight, as did the many guests who visited her Alameda, California, home. She decided that it was time to find a less fattening way to tantalize the tastebuds and put a fine finish on a meal. The solution, Amy discovered, was fruit desserts.

I have never been a sugar addict the way some people are, but I have always loved desserts. I felt that dinner wasn't complete without a rich encore—a chocolate torte, for example, or deep-dish apple pie topped with ice cream.

I still like rich desserts, but I have to be honest. Ever since I turned 31, they don't like me. I just can't eat the same foods and amounts without putting on weight.

I love cooking and having people over, and I wasn't about to stop. I realized that just changing the dessert menu would cut out a lot of calories. I wasn't sure where to begin, so I started reading magazines about low-fat cooking, and I kept a file of recipes that I cut out. One day, on a whim, I bought a book about cooking with fruit. That's when the lightbulb came on. Living in California's Bay Area, I have access to an incredible variety of seasonal fruits. Mangoes, kiwifruit, kumquats, blueberries, strawberries—all fresh and nearly bursting with flavor.

At first, I was a little disappointed. Fruits may have a lot of natural sugar, but fruit desserts don't automatically have that rich texture that makes things like chocolate so appealing. I gradually learned a few tricks, like pureeing dates or prunes and using them as a chocolate and butter substitute. They add a lot of richness and a nice, deep color. And they're totally healthy.

The more I experimented, the more I began focusing on just the fruits. My tastes have changed. I don't crave that heavy richness the way I used to. I find that a fresh fruit salad with yogurt or a warm apple crisp is just as satisfying. I like keeping things simple. Maybe I'll bake pears and top them with brown sugar. Or I'll make mango pudding using 2 percent milk and fresh mango.

I was pleasantly surprised to discover that fruit desserts are very fast to make. They don't require a lot of ingredients, and all of my guests seem to love them.

It's interesting, but I don't think about calories and fat as much any more. I've come to appreciate fruits for the tastes alone. And with so much variety, I'm never going to run out of ideas to try next.

Raspberry Jelly Roll

1 c all-purpose flour
1 tsp baking powder
¼ tsp salt
4 eggs
¾ c sugar
¼ cup cold water
1 tsp vanilla extract
2 tsp confectioners' sugar
¾ c seedless raspberry all-fruit spread

Preheat the oven to 375°F. Generously coat a 15" × 10" nonstick jelly-roll pan with nonstick spray and dust with flour.

In a small bowl, combine the flour, baking powder, and salt.

In a large bowl, beat the eggs with an electric

mixer at the highest speed for 5 minutes, or until thick and lemon-colored. Add the sugar, 1 tablespoon at a time, beating constantly until light and fluffy. Stir in the water and vanilla extract. Add the flour mixture and blend at low speed just until the dry ingredients are incorporated.

Spoon the batter into the prepared pan and smooth it evenly. Bake for 8 to 12 minutes, or just until the top springs back when lightly touched in the center.

While the cake bakes, cut a length of paper towel about 20" long. Sprinkle evenly with 1 teaspoon of the confectioners' sugar.

Loosen the edges of the baked cake and immediately invert onto the towel. Roll up, starting from a short end, rolling the towel into the cake. Cool on a rack. Carefully unroll the cake and remove the towel. Spread the inside of the cake with the fruit spread and reroll the cake. Wrap in plastic wrap or foil and refrigerate. Dust with the remaining 1 teaspoon confectioners' sugar before serving.

Makes 12 servings
Per serving: 165 calories, 2 g fat

Dried-Fruit Truffles

½ c dried pitted prunes
½ c pitted dates
½ c dried apricots
1 Tbsp dried lemon peel
2 Tbsp butter
½ c sugar
1 Tbsp honey
2 Tbsp frozen orange juice concentrate, thawed
1 tsp ground cinnamon
1½ c crispy rice cereal
2 Tbsp confectioners' sugar

In a food processor, combine the prunes, dates, apricots, and lemon peel. Process until finely chopped.

In a heavy saucepan over medium-low heat, combine the butter, sugar, honey, orange juice concentrate, and cinnamon. Cook, stirring occasionally, until the sugar is dissolved. Add the fruit mixture and cereal. Stir to coat. Remove from the heat and set aside to cool.

When cooled, pinch off small pieces of the mixture and roll into 1" balls. Place the confectioners' sugar in a shallow bowl or pie plate. Roll the balls in the sugar and set on waxed paper to dry.

Makes 36
Per truffle: 46 calories, 1 g fat

Crunchy Peanut Butter Cookies

¾ c packed brown sugar
¼ c sugar
6 Tbsp butter, softened
¼ c crunchy peanut butter
1 tsp vanilla extract
1 egg white
3 Tbsp water
1¾ c all-purpose flour
¾ tsp baking soda
¼ tsp salt

Preheat the oven to 350°F. Coat nonstick baking sheets with nonstick spray or line with parchment paper.

In a medium bowl, combine the brown sugar, sugar, butter, and peanut butter until smooth. Add the vanilla extract, egg white, and water. Beat until fluffy.

In another medium bowl, combine the flour, baking soda, and salt. Stir into the peanut butter mixture.

(continued)

Shape the batter into 1" balls and place on the prepared baking sheets, leaving 2" between cookies. Using a fork that has been dipped in water, flatten the cookies. Bake for 10 to 12 minutes, or just until the cookies are set. Cool on the sheets for 2 minutes. Remove the cookies to a rack and cool completely.

Makes 30
Per cookie: 45 calories, 2 g fat

Poached Bananas in Vanilla Sauce

    2 c apple juice
    3 Tbsp raisins
    1 tsp vanilla extract
    ¾ tsp ground cinnamon
    ⅛ tsp ground nutmeg
    4 bananas, sliced
    ¼ c fat-free vanilla yogurt

In a medium saucepan, combine the apple juice, raisins, vanilla extract, cinnamon, and nutmeg. Bring to a boil over medium-high heat. Reduce the heat to low and simmer for 5 minutes.

Add the bananas, cover, and simmer for 10 minutes, or until the bananas are plump and softened. Remove the pan from the heat. Using a slotted spoon, carefully remove the bananas and divide among 4 dessert bowls. Set aside.

Stir the yogurt into the juice mixture to make a sauce. Spoon over the bananas. Serve warm.

Makes 4 servings
Per serving: 196 calories, 1 g fat

Banana-Mango Mousse

    2 mangoes, peeled and coarsely chopped
    ½ c fat-free vanilla yogurt

    1 small banana
    2 tsp honey
    2 drops vanilla extract
    3 ice cubes
    4 mint sprigs

In a food processor or blender, combine the mangoes, yogurt, banana, honey, vanilla extract, and ice cubes. Process with on/off turns until the ice is broken up. Process until smooth. Remove any remaining large pieces of ice.

Divide the mixture among 4 dessert dishes. Garnish with the mint. Serve immediately.

Makes 4 servings
Per serving: 127 calories, 0.5 g fat

HEALTH BONUS

Gourmet Honey: The Best of All

Every drop of honey has a smidgen of healing antioxidants. But some honeys found in gourmet shops and health food stores have far more than others.

Buckwheat honey. You either love the robust flavor or you don't. But you have to love what it offers: about eight times more antioxidants than the amount in common clover honey.

Hawaiian Christmas berry honey. It has a butterscotch flavor, with almost three times the antioxidants in clover honey.

Sunflower honey. It has a bold flavor, and it has three times the antioxidants of clover honey.

Florida Tupelo honey. It is extremely sweet and has more than twice the antioxidants of clover honey.

Peach Crunch

½ c fat-free plain yogurt

1 Tbsp apple pie spice

1 tsp margarine

½ c Grape-Nuts cereal

2 tsp honey

1 package (16 oz) frozen unsweetened peach slices or 3½ c peeled, pitted, and sliced fresh peaches

In a small bowl, stir together the yogurt and 1½ teaspoons of the apple pie spice. Cover and refrigerate until ready to serve.

Coat a small skillet with nonstick spray. Add the margarine and warm over medium heat until melted.

Meanwhile, in another small bowl, combine the cereal, honey, and the remaining 1½ teaspoons apple pie spice.

Add the cereal mixture to the skillet. Cook and stir for 2 minutes, or until the margarine is absorbed. Remove the skillet from the heat.

To serve, spoon the peaches into 4 individual dessert bowls. Top each with 2 tablespoons of the yogurt mixture and sprinkle with 2 tablespoons of the cereal mixture.

Makes 4 servings

Per serving: 139 calories, 1.5 g fat

PART THREE

Make-
Ahead
Meals

Casseroles: Lovin' from the Oven

Casseroles are the perfect antidote for women with health on their minds and no time on their hands. Fill a Dutch oven or baking dish with vegetables, grains, pasta, and a little meat. Put a lid on it and let it bake slowly for an hour. The result is a wonderful melding of flavors as the ingredients tenderize and commingle—and there's only one pot to wash when you're done.

Casseroles are nearly foolproof because the food cooks slowly in hot steam. It won't burn as long as you add enough liquid. And because casseroles get their unique flavors from a panoply of flavorful ingredients, seasoning is a snap.

Here are a few easy ways to make these healthy, flavorful meals even better.

Use anything and everything. Casseroles are the perfect way to use leftovers, or some of those canned vegetables and beans at the back of the pantry. You don't need a recipe. Just fill the pan with a variety of ingredients, raw or cooked, and put it in the oven. Set a fresh salad and maybe some bread on the table, and you have a ready-to-go meal.

Use just a little meat. You don't need a lot of meat to flavor a casserole. You'll discover that a few slices of leftover pot roast or a chicken thigh or two will give a lot of taste without a lot of fat and calories, says Sue Snider, Ph.D., food and nutrition specialist at the University of Delaware's department of animal and food sciences in Newark.

Brown fresh meats and vegetables. It's not essential, but browning meats before starting the casserole will seal the surface and lock in flavors and tenderness. Celery, carrots, and onions will also benefit from browning. Don't bother using a separate pot. Brown the meat and vegetables in the casserole dish, using just a little oil, then add the rest of the ingredients.

Blend in whole grains. Even people who don't care for the strong flavors of whole grain noodles or brown rice will enjoy a casserole that's loaded with them. The blending of flavors that occurs in casseroles takes the edge off whole grain tastes so that they don't overwhelm the dish, says Katherine B. Goldberg, R.D., a culinary arts specialist at the University of

WOMAN TO WOMAN
Diary of a Sunday Cook

While her friends spend Sundays relaxing, Margo Donohue of Brooklyn, New York, is busy cooking. It's not that Margo, a 30-year-old public relations specialist, is passionate about cooking. She does it because she has found that it's the only way to have healthy, home-cooked meals in a city that's not known for either its leisure or its healthy habits. Here's how she does it.

When I moved to New York City 4 years ago, I was making only a meager wage. You can eat pretty cheaply in New York, and most days, I just grabbed a sandwich at lunch. I'd do the same thing at night sometimes. Even though I'm single and don't have kids, I was always too tired after working all day and commuting home to do any decent cooking.

After a while, I got tired of eating the same things all the time. I also got tired of spending the money. So I talked to my mom. She suggested that I do all of my cooking—and she meant all of it—on Sunday. By making a lot of food on Sunday, she explained, I'd always have something quick and nutritious to eat, and it would cost a heck of a lot less than the sandwiches that I'd been buying.

So the very next Sunday, and most every Sunday since then, I did it. At first, I set aside a lot of time, but I soon discovered that it doesn't take any longer to make big batches of food than it does to make a single meal. Whatever I was making—roasted chicken, pasta salad—I made extra.

I really take advantage of the freezer. Whenever I make soup, for example, I freeze half of it. I have also become an expert in reusing leftovers. Roasted chicken is great because there's always plenty left. I might slice up the white meat and use it for chicken sandwiches. Or I'll cube it for chicken salad. I usually use the leftover carcass to make chicken stock. That becomes chicken soup with noodles and vegetables.

I'm real big on pesto sauce. Since all you have to do is put fresh basil, Parmesan cheese, olive oil, and garlic in a blender, it's really fast. I use it to dress up pasta, steamed vegetables, and the packaged tortellini that I make sometimes.

One reason why I've stuck with this system is that it allows me to eat a lot healthier. If I don't keep good food in my apartment, I'll have to grab anything, and it's usually not going to be healthy.

I started cooking on Sundays out of necessity, but I've come to really enjoy it. I like home-cooked food a lot better than the processed stuff. And I'm saving so much time! If I ever have kids, I'm sure that I'll continue my Sunday ritual. It will make it so much easier to come home and put dinner on the table for my family.

Michigan's M-Fit Health Promotion Program in Ann Arbor, and co-author of *The High Fit–Low Fat Vegetarian Cookbook*.

Thicken the mix. Because casseroles cook in a high-moisture environment, you may want to thicken the mix after it is cooked to keep the dish from being too watery. Traditional chefs use a high-fat thickener called a roux, which is made by whisking together butter and flour in a saucepan and cooking until brown. You can get the same result without the additional fat by whisking together 1 tablespoon of cornstarch or flour and 1 tablespoon of cold water. Add to the warm casserole and bring it back to a gentle boil to allow thickening.

Add instant texture. A faster way to thicken a casserole and add layers of flavor is to pour in a can of low-fat cream of mushroom, cream of chicken, cream of tomato, or cream of celery soup, Goldberg says.

Tuna Noodle Casserole

8 oz whole wheat noodles

1 package (16 oz) frozen broccoli florets, thawed

1 can (12 oz) water-packed white tuna, drained and flaked

1 can (10¾ oz) fat-free condensed cream of mushroom soup

1 c 1% milk

1 c shredded reduced-fat Monterey Jack cheese

8 oz fat-free plain yogurt

½ tsp ground black pepper

¼ tsp celery seeds

¼ tsp crushed red-pepper flakes

½ c crushed saltines

¼ c grated Parmesan cheese

Preheat the oven to 350°F.

Coat a 13" × 9" baking dish with nonstick spray.

Cook the noodles according to package directions. Drain and return to the pot. Remove from the heat. Toss with the broccoli and tuna.

In a large bowl, mix the soup, milk, Monterey Jack, yogurt, black pepper, celery seeds, and red-pepper flakes. Pour over the noodle mixture and carefully stir. Transfer to the prepared baking dish.

In a small bowl, mix the crackers and the Parmesan. Sprinkle over the casserole. (If freezing, reserve the topping step until baking time to avoid sogginess. Bake for 60 minutes in a 370° oven until the center is hot.) Refrigerate the casserole until ready to bake.

Bake for 30 minutes, or until lightly browned.

Makes 4 servings
Per serving: 563 calories, 13 g fat

Quick Cassoulet

1 can (15½ oz) small white beans, rinsed and drained

4 boneless, skinless chicken breast halves

¼ tsp ground black pepper

1 Tbsp olive oil

6 oz turkey kielbasa, sliced ¼" thick

½ c chicken broth

1 c chopped onions

¾ c seasoned bread crumbs

¼ c dry-pack sun-dried tomatoes, thinly sliced

2 Tbsp chopped fresh basil or 2 tsp dried

Preheat the oven to 350°F. Spread half of the beans in a 2-quart baking dish.

Season the chicken on both sides with the pepper. In a large skillet over medium heat, brown the chicken in the oil for 5 minutes, turning once. Transfer the chicken to the baking dish. Top with the kielbasa, the remaining beans, and broth.

In the same skillet, cook the onions for 4 minutes, stirring to loosen any browned bits from the pan. Stir in the bread crumbs, tomatoes, and basil. Cook, stirring, for 2 minutes. Spread over the beans, patting to create a thick crust.

Cover and bake for 10 minutes. Uncover and bake for 15 minutes longer, or until the crust is browned. (The casserole can be frozen at this point. To serve, thaw first, then reheat in a 350°F oven for 25 minutes, or until heated through.)

Makes 4 servings
Per serving: 376 calories, 6.5 g fat

Turkey Potpie

1 onion, thinly sliced

1 Tbsp chopped fresh garlic

1 Tbsp flour

1 can (12 oz) fat-free evaporated milk

¼ tsp ground black pepper

2 Tbsp chopped fresh tarragon or 2 tsp dried

1 lb cooked turkey breast, cut into 1" cubes

3 small red potatoes, cubed

1 small sweet potato, cubed

2 small parsnips, thinly sliced

½ c frozen crinkle-cut carrots, thawed

1 c buttermilk biscuit mix

¼ c fat-free milk

Preheat the oven to 350°F. Coat a large skillet with nonstick spray and place over medium heat. Add the onion and garlic; cook for 4 minutes. Stir in the flour; cook, stirring, for 30 seconds. Whisk in the evaporated milk; cook, stirring, for 3 to 5 minutes, or until slightly thickened. Season with the pepper and half of the tarragon.

Stir in the turkey, red potatoes, sweet potato, parsnips, and carrots. Transfer to a 2-quart casserole. Cover and bake for 30 minutes, or until the vegetables are tender. (If freezing, combine all the ingredients to this point and bake, but do not make the biscuit topping. To serve, thaw first, then bake in a 350°F oven for 30 minutes, or until piping hot. Follow instructions for the biscuit topping and bake for 10 to 15 minutes longer.)

In a small bowl, stir together the biscuit mix, fat-free milk, and the remaining tarragon. Drop 4 biscuits on top of the filling. Bake for 10 to 15 minutes, or until the biscuits are golden brown and the vegetables are tender.

Makes 4 servings

Per serving: 428 calories, 8 g fat

WOMEN ASK WHY

Why do beans give me gas?

Beans are loaded with dietary fiber and complex carbohydrates, and people lack all the enzymes needed to digest them completely. This means that tiny little bean units float around the digestive tract, providing fodder for bacteria. As it turns out, bacteria produce gas, too. Their gas turns into our gas, and it has to go somewhere, either upward in the form of a belch or down the other way.

Beans aren't all the same on the gas meter. Soybeans are the worst offenders, followed by navy beans, black beans, and pinto beans. Presoaking beans appears to reduce gas somewhat. It's also a good idea not to eat beans along with other gas-producing vegetables, such as cabbage, broccoli, onions, and peppers.

If you find that you're avoiding beans—and all the wonderful nutrients they contain—because of gas, you may want to try an over-the-counter supplement called Beano. It contains an enzyme called alpha-D-galactosidase, which breaks down the indigestible parts of beans while they're still in your stomach. This keeps them out of the intestine, where gas occurs.

Beans are such a nutritious food that it would be unfortunate if anyone stopped eating them. What's a little noise? We should all have more of a sense of humor about it. Remember the whoopee cushion?

Expert Consulted
Gail C. Frank, R.D., Dr.P.H.
Professor of nutrition
California State University
Long Beach

FREEZING FOR FRESHNESS

The great thing about casseroles is that it's just as easy to make 10 servings as it is to make 2. Most casseroles freeze well, which means that you can load the freezer with ready-to-eat meals. As long as you wrap them well, they'll last a month or longer. Various foods behave differently in the freezer, however, says Sue Snider, Ph.D., food and nutrition specialist at the University of Delaware's department of animal and food sciences in Newark. Here are her tips for successful freezing.

- Rice-based casseroles freeze extremely well, but potatoes develop a slightly grainy texture. Cooked pasta doesn't hold up well during freezing either.

- Anything with mayonnaise tends to break down in the freezer, and white sauces often get runny. Sometimes you can blend everything back together, but sometimes you can't.

- One way to freeze a creamy casserole successfully is to prepare it with sweet rice flour (also called waxy rice starch). Available in Asian groceries, it makes the dish just as creamy as the usual ingredients but will help the casserole maintain its texture in the freezer.

- Garlic and peppers tend to get stronger in flavor when they're frozen, and spices such as sage and clove may turn bitter.

- Casserole toppings such as crumbled crackers or potato chips invariably get soggy during freezing. It's best to add these ingredients after you've reheated a casserole.

Incidentally, the faster a casserole is frozen, the more palatable it will be and the better its texture. To cool your casserole quickly, put the hot cooking pot in a sink partially filled with cold water. Allow the water to come to within 1 inch of the top of the pot. Adding ice cubes to the water will cause the casserole to cool even faster.

Baked Rigatoni and Vegetables

8 oz rigatoni
1 jar (26 oz) fat-free pasta sauce
1 can (14½ oz) diced tomatoes
1 package (16 oz) frozen broccoli, red pepper, onion, and mushroom mix (or similar vegetable mixture)
1 package (10 oz) frozen broccoli florets
6 oz frozen, pre-browned, all-vegetable burger crumbles
1 tsp dried basil
¼ tsp fennel seeds
1 bag (4 oz) shredded reduced-fat mozzarella cheese

Preheat the oven to 400°F.

Cook the pasta according to package directions.

In a 13" × 9" baking dish, combine the pasta, pasta sauce, tomatoes (with juice), frozen vegetable mix, broccoli, burger crumbles, basil, fennel seeds, and cheese.

Bake for 20 minutes, or until heated through.

If freezing, the casserole can be placed in the freezer after the ingredients are combined. Thaw before baking. Bake in a 350°F oven for 20 minutes, or until heated through.

Makes 6 servings
Per serving: 398 calories, 7.5 g fat

Creamy Asparagus Chicken

1 boil-in-bag rice

1 package (9 oz) frozen chopped onion

1 Tbsp Poultry Seasoning (page 15)

1 lb boneless, skinless chicken breast halves, cut into strips

2 packages (10 oz each) frozen asparagus tips

1 can (10¾ oz) fat-free cream of mushroom soup

¼ c white wine or nonalcoholic white wine

¼ c chicken broth or water

2 Tbsp grated Parmesan cheese

Preheat the oven to 400°F.

Cook the rice according to package directions; drain. Place in an 11" × 7" baking dish. Add the onion and poultry seasoning. Spread the mixture in the dish.

Arrange the chicken over the rice mixture. Place the asparagus over the chicken.

In a small bowl, combine the soup, wine, and broth or water. Spoon over chicken mixture. Sprinkle with the cheese and bake for 25 minutes, or until the chicken is cooked through and no longer pink, and the mixture is bubbly.

The casserole can be frozen after the ingredients are combined. Thaw overnight and bake in a 400°F oven for 20 minutes, or until heated through.

Makes 6 servings
Per serving: 259 calories, 6 g fat

Vegetable Chili

2 Tbsp olive oil

1½ c chopped onions

2 Tbsp minced garlic

2 c finely chopped red bell pepper

2 tsp finely chopped jalapeño chile pepper (wear plastic gloves when handling)

2½ tsp chili powder

1 tsp ground cumin

⅛ tsp dried basil

1 can (28 oz) whole tomatoes

1 c beef broth

½ c mild or medium salsa

1 can (19 oz) red kidney beans, rinsed and drained

1½ c corn

Heat the oil in a large, heavy saucepan over medium-high heat. Add the onions and garlic. Cook, stirring occasionally, for 3 to 4 minutes, or until softened.

Stir in the bell pepper and chile pepper. Cook, stirring occasionally, for 3 to 4 minutes, or until softened.

Add the chili powder, cumin, and basil. Cook, stirring occasionally, for 1 minute.

Drain the tomatoes, reserving ½ cup of the juice. Add the juice to the pan. Crush the tomatoes (or cut with scissors) and add to the pan along with the broth and salsa. Bring to a boil.

Reduce the heat to medium-low and simmer, stirring occasionally, for 10 minutes, or until the mixture has thickened slightly.

Add the beans and corn. Raise the heat to medium and simmer for 6 to 8 minutes, or until the beans and corn are heated.

If freezing, spoon the chili into a large freezer container. Thaw and reheat it in a large saucepan over low heat.

Makes 4 servings
Per serving: 320 calories, 9 g fat

Mexican Cornbread Casserole

- 1 can (16 oz) red kidney beans, rinsed and drained
- 1 can (16 oz) black beans, rinsed and drained
- 1 c frozen chopped green bell pepper, thawed
- 1 c frozen corn kernels, thawed
- 1 can (14½ oz) chunky tomatoes
- 1 c low-fat cheese-and-salsa dip
- ¼ c shredded reduced-fat Cheddar cheese
- 1 Tbsp Mexican Spice Mix (page 15)
- 1 package (6½ oz) low-fat cornbread mix
- ¼ c liquid egg substitute or 1 egg
- ⅓ c fat-free milk
- 1 Tbsp canola oil

Preheat the oven to 400°F.

In an 8" × 8" baking dish, combine the kidney beans and black beans with the pepper, corn, tomatoes (with juice), dip, cheese, and spice mix.

In a medium bowl, stir together the cornbread mix, egg substitute or egg, milk, and oil. Spoon evenly over the bean mixture. (If freezing, combine all the ingredients, but reserve the biscuit topping step until ready to bake.)

Bake for 25 to 30 minutes, or until heated through and the cornbread topping is lightly browned.

Makes 6 servings
Per serving: 324 calories, 2 g fat

Sensational Soups and Stews

Soups and stews provide the equivalent of culinary flextime. You can prepare them days or weeks ahead of time, then reheat them at your convenience. They actually improve the longer they sit, as the flavors blend and mingle. Best of all, they freeze well. You can make large batches, then freeze them in ready-to-eat meal-size containers.

"I'll make a big pot on the weekend, then refrigerate or freeze it. Every time I serve it, I may add different things just to vary the taste," says Barbara Pool Fenzl, owner of Les Gourmettes Cooking School in Phoenix.

Stock up on stock. Soups and stews are only as good as the liquids, called stocks or broths, that they're cooked in. You can make excellent stocks by gently simmering meat or poultry with vegetables, then straining out the ingredients when the stocks are done. Fenzl recommends using chicken or turkey carcasses. Or you can save up small bones from meat and poultry, freeze them, and then make a stock when you have enough.

Stocks need to simmer for hours, but they don't need any attention on your part. Just let them simmer on low heat, strain the coarse material, then refrigerate them overnight so that the fat congeals on the surface, where it's easy to remove. Stock freezes extremely well, so you'll always have some ready.

Add flavor with canned stock. You don't need fresh-made stock to get great taste. In fact, many chefs have dispensed altogether with making their own stock, choosing instead to use canned stock. Use a stock that doesn't have added salt, Fenzl advises. "The flavor should come from the herbs in the soup or stew, not from the saltiness of the broth."

Add flavor with a vegetable sauté. Before cooking soups and stews, take a moment to sauté a mixture of vegetables, using the same pot that you're going to cook the soup in. Sautéing the vegetables first—as opposed to just dropping them into the stock—releases deep, long-lasting flavors.

Choose your texture. Vegetables are the foundation of most soups and stews, and how you prepare them will determine the character of the meal. Many people prefer small pieces of vegetables—coarsely chopped onions, carrots,

Use lean, trimmed meats. The high temperatures of soups and stews cause fats to thin and spread out, so even tiny amounts go a long way. It's important for taste as well as health to trim meats well before adding them to the pot. Take the skin off poultry, too.

Stew meats, which are purchased in easy-to-use chunks, aren't a good choice because they aren't trimmed thoroughly and may contain a lot of fat.

Add dried herbs early, fresh herbs late. Great soups and stews usually include a lot of herbs and spices. Timing is important. Fresh herbs give up their flavors easily, so it's best to add them toward the end of the cooking time. Dried herbs and spices hold on to their flavors. They require a lot of cooking to coax the flavors out.

Salt, incidentally, should always be added late in the cooking time. The soup's flavors swell and magnify over time. You can't taste it a half-hour after starting and assume that it needs extra help. Taste the soup or stew when it's almost done, then add salt if you think it needs it.

If you accidentally add too much salt to a soup, you can correct the flavor by dropping in several large chunks of raw potato, which will help absorb the salt. Discard them after about 15 minutes.

and celery, for example, with maybe a bag or two of frozen vegetables thrown in. (To make life really easy, you can make soups and stews using only frozen vegetables or vegetables ready-cut from the supermarket.) Another option is to run some of the vegetables through a food processor. This will give soups and stews more body.

Vegetable, Beef, and Barley Soup

1 Tbsp olive oil
8 oz beef, cut into ¼" strips
1 c chopped onions
1½ c quick-cooking barley
1 package (10 oz) shredded carrots
8 oz cole slaw mix
3 cans (14½ oz each) beef broth
1 can (14½ oz) vegetable broth

1 can (14½ oz) diced tomatoes
1 tsp sugar
2 Tbsp lemon juice
  Ground black pepper
1 green apple, finely chopped
  Chopped fresh parsley

Warm the oil in a nonstick Dutch oven over high heat. Add the beef and cook, stirring constantly, for 4 minutes, or until no longer pink. Remove with a slotted spoon and set aside.

Add the onions and barley and cook, stirring constantly, for 5 minutes. Add a little water if the onions start to stick.

Add the carrots and cole slaw mix and cook, stirring constantly, for 5 minutes. Stir in the beef broth, vegetable broth, tomatoes (with juice), and sugar. Bring to a boil. Reduce the heat to low, cover, and simmer for 10 to 15 minutes. Stir in the lemon juice and beef (with any drippings). Season with pepper to taste. Serve sprinkled with apples and parsley.

Makes 8 servings
Per serving: 231 calories, 6 g fat

Oyster and Corn Chowder

1 Tbsp olive oil
¼ c chopped onion
1 small green bell pepper, finely chopped
1 pint shucked frying oysters
2 large potatoes, peeled and finely chopped
¼ tsp dried thyme
¼ tsp salt
3 c canned corn kernels, drained
3 c 1% milk
½ c nonfat dry milk
¼ c superfine flour (such as Wondra)
  Ground black pepper
  Ground red pepper

Warm the oil in a soup pot over medium heat. Add the onion and bell pepper; sauté for 3 minutes.

Drain the oysters, reserving the liquid; set the oysters aside. Add enough water to the liquid to make 1 cup; add to the pot. Add the potatoes, thyme, and salt. Bring to a boil over medium-high heat, cover, and simmer for 7 minutes. Lightly mash the potatoes with a wooden spoon or potato masher. Add the corn and simmer for 5 minutes.

In a large bowl, whisk together the 1% milk, dry milk, and flour. Pour the mixture into the pot. Bring the soup to a boil, stirring constantly. Reduce the heat to low and simmer for 1 minute. Add the oysters and simmer for 3 minutes, or until the edges curl. Season with black pepper and red pepper to taste.

Makes 6 servings
Per serving: 250 calories, 5 g fat

Lentil Soup with Sun-Dried Tomatoes

1 c very small shell pasta
1 Tbsp olive oil
1 large onion, chopped
2 garlic cloves, minced, or 1 tsp prepared minced garlic
4 c chicken broth
3 c water
2 c dried lentils, rinsed
1 c sliced carrots
¾ tsp Italian Herb Blend (page 15)
¼ tsp ground black pepper
½ c oil-packed sun-dried tomatoes, drained and slivered
2 Tbsp balsamic vinegar plus additional for seasoning
  Salt (optional)

Cook the pasta according to package directions.

Meanwhile, warm the oil in a soup pot over medium heat. Add the onion and garlic and sauté for 3 minutes. Add the broth, water, lentils, carrots, herb blend, and pepper. Bring to a boil. Reduce the heat, cover, and simmer, stirring occasionally, for 20 minutes. Add the tomatoes. Simmer, stirring often, for 15 minutes, or until the lentils are tender. Stir in the vinegar. Season with salt, if using, and more vinegar, if desired.

Stir the pasta into the soup.

Makes 8 servings
Per serving: 312 calories, 7 g fat

Chicken Stew with Dumplings

Stew
4 c chicken broth
1 bay leaf
2 c baby carrots
½ c sliced celery
1 c frozen small whole onions
1 c frozen or drained canned peas
½ c flour
1 tsp Poultry Seasoning (page 15)
⅔ c fat-free milk
1¾ c cubed cooked chicken breast

Dumplings
1¼ c fat-free biscuit mix
⅓ c fat-free milk

To make the stew: In a medium saucepan, bring the broth and bay leaf to a boil over medium-high heat. Add the carrots and celery. Cook for 5 minutes. Add the onions and cook

for 2 minutes. Add the peas and cook for 2 minutes, or until tender.

Strain the vegetables and set aside. Collect the liquid; add broth or water to make 4 cups. Remove and discard the bay leaf. Return the liquid to the saucepan.

In a small bowl, whisk together the flour, poultry seasoning, and milk. Whisk into the broth. Cook, whisking, over medium heat for 2 minutes, or until thickened. Stir in the chicken and reserved vegetables.

To make the dumplings: In a small bowl, stir the biscuit mix and milk to form a soft dough. Drop by tablespoonfuls onto the simmering stew; stir occasionally. The dumplings will be cooked through in about 5 minutes.

Makes 6 servings
Per serving: 258 calories, 4.5 g fat

Sweet Pepper and Corn Soup

⅛ c finely chopped turkey bacon
2 c finely chopped onions
1 c finely chopped celery
2 garlic cloves, minced, or 1 tsp prepared minced garlic
3 c finely chopped potatoes
1 can (14½ oz) vegetable or chicken broth
2 Tbsp Dijon mustard
½ tsp dried thyme
⅛ tsp ground black pepper
1 bay leaf
½ c sliced carrots
1 red or green bell pepper, finely chopped
2 c drained canned corn kernels
1 can (28 oz) whole tomatoes

In a soup pot over medium-high heat, sauté the bacon for 5 minutes, or until browned. Add the onions, celery, and garlic. Cook, stirring often, for 5 minutes; do not brown. Add the potatoes, broth, mustard, thyme, black pepper, and bay leaf. Mix well.

Bring to a boil. Cover, reduce the heat to low, and simmer for 10 minutes, or until the potatoes are tender. Remove and discard the bay leaf. Add the carrots, bell pepper, and corn.

Pour the tomatoes (with juice) into a blender and chop with 2 or 3 on/off turns; stir into the soup. Bring to a boil over medium-high heat. Cover, reduce the heat to low, and simmer for 15 minutes, or until the carrots are tender.

Makes 7 servings

Per serving: 182 calories, 2.5 g fat

Salmon Bisque

    2 tsp olive oil
    1 onion, diced
 1½ Tbsp all-purpose flour
    2 c chicken broth
    1 c tomato puree
    1 tsp lemon juice
    1 salmon fillet (12 oz), cut into ½" chunks
    1 Tbsp minced fresh parsley or 1 tsp dried
    2 tsp minced fresh dill or ½ tsp dried
 1½ c fat-free evaporated milk

In a medium saucepan over medium heat, warm the oil. Add the onion and sauté for 5 minutes, or until soft. Add the flour and cook for 3 minutes, or until light brown.

Add the broth, tomato puree, lemon juice, salmon, parsley, and dill. Simmer for 10 minutes. Add the milk and heat until the fish flakes easily.

Makes 4 servings

Per serving: 251 calories, 5.5 g fat

WOMEN ASK WHY

Why does eating soup make my nose run?

Everyone has heard that chicken soup is good for colds, but almost any kind of hot soup probably helps. When you eat soup, the steam swirls into your mouth and up the back of your palate, and the heat is transferred to your sinuses. The combination of heat and steam loosens congestion by making mucus more fluid, and fluid, of course, runs downhill. Hence, the runny nose.

It's not just the steam that makes noses run. Soups seasoned with spicy ingredients can cause a major increase in secretions. Jalapeño chiles, ground red pepper, and their fiery kin contain a compound called capsaicin. This compound, which is similar to a drug in cold and flu medications, causes the nose to run freely.

You may not appreciate the runny nose, but it's probably good for your long-term health. Mucus in the nose traps dust and allergens, which are flushed away when your nose runs. In addition, people with dry mucous membranes are more vulnerable to colds and other upper respiratory infections. The steam from soup adds moisture and may help keep you from getting sick.

Expert Consulted
Mary Ellen Camire, Ph.D.
Associate professor
Department of food science
*   and human nutrition*
University of Maine
Orono

CREAMY SOUPS
WITHOUT THE FAT

Want the texture of cream without using fatty butter-and-flour bases? All you have to do is puree a cup of vegetables with broth and add it to the soup. Cooked carrots, leeks, asparagus, beans, celery, and winter squash are good choices.

Or use potatoes. Blending potatoes with canned low-fat broth makes a fast, creamy foundation for frozen or canned tomatoes, peas, corn, or carrots. Grains such as barley and rice work nicely, too.

For milk-based soup, heat some low-fat milk separately and add it to the warmed soup. Stir it in just before serving to keep the milk from curdling.

Black Bean Chili with Turkey

    1 pound ground turkey
    1 c coarsely chopped onions
    1 red bell pepper, coarsely chopped
    2 jalapeño chile peppers, seeded and finely chopped (wear plastic gloves when handling)
    2 Tbsp minced garlic
    1 can (28 oz) tomatoes, coarsely chopped
    1 can (16 oz) black beans, rinsed and drained
    2 Tbsp Mexican Spice Mix (page 15)
    ½ c coarsely chopped and loosely packed fresh cilantro or parsley
       Salt (to taste)

In a large saucepan over medium heat, cook the turkey, onions, bell pepper, chile peppers, and garlic for 8 minutes, or until the turkey is no longer pink and the vegetables are tender.

Stir in the tomatoes (with juice), beans, and spice mix. Raise the heat to medium-high and bring to a gentle boil. Reduce the heat to medium-low, cover, and simmer for 5 minutes. Stir in the cilantro or parsley and season to taste with salt.

Makes 4 servings
Per serving: 312 calories, 4 g fat

Cheese Tortellini Soup

    3 c beef broth
    1 c frozen cheese tortellini
    1 c frozen peas
    2 Tbsp chopped sun-dried tomatoes
    1 Tbsp Italian Herb Blend (page 15)

In a medium saucepan, combine the broth, tortellini, peas, tomatoes, and herb blend. Cover and bring to a boil over medium-high heat, then reduce the heat to medium-low. Simmer for 5 to 6 minutes, or until the tortellini are tender.

Makes 4 servings
Per serving: 107 calories, 2 g fat

HEALTH BONUS

Oysters: Immunity on the Half-Shell

Forget pearls. The real payload in oysters is immunity-boosting zinc. These nutrient-rich mollusks are also packed with iron, copper, vitamin B_{12}, and selenium. When you buy oysters, be sure to ask for some of the liquid that they're packed in, which also contains these valuable nutrients.

Chicken Vegetable Soup with Shells

6 c chicken broth

12 oz boneless, skinless chicken breasts, cut into 1" pieces

1 large onion, thinly sliced

1 tsp Poultry Seasoning (page 15)

¼ tsp ground black pepper

¾ c tiny shell pasta

3 c frozen mixed broccoli, cauliflower, and carrots or other mixed vegetables

In a medium saucepan, combine the broth, chicken, onion, poultry seasoning, and pepper. Cover and bring to a boil over medium-high heat. Reduce the heat to medium-low and simmer, stirring occasionally, for 10 minutes.

Stir in the pasta. Raise the heat to medium-high and return to a boil. Reduce the heat to medium-low. Cover and simmer, stirring occasionally, for 5 minutes.

Stir in the vegetables. Raise the heat to medium-high and return to a boil. Reduce the heat to medium-low. Cover and simmer, stirring occasionally, for 5 minutes, or until the vegetables are crisp-tender.

Makes 4 servings

Per serving: 296 calories, 4.5 g fat

HEALTH BONUS

Start with Soup

Researchers at Johns Hopkins University in Baltimore found that people who began a meal with a soup appetizer consumed 25 percent fewer calories over the course of the meal than those who had a cheese-and-crackers appetizer. The researchers theorize that soup fills you up better than other foods so that you don't feel like eating as much. Just be sure to avoid soups that begin with the words *cream of.*

Crock-Pots: Hands-Off Cooking

If you got married in the 1970s or early 1980s, you probably got a Crock-Pot or another type of slow cooker as a wedding present. You may have even gotten two or three. Like most women, you probably used them for a while, then put them out of sight under a counter along with the fondue pot.

Well, it's time to haul them out and dust them off. What began as a fad has become an indispensable time-saver for today's busy women. Slow cooking may be at the opposite end of the spectrum from gourmet cooking, but it's arguably the easiest cooking technique ever developed.

Load a cold Crock-Pot with beans, rice, meat, potatoes, tomato juice, chicken broth, or whatever you have a taste for, turn it on, and go shopping for the rest of the day. When you come back, the house will smell as though you've been cooking all day, and the ingredients will be so tender that you won't even need a knife.

The advantage of slow cookers is that they provide a steady wraparound heat that cooks food slowly and evenly, says Babs Carlson, R.D., Ph.D., a registered dietitian at Chesa-

peake General Hospital's Lifestyle Fitness Center in Chesapeake, Virginia. This means no hot spots, virtually no supervision, and, unless the cooker runs completely dry, almost no risk of burning. To get the best results, according to Dr. Carlson, here are a few things that you'll want to do.

Go from tough to tender. Slow cookers are hottest at the bottom of the pot and coolest at the top. You'll want to put tougher, slower-cooking ingredients, like carrots, parsnips, and potatoes, in first and faster-cooking ingredients, like onions, higher up.

Cook lean meats long and slow. Game meats and lean cuts of beef such as flank steak don't benefit from the natural tenderizing effect of fat. They need to cook for a long time—up to 8 hours or more—at the lowest heat. Poultry tends to cook quickly, however, so you may want to cut it into chunks and freeze it before adding it to the pot.

Cook drier than usual. Stews prepared in slow cookers retain more liquid than those made on the stove top. Adding too much water will make them thin and watery. You can either use

REAL-LIFE SCENARIO

That Old Cookbook Isn't Working Anymore

You can tell how Shea feels about her Crock-Pot just by looking at her ancient slow-cooker cookbook: It's torn, splattered with gravy, and barely holding together. As a researcher who works long and irregular hours, Shea has found that the slow cooker is the only thing that allows her to give her family regular meals. She loves the idea that dinner is cooking even when she's gone, and she loves the aroma when she walks in the door. Pot roast—what could be easier! Pork and sauerkraut, beef and kidney casserole, chicken and dumplings, and sausage stew are all family favorites. It's not exactly health food, but Shea tries to make up for it on nights when she actually has time to cook. The family gets chicken and fish at least once a week, and there's always shredded lettuce and dressing on the table. But Shea realizes that her system isn't working. Yesterday, her husband, Stan, came back from the doctor with a bad report card: His cholesterol is over 250 milligrams per deciliter, and he's 30 pounds overweight. He needs her help, but what can she do?

The Crock-Pot isn't the problem. It's what Shea is putting in it.

For instance, if she is cooking chicken and dumplings and leaving the skin on the chicken, she is substantially increasing the fat content without doing a thing for the flavor, and it certainly isn't doing Stan any good. Slow cookers are great for convenience, and she should keep using hers. She just has to watch the ingredients with an eye toward lowering fat. Forget kidney casse-role—there's no way she's going to make that healthy. She needs to be using more lean meats, like flank steak or sirloin tips.

Then there's that old, battered cookbook. Fifteen years ago, no one was thinking very much about fat and cholesterol. Shea needs to get a cookbook that incorporates the latest knowledge about healthy cooking. Some of the best cookbooks rework traditional recipes, giving the same tastes but with a lot less fat.

If Shea finds that cooking leaner doesn't satisfy Stan's tastes—and this happens with a lot of people—she's going to want to pump up the flavors. This is as simple as adding more herbs, spices, or flavored liquids.

The lettuce that she's using sounds like iceberg, which has fewer nutrients than darker greens such as spinach and romaine. These and other salad greens taste just as good (actually, they taste better) and also provide a nutritional payload. She should also use a low-fat dressing.

Shea needs to take her husband's cholesterol problem seriously, and cutting back on fat—mainly in meat, salad dressings, and dairy products—may be the way to do it. So she should throw out that old cookbook and buy a new one.

Expert Consulted

Sue Snider, Ph.D.
Food and nutrition specialist
Department of animal and food
  sciences
University of Delaware
Newark

less liquid to begin with or thicken the liquid with a teaspoon of quick-cooking tapioca.

Use extra spices. The long cooking time required by slow cookers means that herbs and spices tend to give up the ghost before the meal is done. You can compensate by adding about 25 percent more herbs and spices than you would if you were cooking in the oven or on the stove.

THE BEST AND WORST INGREDIENTS FOR SLOW COOKERS

Some foods taste best when they're cooked quickly in the oven or on the stove. Others grow richer and more tender with slow cooking. You'll want to experiment to find your own favorites, but here are a few of the proven winners—and losers.

The Best

- Beans
- Brown rice, barley, and other whole grains
- Lean meats, especially pork and beef roasts and tenderloins
- Potatoes, turnips, and other root vegetables
- Poultry, especially thighs, legs, and whole birds
- Rhubarb and celery

The Worst

- Boneless chicken breasts and chicken tenders
- Broccoli, spinach, and other vegetables that can fall apart
- Fish
- Milk, cheese, and eggs
- Pasta

Save time with patience. Each time you open the lid, built-up steam escapes. This can cost you about 20 minutes in cooking time. There's no need to look under the hood anyway. The great thing about slow cooking is that it takes care of itself.

Crock-Pot Baked Beans

    3 cans (15–16 oz each) low-sodium navy or great Northern beans, rinsed and drained
    ½ c hickory-flavored barbecue sauce
    ½ c reduced-sodium ketchup
    ½ c packed brown sugar
    1 tsp mustard powder
    1 green or red bell pepper, finely chopped
    1 large onion, finely chopped
    4 oz lean reduced-sodium ham, chopped

In a 4-quart slow cooker, mix the barbecue sauce, ketchup, brown sugar, and mustard powder until smooth.

Stir in the beans, pepper, onion, and ham. Cover and cook on high for 3 to 4 hours or on low for 8 to 12 hours, or until thick.

Makes 12 servings
Per serving: 138 calories, 1.5 g fat

Easy Barbecued Beef Stew

    1 large onion, finely chopped
    1 lb boiling potatoes, cut into ¾" cubes
    1½ c green beans cut into 1¼" pieces or 2 c coarsely shredded cabbage
    1 large carrot, sliced
    1 large celery rib, sliced
    1 large garlic clove, minced
    1 lb very lean stew beef, trimmed of all visible fat and cut into bite-size pieces
    1 c defatted beef broth
    1 can (8 oz) tomato sauce
    ½ c ketchup
    2 Tbsp packed light brown sugar
    1 Tbsp apple cider vinegar
    1 tsp dried thyme leaves
    1 tsp Dijon mustard
    ¼ tsp ground allspice
    ¼ tsp ground black pepper

In a large Crock-Pot or other slow cooker, combine the onion, potatoes, beans or cabbage, carrot, celery, and garlic. Mix well. Top with the meat.

In a medium bowl, stir together the broth, tomato sauce, ketchup, brown sugar, vinegar, thyme, mustard, allspice, and pepper. Pour the mixture over the meat and vegetables.

Cover the slow cooker. Cook on high for 4 to 4½ hours, or until the meat and vegetables are tender. Stir well after the first 3 hours. (An alternate method is to cook the vegetables and meat in the slow cooker on high for 1 hour, then reduce the temperature to low and cook for 6 to 7 hours longer.)

Makes 5 servings
Per serving: 311 calories, 6.5 g fat

Italian Sausage and White Bean Stew

 1 c frozen chopped onions
 4 oz frozen low-fat hot Italian turkey sausage, chopped
 1 c frozen chopped carrots
 1 c frozen diced potatoes
 1 c frozen cooked navy beans
 4 large garlic cloves, minced
 ¼ c all-purpose flour
 3 c defatted chicken broth
 ½ tsp dried thyme
 ½ tsp ground black pepper
 ¼ tsp salt
 ½ c fat-free sour cream

Coat a Crock-Pot or other slow cooker with nonstick spray and set on high heat until hot. Add the onions and sausage. Cook, stirring, for 5 minutes, or until the onions are soft and the sausage is browned. Add the carrots, pota-toes, beans, garlic, flour, and broth. Cook, stirring, for 2 minutes. Add the thyme. Bring to a boil.

Reduce the heat to low and cook for 4 to 5 hours, or until the stew is thick and the sausage is no longer pink in the center. Add the pepper and salt. Stir to combine. Top each serving with sour cream.

Makes 6 servings
Per serving: 176 calories, 1.5 g fat

Chicken and Barley Stew

 4 skinless chicken thighs
 ½ c barley
 5½ c chicken broth
 1 celery rib, chopped
 3 small carrots, sliced
 1 large tomato, peeled and chopped
 2 garlic cloves, minced
 1 Tbsp tamari
 ½ tsp dried basil
 ⅛ tsp dried oregano
 ⅛ tsp dried thyme
    Dash of ground red pepper
 2 Tbsp finely chopped fresh parsley

In a Crock-Pot or other slow cooker, layer the chicken, barley, broth, celery, carrots, tomato, garlic, tamari, basil, oregano, thyme, and pepper.

Set the cooker on low and cook for 4 to 6 hours, stirring occasionally.

Remove the chicken thighs from the stew. When they have cooled slightly, remove the meat from the bones, cutting it in bite-size pieces if necessary. Return the meat to the stew.

Cook for 30 minutes longer, stir in the parsley, and serve.

Makes 4 servings
Per serving: 223 calories, 3.5 g fat

Mexican Corn Stew

1 c chopped onions

½ c thinly sliced carrot

½ c thinly sliced celery

1 small red or green bell pepper, finely chopped

3 small jalapeño chile peppers, seeded and finely chopped (wear plastic gloves when handling)

1 Tbsp minced garlic

2 c whole kernel corn

1 c dried pinto beans

3 Tbsp minced fresh parsley or cilantro

2 tsp ground cumin

2 tsp ground coriander

½ tsp ground red pepper

6 c fat-free chicken broth

⅛ tsp salt

⅛ tsp ground black pepper

In a Crock-Pot or other slow cooker, layer the onions, carrot, celery, bell pepper, chile peppers, and garlic. Add the corn, beans, parsley or cilantro, cumin, coriander, and red pepper. Pour the chicken broth over the top. Bring to a boil on high. Reduce the heat to low. Cover and cook for 5 to 6 hours, or until the beans are tender and the stew is thick. Add the salt and black pepper.

Makes 6 servings
Per serving: 214 calories, 2 g fat

Russian Potato and Green Bean Stew

3 russet potatoes, cubed

1 large onion, thinly sliced

8 oz green beans, cut into 1" pieces

½ c water or apple juice

5 c fat-free chicken broth

1 can (10¾ oz) condensed cream of chicken soup

¾ c reduced-sodium sauerkraut, rinsed and drained

½ tsp dried dillweed

¾ tsp ground black pepper

In a Crock-Pot or other slow cooker, layer the potatoes, onion, and beans. Combine the water or juice, broth, and soup. Pour over the vegetables. Add the sauerkraut and dillweed. Cook on low for 4 to 6 hours, or until the mixture is thickened. Sprinkle with the pepper before serving.

Makes 4 servings
Per serving: 197 calories, 4 g fat

Chili Con Carne

1 Tbsp vegetable oil

1 onion, chopped

1 garlic clove

1–2 Tbsp chopped canned jalapeño chile peppers (to taste)

1 red or green bell pepper, chopped

2 lb lean ground beef

8 tomatoes, chopped

1½ c tomato puree

2–3 Tbsp chili powder

1 Tbsp Worcestershire sauce

2 Tbsp soy sauce

½ tsp ground black pepper

4 c cooked kidney beans

Heat the oil in a large Crock-Pot or other slow cooker set to high. Add the onion, garlic, chile peppers, and bell pepper and cook, stirring occasionally, for 5 minutes, or until soft.

Add the beef and cook for 5 minutes, or until well-browned. Add the tomatoes, tomato puree,

WOMAN TO WOMAN
Crock-Pot Saves the Day

Shannon Entin of Lambertville, New Jersey, first discovered the convenience of Crock-Pot cooking when she was in college. When she left college and went to work, however, the Crock-Pot was mainly forgotten, until Shannon, a 30-year-old journalist , started her own business in 1996. Now the Crock-Pot is a kitchen essential.

Once I started my own business publishing and editing a Web site, I found that I didn't have a lot of time left for cooking at the end of the day. In fact, I don't always *have* an end of the day. I work at home, and I always feel a little guilty when I'm in the kitchen instead of at my desk working.

To be perfectly honest, cooking is often the last thing that I want to do. I used to ruin a lot of meals because I'd put something on the stove, then get caught up in my work. It was sometimes a half-hour before I remembered the pasta boiling on the stove. By then, of course, it would be a soggy mess.

After one especially hectic day, I decided to dust off the Crock-Pot. I loved it when I was in college because it was so easy, and my schedule then was nothing compared to what it is today. So I decided to start using the Crock-Pot again.

There's nothing easier than Crock-Pot cooking. No standing over a stove. No stirring. No adjusting the heat. You just spend a few minutes cutting up the ingredients, throw them in the pot, put the lid on, and walk away. About 6 hours later, dinner is ready. And no dirty pots to deal with. To clean the Crock-Pot, I fill it with water and let it soak overnight. In the morning, I sponge it out, then fill it up again.

Like everyone else these days, I'm trying to eat less fat and fewer calories. Slow cookers make this easy. The food is cooked with steam and moistened in its own juices. You don't have to add any oil. My favorite dish is sweet-and-sour chicken. My husband loves corned beef and potatoes. Okay, it's not exactly low-fat, but it tastes great, and we don't have it all that often.

My friends probably get tired of hearing me talk about the Crock-Pot, but I can't help it. It has worked so well for me, I can't imagine anyone doing without it.

---

2 tablespoons of the chili powder, Worcestershire sauce, soy sauce, black pepper, and beans.

Reduce the heat to low, cover, and cook for 4 to 6 hours. (Uncover for the last 10 minutes of cooking if a thicker consistency is desired.)

Taste and add more chili powder if you would like more heat.

Makes 12 servings
Per serving: 306 calories, 15 g fat

Index

Underscored page references indicate boxed text.

A

Antipastos, 31, 88
Apples
  Pork Cutlets with Apple Slices,
    68–69
  Rice-Raisin Pudding, 101
Artichokes
  Vegetarian Paella, 77
Asian-style dishes
  Fusilli Primavera in Spicy
    Peanut Sauce, 44–45
  Ginger Chicken, 48
  Pork and Cabbage Roll-Ups, 96
  Quick-Fry with Tofu and
    Vegetables, 78
  Sesame Turkey Cutlets, 53
  Teriyaki Swordfish Kabobs,
    89–90
  Thai Chicken Kabobs, 50
  Thai Tuna Wraps, 97
Asparagus
  Asparagus and Orange
    Linguine, 44
  Asparagus Quesadillas, 97–98
  Creamy Asparagus Chicken,
    125
  Pasta Primavera with Tomato-
    Basil Sauce, 40–41
Avocados, 30
  Bean Burritos, 96
  Crab Salad with Avocado and
    Mango, 35
  Wagon Wheels with Mexican
    Salsa, 79

B

Baked goods, reducing fat in, 111
Bananas, 110
  Banana-Mango Mousse, 116
  Banana-Raspberry Rice
    Pudding, 112
  Poached Bananas in Vanilla
    Sauce, 116

Barley
  Chicken and Barley Stew, 137
  Vegetable, Beef, and Barley
    Soup, 128–29
Basil
  Creamy Tomato Sauce, 40
  Pasta Primavera with Tomato-
    Basil Sauce, 40–41
  Quick Tomato Sauce, 40
  Red, White, and Green Pizza,
    78–79
  Stuffed Tomatoes, 106
  Tofu Layered with Three
    Cheeses, 77–78
Bass, sea
  Broiled Barbecued Sea Bass, 62
Beans, dried. _See also specific beans_
  Bangers and Beans, 68
  Bean Burritos, 96
  canned, 14, 72, 100
  digestibility of, 123
  in healthy diet, 6, 9
  preparing, 72
Beans, green. _See_ Green beans
Beef
  Beef and Noodle Paprikash,
    66–67
  Beefy Tortilla Stack, 96–97
  Chili Con Carne, 138–39
  cooking methods, 25–26,
    64–65, 120, 134
  Corned Beef Hash, 67
  cuts of, 14, 17, 69
  Easy Barbecued Beef Stew,
    136–37
  freezing, 17, 66
  French Beef and Rice, 68
  in healthy diet, 14
  herb blends for, 15
  Indian Beef and Rice, 68
  marinating, 20, 25–26, 82–83
  Mexican Beef and Rice, 68
  Mushroom-Onion Burgers, 86
  Pepper-Marinated Flank Steak,
    83–84

  in salads, 28–29, 36
  salmonella in, 52
  Savory Beef Rolls, 70
  Skillet Beef and Rice, 68
  Sloppy Burger Sandwiches, 70
  spice rubs for, 83
  trimming fat from, 66, 69, 128
  Vegetable, Beef, and Barley
    Soup, 128–29
Bell peppers, 85
  Black Bean Chili with Turkey,
    132
  Chili Con Carne, 138–39
  Creamy Tomato Sauce, 40
  Crock-Pot Baked Beans, 136
  French Beef and Rice, 68
  Indian Beef and Rice, 68
  Linguine with Mushrooms and
    Peppers, 42–43
  Meatless Sloppy Joes, 98–99
  Mexican Beef and Rice, 68
  Mexican Cornbread Casserole,
    126
  Mexican Corn Stew, 138
  Penne with Mediterranean
    Vegetables, 39
  Poached Sole with Italian
    Vegetables, 60
  Quick-Fry with Tofu and
    Vegetables, 78
  Red, White, and Green Pizza,
    78–79
  Roasted Vegetable Medley, 104
  Skillet Beef and Rice, 68
  Stuffed Spaghetti Squash,
    79–80
  Sweet Pepper and Corn Soup,
    130–31
  Teriyaki Swordfish Kabobs,
    89–90
  Thai Chicken Kabobs, 50
  Thai Tuna Wraps, 97
  Turkey and Sausage Jambalaya,
    54
  Vegetable Chili, 125

Bell peppers *(continued)*
  Vegetarian Paella, 77
  White Beans and Sausage with
    Greens, 32
Berries, 13. *See also specific berries*
Bisque
  Salmon Bisque, 131
Black beans
  Beefy Tortilla Stack, 96–97
  Black Bean Chili with Turkey,
    132
  Black Bean Citrus Salad, 33–34
  Cuban Black Beans and Rice,
    101
  Mexican Cornbread Casserole,
    126
  Wagon Wheels with Mexican
    Salsa, 79
Black pepper
  Basic Barbecue Dry Rub, 83
  Pepper Blend Rubs, 83
  Pepper-Marinated Flank Steak,
    83–84
Blueberries, 104
  Peach and Blueberry Sauce,
    109
Bow-tie pasta
  Warm Pasta Salad with
    Chicken, 31–32
Braising, 64
Broccoli, 79
  Baked Rigatoni and Vegetables,
    124
  Rice and Broccoli Salad, 101
  Tuna Noodle Casserole, 122
  Turkey Divan with Peaches, 55
  Warm Steak Salad, 84
Broth, 62, 127
Brownies
  10-Minute Brownies, 112–13
Browning, 120
Brussels sprouts
  Brussels Sprouts with Dill,
    103–4
Bulgur
  Curried Bulgur and Ham
    Salad, 31
  Sloppy Burger Sandwiches, 70
Burgers
  Mushroom-Onion Burgers, 86
Burritos
  Bean Burritos, 96

C

Cabbage, 102
  Crunchy Cabbage Slaw, 106
  Easy Barbecued Beef Stew,
    136–37
  Key West Crab Salad, 35–36
  Pork and Cabbage Roll-Ups,
    96
  Quick-Fry with Tofu and
    Vegetables, 78
  Vegetable, Beef, and Barley
    Soup, 128–29
Cakes
  Raspberry Jelly Roll, 114–15
Carrots, 85
  Chicken and Barley Stew, 137
  Chicken Stew with Dumplings,
    130
  Court Bouillon, 62
  Crunchy Cabbage Slaw, 106
  Italian Sausage and White
    Bean Stew, 137
  Lentil Soup with Sun-Dried
    Tomatoes, 129–30
  Maple-Glazed Carrots with
    Radishes, 106
  Pasta Primavera with Tomato-
    Basil Sauce, 40–41
  Turkey Potpie, 123
  Vegetable, Beef, and Barley
    Soup, 128–29
Casseroles, 120–22, 124
  Baked Rigatoni and Vegetables,
    124
  Creamy Asparagus Chicken,
    125
  Mexican Cornbread Casserole,
    126
  Quick Cassoulet, 122
  Tuna Noodle Casserole, 122
  Turkey Potpie, 123
  Vegetable Chili, 125
Catfish
  Blackened Catfish, 59
Cheddar cheese
  Bean Burritos, 96
  French Beef and Rice, 68
  Indian Beef and Rice, 68
  Mexican Beef and Rice, 68
  Mexican Cornbread Casserole,
    126

Skillet Beef and Rice, 68
  Spinach-Cheese Quesadillas,
    98
Cheese, 17, 38. *See also specific
    cheeses*
Chicken
  Apricot-Glazed Chicken
    Breasts, 47–48
  buying, 9, 16, 47
  Chicken and Barley Stew, 137
  Chicken and Grape Salad in
    Pitas, 51
  Chicken and Waffles, 51
  Chicken Fingers Parmesan, 41
  Chicken Pesto Pasta, 42
  Chicken Provençal with Garlic
    Potatoes, 49–50
  Chicken Stew with Dumplings,
    130
  Chicken Vegetable Soup with
    Shells, 133
  cooking methods, 25–26,
    46–47, 51, 81, 134
  Creamy Asparagus Chicken,
    125
  defrosting, 46
  Fast Chicken Curry, 53
  fat in, 16, 26, 47, 53
  freezing, 16, 46
  Ginger Chicken, 48
  in healthy diet, 14
  herb blends for, 15
  marinating, 25–26
  Mushroom-Onion Burgers, 86
  Quick Cassoulet, 122
  in salads, 28–29, 36
  salmonella in, 47, 52
  spice rubs for, 83
  Thai Chicken Kabobs, 50
  Tuscan Chicken Legs with
    Spinach Fettuccine, 48
  Warm Pasta Salad with
    Chicken, 31–32
  Zesty Barbecued Chicken
    Breasts, 86
Chile peppers
  Beefy Tortilla Stack, 96–97
  Black Bean Chili with Turkey,
    132
  Broiled Barbecued Sea Bass, 62
  Chili Con Carne, 138–39
  Creamy Tomato Sauce, 40

Jamaican Pork, 87
Mexican Corn Stew, 138
Vegetable Chili, 125
Wagon Wheels with Mexican
Salsa, 79
Chili
Black Bean Chili with Turkey,
132
Chili Con Carne, 138–39
Vegetable Chili, 125
Chives
Brussels Sprouts with Dill,
103–4
Crunchy Cabbage Slaw, 106
Fettuccine Alfredo, 41
Grilled Tuna Steaks with Chive
and Dill Sauce, 88
Chocolate
Chocolate Mousse, 113
Italian Biscotti Parfaits, 112
10-Minute Brownies, 112–13
Chowders
Oyster and Corn Chowder, 129
Clams
Pasta with Red Clam Sauce, 43
Cod
Baked Cod with Crumb
Topping, 61
Condiments, 18, 75, 84. *See also*
mustard
Convenience foods
precooked meats, 29
precooked poultry, 9, 29
precut vegetables, 8–9, 72
Cookies
Crunchy Peanut Butter
Cookies, 115–16
Cooking methods
braising, 64
browning, 120
grilling, 25–26, 81–82, 85, 87
poaching, 23–24, 57, 62
sautéing, 21–23, 74–75
steaming, 21, 24–25, 74
stir-frying, 19–21, 91–93, 93
Cookware, 19–25, 22–23, 100
Corn, 85
Corn and Spinach Fritters, 103
Mexican Cornbread Casserole,
126
Mexican Corn Stew, 138
Oyster and Corn Chowder, 129

Quick-Fry with Tofu and
Vegetables, 78
Sweet Pepper and Corn Soup,
130–31
Vegetable Chili, 125
Vegetarian Paella, 77
Wagon Wheels with Mexican
Salsa, 79
Cottage cheese
Creamy Tomato Sauce, 40
Dill Sauce, 61
Couscous
Couscous Salad Niçoise, 30
Stuffed Spaghetti Squash,
79–80
Vegetarian Paella, 77
Crabmeat
Crab Cakes, 58
Crab Salad with Avocado and
Mango, 35
Key West Crab Salad, 35–36
Cranberries
Cranberry-Glazed Pork Chops,
69
Crock-Pots, 64–65, 134–36, 136.
See also Slow cooker recipes
Crusts, pie, 110–11
Cucumbers
Black Bean Citrus Salad, 33–34
Thai Tuna Wraps, 97
Curry powder
Curried Bulgur and Ham
Salad, 31
Curried French Vinaigrette, 32
Fast Chicken Curry, 53
Indian Beef and Rice, 68
Lamb Curry with Rice, 70–71

D

Dairy foods, 7–8, 17, 75
Defrosting, 21, 46
Desserts, 108, 110–11
Banana-Mango Mousse, 116
Banana-Raspberry Rice
Pudding, 112
Chocolate Mousse, 113
Creamy Strawberry Sauce, 109
Crunchy Peanut Butter
Cookies, 115–16
Dried-Fruit Truffles, 115
Italian Biscotti Parfaits, 112

Key Lime Pie, 112
Peach and Blueberry Sauce, 109
Peach Crunch, 117
Poached Bananas in Vanilla
Sauce, 116
Raspberry Dessert Sauce, 109
Raspberry Jelly Roll, 114–15
Rice-Raisin Pudding, 101
10-Minute Brownies, 112–13
Dill
Brussels Sprouts with Dill,
103–4
Dill Sauce, 61
Grilled Tuna Steaks with Chive
and Dill Sauce, 88

E

Eggplant, 85
Lamb Curry with Rice, 70–71
Penne with Mediterranean
Vegetables, 39
Eggs, 67, 78
Potato Pancakes, 102
Spinach and Mushroom
Frittata, 76–77

F

Fat, dietary, 7, 12, 17, 29, 30, 33,
44, 59
in beef cuts, 17, 66, 69, 128
in canned fish, 14, 63
in cooking oils, 17–18
in game birds, 53
in margarine, 44
in nuts, 107
in peanut butter, 12
in pork, 71
in poultry, 16, 26, 47, 53
substitutes, for baked goods, 111
substitutes, for creamy soups,
132
in vegetarian cooking, 75
Feta cheese
Greek Salad with Shrimp,
32–33
Stuffed Spaghetti Squash, 79–80
Fettuccine
Chicken Pesto Pasta, 42
Fettuccine Alfredo, 41
Pasta with Red Clam Sauce, 43

Fettuccine *(continued)*
    Tuscan Chicken Legs with
        Spinach Fettuccine, 48
Fish. *See also* Shellfish
    Baked Cod with Crumb
        Topping, 61
    Blackened Catfish, 59
    Broiled Barbecued Sea Bass, 62
    buying, 56
    canned, 14, 63
    cooking methods, 21, 57
    Couscous Salad Niçoise, 30
    Crispy Fish Fillets, 58
    freezing, 16, 56
    Grilled Tuna Steaks with Chive
        and Dill Sauce, 88
    in healthy diet, 9, 14, 63
    herb blends for, 15
    Poached Sole with Italian
        Vegetables, 60
    poaching broth for, 62
    Roasted Swordfish with
        Herbed Crust, 59–60
    Roast Salmon with Ginger and
        Garlic, 58
    in salads, 36
    Salmon Bisque, 131
    spice rubs for, 83
    Teriyaki Swordfish Kabobs,
        89–90
    Thai Tuna Wraps, 97
    toppings for, 61
    Tuna Noodle Casserole, 122
Flounder
    Crispy Fish Fillets, 58
Freezing
    bread, 12
    casseroles, 124
    cheese, 17
    fish, 16, 56
    meat, 17, 66
    pie crusts, 110–11
    poultry, 16, 46
Frittata
    Spinach and Mushroom
        Frittata, 76–77
Fritters
    Corn and Spinach Fritters, 103
Fruit. *See also specific fruits*
    for dessert, 108, 110
    Dried-Fruit Truffles, 115
    frozen, 105, 108

in healthy diet, 6
as side dish, 102
in well-stocked kitchen, 13
Fusilli
    Fusilli Primavera in Spicy
        Peanut Sauce, 44–45

G

Garlic, 8–9, 13
    Apricot-Glazed Chicken
        Breasts, 47–48
    Black Bean Chili with Turkey,
        132
    Chicken and Barley Stew, 137
    Chicken Provençal with Garlic
        Potatoes, 49–50
    Creamy Tomato Sauce, 40
    Easy Barbecued Beef Stew,
        136–37
    French Beef and Rice, 68
    Garlic Vinaigrette, 32
    Grilled Sea Scallop Kabobs, 89
    Indian Beef and Rice, 68
    Italian Sausage and White
        Bean Stew, 137
    Lentil Soup with Sun-Dried
        Tomatoes, 129–30
    Mexican Beef and Rice, 68
    Pasta Primavera with Tomato-
        Basil Sauce, 40–41
    Penne with Mediterranean
        Vegetables, 39
    Pepper-Marinated Flank Steak,
        83–84
    Quick Tomato Sauce, 40
    Roasted Vegetable Medley, 104
    Roast Salmon with Ginger and
        Garlic, 58
    Skillet Beef and Rice, 68
    Stuffed Spaghetti Squash, 79–80
    Sweet Pepper and Corn Soup,
        130–31
    Turkey Piccata, 54–55
    Warm Steak Salad, 84
    Zucchini Marinara, 106–7
Ginger
    Asparagus and Orange
        Linguine, 44
    Crunchy Cabbage Slaw, 106
    Fast Chicken Curry, 53
    Ginger Chicken, 48

Jamaican Pork, 87
    Quick-Fry with Tofu and
        Vegetables, 78
    Roast Salmon with Ginger and
        Garlic, 58
    Teriyaki Swordfish Kabobs,
        89–90
    Warm Steak Salad, 84
Grains. *See also specific grains*
    in casseroles, 120–21
    cooking methods, 72, 100
    in healthy diet, 6
    in well-stocked kitchen, 10–12
Grapes
    Chicken and Grape Salad in
        Pitas, 51
    Summer Fruit Salad with
        Honey-Lime Dressing, 35
Green beans
    Couscous Salad Niçoise, 30
    Easy Barbecued Beef Stew,
        136–37
    Roasted Vegetable Medley, 104
    Russian Potato and Green Bean
        Stew, 138
Greens. *See specific greens*
Grilled dishes
    Grilled Sea Scallop Kabobs, 89
    Grilled Tuna Steaks with Chive
        and Dill Sauce, 88
    Jamaican Pork, 87
    Mushroom-Onion Burgers, 86
    Pepper-Marinated Flank Steak,
        83–84
    Teriyaki Swordfish Kabobs,
        89–90
    Warm Steak Salad, 84
    Zesty Barbecued Chicken
        Breasts, 86
Grilling, 25–26, 81–82, 85, 87

H

Ham, 65–66
    Crock-Pot Baked Beans, 136
    Curried Bulgur and Ham
        Salad, 31
Hash
    Corned Beef Hash, 67
    Turkey Hash, 55
Herbs, 15, 128, 135. *See also
    specific herbs*

Honey, <u>116</u>
Horseradish
  Bangers and Beans, 68
  Creamy Horseradish Sauce, 61

K

Kabobs, <u>88</u>
  Grilled Sea Scallop Kabobs, 89
  Teriyaki Swordfish Kabobs,
    89–90
  Thai Chicken Kabobs, 50
Kidney beans
  Black Bean Citrus Salad, 33–34
  Chili Con Carne, 138–39
  Mexican Cornbread Casserole,
    126
  Vegetable Chili, 125

L

Lamb
  Lamb Curry with Rice, 70–71
Lentils
  Lentil Soup with Sun-Dried
    Tomatoes, 129–30
Lettuce, 28
  Bean Burritos, 96
  Chicken and Grape Salad in
    Pitas, 51
  Couscous Salad Niçoise, 30
  Crab Salad with Avocado and
    Mango, 35
  Greek Salad with Shrimp, 32–33
  Key West Crab Salad, 35–36
  Sloppy Burger Sandwiches, 70
  Summer Fruit Salad with
    Honey-Lime Dressing, 35
  Thai Tuna Wraps, 97
  White Beans and Sausage with
    Greens, 32
Limes
  Key Lime Pie, 112
  Summer Fruit Salad with
    Honey-Lime Dressing, 35
Linguine
  Asparagus and Orange
    Linguine, 44
  Linguine with Mushrooms and
    Peppers, 42–43
Liver, <u>67</u>
Lycopene, 13, <u>43</u>

M

Mangoes
  Banana-Mango Mousse, 116
  Crab Salad with Avocado and
    Mango, 35
Margarine, <u>44</u>
Marinating, <u>20</u>, 25–26, 64,
    82–83
Meat. *See* Beef; Lamb; Pork
Meatballs
  Turkey Meatballs, 39
Melon
  Summer Fruit Salad with
    Honey-Lime Dressing, 35
Monterey Jack cheese
  Asparagus Quesadillas, 97–98
  Beefy Tortilla Stack, 96–97
  Spinach-Cheese Quesadillas,
    98
  Tuna Noodle Casserole, 122
Mousse
  Banana-Mango Mousse, 116
  Chocolate Mousse, 113
Mozzarella cheese
  Baked Rigatoni and Vegetables,
    124
  Chicken Fingers Parmesan, 41
  Corn and Spinach Fritters, 103
  Red, White, and Green Pizza,
    78–79
  Tofu Layered with Three
    Cheeses, 77–78
Mushrooms, <u>85</u>
  Beef and Noodle Paprikash,
    66–67
  Chicken and Waffles, 51
  Chicken Provençal with Garlic
    Potatoes, 49–50
  French Beef and Rice, 68
  Indian Beef and Rice, 68
  Linguine with Mushrooms and
    Peppers, 42–43
  Mexican Beef and Rice, 68
  Mushroom-Onion Burgers, 86
  Poached Sole with Italian
    Vegetables, 60
  Quick-Fry with Tofu and
    Vegetables, 78
  Skillet Beef and Rice, 68
  Spinach and Mushroom
    Frittata, 76–77

Mustard
  Bangers and Beans, 68
  Creamy Horseradish Sauce, 61
  Dijon Mustard Vinaigrette, 32
  Dill Sauce, 61
  Grilled Tuna Steaks with Chive
    and Dill Sauce, 88
  Maple-Glazed Carrots with
    Radishes, 106

N

Noodles
  Beef and Noodle Paprikash,
    66–67
  Tuna Noodle Casserole, 122
Nuts, 29, <u>36</u>, <u>107</u>

O

Oils, cooking, 17–18, <u>29</u>, <u>33</u>
Olives, <u>36</u>
  Chicken Provençal with Garlic
    Potatoes, 49–50
  Roasted Vegetable Medley, 104
Oranges
  Asparagus and Orange
    Linguine, 44
  Black Bean Citrus Salad,
    33–34
  Key West Crab Salad, 35–36
Orzo
  Stuffed Red Tomatoes, 75–76
Oysters, <u>132</u>
  Oyster and Corn Chowder, 129

P

Paella
  Vegetarian Paella, 77
Pancakes
  Potato Pancakes, 102
Pantry foods
  beans, 14
  cooking oils, 17–18
  dairy, 17
  fish and meats, 14, 16–17
  fruits and vegetables, 8–9,
    13–14, 72
  grains and breads, 10–12
  poultry, 9, 16
  spices and condiments, 18

Paprika
  Basic Barbecue Dry Rub, 83
  Beef and Noodle Paprikash,
    66–67
  Cajun Spice Rub, 83
  Fast Chicken Curry, 53
  Pepper Blend Rubs, 83
Parfaits
  Italian Biscotti Parfaits, 112
Parmesan cheese
  Chicken Fingers Parmesan, 41
  Creamy Tomato Sauce, 40
  Fettuccine Alfredo, 41
  Penne with Mediterranean
    Vegetables, 39
  Stuffed Tomatoes, 106
  Tofu Layered with Three
    Cheeses, 77–78
  Turkey Hash, 55
Pasta, 11–12, 37–38, 42, 102
  Asparagus and Orange
    Linguine, 44
  Baked Rigatoni and Vegetables,
    124
  Beef and Noodle Paprikash,
    66–67
  Cheese Tortellini Soup, 132
  Chicken Fingers Parmesan, 41
  Chicken Pesto Pasta, 42
  Chicken Vegetable Soup with
    Shells, 133
  Fettuccine Alfredo, 41
  Fusilli Primavera in Spicy
    Peanut Sauce, 44–45
  Lentil Soup with Sun-Dried
    Tomatoes, 129–30
  Linguine with Mushrooms and
    Peppers, 42–43
  Pasta Primavera with Tomato-
    Basil Sauce, 40–41
  Pasta with Red Clam Sauce,
    43
  Penne with Mediterranean
    Vegetables, 39
  Stuffed Red Tomatoes, 75–76
  Tuna Noodle Casserole, 122
  Tuscan Chicken Legs with
    Spinach Fettuccine, 48
  Wagon Wheels with Mexican
    Salsa, 79
  Warm Pasta Salad with
    Chicken, 31–32

Peaches
  Peach and Blueberry Sauce,
    109
  Peach Crunch, 117
  Summer Fruit Salad with
    Honey-Lime Dressing, 35
  Turkey Divan with Peaches, 55
Peanut butter, 12
  Crunchy Peanut Butter
    Cookies, 115–16
  Fusilli Primavera in Spicy
    Peanut Sauce, 44–45
Peas
  Cheese Tortellini Soup, 132
  Chicken Stew with Dumplings,
    130
  Fusilli Primavera in Spicy
    Peanut Sauce, 44–45
  Pasta Primavera with Tomato-
    Basil Sauce, 40–41
  Stuffed Spaghetti Squash,
    79–80
  Vegetarian Paella, 77
Penne pasta
  Pasta Primavera with Tomato-
    Basil Sauce, 40–41
  Penne with Mediterranean
    Vegetables, 39
Phyllo crusts, 110
Pie
  crusts, 110–11
  Key Lime Pie, 112
Pineapple
  Summer Fruit Salad with
    Honey-Lime Dressing, 35
  Teriyaki Swordfish Kabobs,
    89–90
Pinto beans
  Mexican Corn Stew, 138
  Sloppy Burger Sandwiches, 70
Pitas
  Chicken and Grape Salad in
    Pitas, 51
Pizza, 88
  Red, White, and Green Pizza,
    78–79
Poaching, 23–24, 57, 62
Pork
  Bangers and Beans, 68
  cooking methods, 64–65
  Cranberry-Glazed Pork Chops,
    69

Crock-Pot Baked Beans, 136
Curried Bulgur and Ham
  Salad, 31
cuts of, 14, 65–66, 71
freezing, 17
Jamaican Pork, 87
Pork and Cabbage Roll-Ups, 96
Pork Cutlets with Apple Slices,
  68–69
in salads, 36
Potatoes, 21, 85, 102, 103
  Chicken Provençal with Garlic
    Potatoes, 49–50
  Corned Beef Hash, 67
  Couscous Salad Niçoise, 30
  Easy Barbecued Beef Stew,
    136–37
  Italian Sausage and White
    Bean Stew, 137
  Oven Fries, 107
  Oyster and Corn Chowder, 129
  Pepper-Marinated Flank Steak,
    83–84
  Potato Pancakes, 102
  Roasted Vegetable Medley, 104
  Russian Potato and Green Bean
    Stew, 138
  Sweet Pepper and Corn Soup,
    130–31
  Turkey Hash, 55
  Turkey Potpie, 123
Potpie
  Turkey Potpie, 123
Poultry. See Chicken; Turkey
Pressure cookers, 100
Puddings
  Banana-Raspberry Rice
    Pudding, 112
  Rice-Raisin Pudding, 101

Q
Quesadillas
  Asparagus Quesadillas, 97–98
  Spinach-Cheese Quesadillas,
    98

R
Radishes
  Maple-Glazed Carrots with
    Radishes, 106

Raisins
  Curried Bulgur and Ham
    Salad, 31
  Herbed Rice, 101
  Rice-Raisin Pudding, 101
Raspberries
  Banana-Raspberry Rice
    Pudding, 112
  Raspberry Dessert Sauce, 109
  Summer Fruit Salad with
    Honey-Lime Dressing, 35
Rice, 11
  Banana-Raspberry Rice
    Pudding, 112
  Bean Burritos, 96
  Blackened Catfish, 59
  Cranberry-Glazed Pork Chops,
    69
  Creamy Asparagus Chicken,
    125
  Cuban Black Beans and Rice,
    101
  Fast Chicken Curry, 53
  French Beef and Rice, 68
  Ginger Chicken, 48
  Herbed Rice, 101
  Indian Beef and Rice, 68
  Lamb Curry with Rice,
    70–71
  Mexican Beef and Rice, 68
  Quick-Fry with Tofu and
    Vegetables, 78
  Quick Pilaf, 101
  Rice and Broccoli Salad, 101
  Rice-Raisin Pudding, 101
  Skillet Beef and Rice, 68
  Speedy Spanish Rice, 104
  Stuffed Tomatoes, 106
  Thai Chicken Kabobs, 50
  Turkey and Sausage Jambalaya,
    54
Ricotta cheese
  Asparagus and Orange
    Linguine, 44
  Tofu Layered with Three
    Cheeses, 77–78
Rigatoni
  Baked Rigatoni and Vegetables,
    124
Romano cheese
  Pasta Primavera with Tomato-
    Basil Sauce, 40–41

Rubs
  Basic Barbecue Dry Rub, 83
  Cajun Spice Rub, 83
  Pepper Blend Rubs, 83

S

Salad dressings, 29. *See also*
  Vinaigrettes
Salads, 28–29, 36
  Black Bean Citrus Salad,
    33–34
  Chicken and Grape Salad in
    Pitas, 51
  Couscous Salad Niçoise, 30
  Crab Salad with Avocado and
    Mango, 35
  Crunchy Cabbage Slaw, 106
  Curried Bulgur and Ham
    Salad, 31
  Greek Salad with Shrimp,
    32–33
  Key West Crab Salad, 35–36
  Rice and Broccoli Salad, 101
  Summer Fruit Salad with
    Honey-Lime Dressing, 35
  Warm Pasta Salad with
    Chicken, 31–32
  Warm Steak Salad, 84
  White Beans and Sausage with
    Greens, 32
Salmon, 14
  Roast Salmon with Ginger and
    Garlic, 58
  Salmon Bisque, 131
Salsas, stir-ins for, 84
Sandwiches. *See also* Wraps
  Chicken and Grape Salad in
    Pitas, 51
  Meatless Sloppy Joes, 98–99
  Mushroom-Onion Burgers, 86
  Sloppy Burger Sandwiches, 70
Sauces
  Creamy Horseradish Sauce, 61
  Creamy Strawberry Sauce, 109
  Creamy Tomato Sauce, 40
  Dill Sauce, 61
  Peach and Blueberry Sauce,
    109
  Quick Tomato Sauce, 40
  Raspberry Dessert Sauce, 109
  Tartar Sauce, 61

Sausage
  Bangers and Beans, 68
  Italian Sausage and White
    Bean Stew, 137
  Quick Cassoulet, 122
  Turkey and Sausage Jambalaya,
    54
  Turkey Meatballs, 39
  White Beans and Sausage with
    Greens, 32
Sautéing, 21–23, 74–75
Scallions
  Asparagus and Orange
    Linguine, 44
  Blackened Catfish, 59
  Crunchy Cabbage Slaw, 106
  Dill Sauce, 61
  Fusilli Primavera in Spicy
    Peanut Sauce, 44–45
  Pasta Primavera with Tomato-
    Basil Sauce, 40–41
  Quick-Fry with Tofu and
    Vegetables, 78
  Stuffed Spaghetti Squash,
    79–80
  Thai Tuna Wraps, 97
  Turkey and Sausage Jambalaya,
    54
Scallops
  Grilled Sea Scallop Kabobs, 89
  Herbed Scallops with
    Tomatoes, 63
Sea bass
  Broiled Barbecued Sea Bass, 62
Sesame seeds
  Fusilli Primavera in Spicy
    Peanut Sauce, 44–45
  Sesame Turkey Cutlets, 53
  Teriyaki Swordfish Kabobs,
    89–90
Shellfish
  Crab Cakes, 58
  Crab Salad with Avocado and
    Mango, 35
  Greek Salad with Shrimp,
    32–33
  Grilled Sea Scallop Kabobs, 89
  Herbed Scallops with
    Tomatoes, 63
  Key West Crab Salad, 35–36
  Oyster and Corn Chowder, 129
  Pasta with Red Clam Sauce, 43

Shell pasta
   Chicken Vegetable Soup with
      Shells, 133
   Lentil Soup with Sun-Dried
      Tomatoes, 129–30
Shrimp, 36, 59
   Greek Salad with Shrimp,
      32–33
Sloppy Joes
   Meatless Sloppy Joes, 98–99
   Sloppy Burger Sandwiches, 70
Slow cooker recipes
   Chicken and Barley Stew, 137
   Chili Con Carne, 138–39
   Crock-Pot Baked Beans, 136
   Easy Barbecued Beef Stew,
      136–37
   Italian Sausage and White
      Bean Stew, 137
   Mexican Corn Stew, 138
   Russian Potato and Green Bean
      Stew, 138
Sole
   Poached Sole with Italian
      Vegetables, 60
Sorbets, homemade, 110
Soups, 127–28, 128, 132, 133. See
   also Stews
   Cheese Tortellini Soup, 132
   Chicken Vegetable Soup with
      Shells, 133
   Lentil Soup with Sun-Dried
      Tomatoes, 129–30
   Oyster and Corn Chowder, 129
   Salmon Bisque, 131
   Sweet Pepper and Corn Soup,
      130–31
   Vegetable, Beef, and Barley
      Soup, 128–29
Southwestern-style dishes
   Asparagus Quesadillas, 97–98
   Bean Burritos, 96
   Beefy Tortilla Stack, 96–97
   Black Bean Chili with Turkey,
      132
   Chili Con Carne, 138–39
   Cuban Black Beans and Rice,
      101
   Mexican Cornbread Casserole,
      126
   Mexican Corn Stew, 138
   Speedy Spanish Rice, 104

Spinach-Cheese Quesadillas, 98
Vegetable Chili, 125
Wagon Wheels with Mexican
   Salsa, 79
Spaghetti, 42
   Chicken Fingers Parmesan, 41
Spaghetti squash
   Stuffed Spaghetti Squash,
      79–80
Spices, 5, 15, 18, 83, 135. See also
   specific spices
Spinach, 11, 104
   Corn and Spinach Fritters, 103
   Key West Crab Salad, 35–36
   Pasta Primavera with Tomato-
      Basil Sauce, 40–41
   Red, White, and Green Pizza,
      78–79
   Spinach and Mushroom
      Frittata, 76–77
   Spinach-Cheese Quesadillas,
      98
   Warm Steak Salad, 84
Squash, 85
   Penne with Mediterranean
      Vegetables, 39
   Pepper-Marinated Flank Steak,
      83–84
   Stuffed Spaghetti Squash,
      79–80
   Warm Pasta Salad with
      Chicken, 31–32
   Zucchini Marinara, 106–7
Steaming, 21, 24–25, 74
Stews, 127–28, 134–35. See also
   Chili
   Chicken and Barley Stew, 137
   Chicken Stew with Dumplings,
      130
   Crock-Pot Baked Beans, 136
   Easy Barbecued Beef Stew,
      136–37
   Italian Sausage and White
      Bean Stew, 137
   Mexican Corn Stew, 138
   Russian Potato and Green Bean
      Stew, 138
Stir-frying, 19–21, 91–93, 93
Stock, 62, 127
Strawberries
   Creamy Strawberry Sauce, 109
Sushi, 60

Sweet potatoes, 85
   Pepper-Marinated Flank Steak,
      83–84
   Turkey Potpie, 123
Swordfish
   Roasted Swordfish with
      Herbed Crust, 59–60
   Teriyaki Swordfish Kabobs,
      89–90

T

Tofu, 21, 76
   Meatless Sloppy Joes, 98–99
   Quick-Fry with Tofu and
      Vegetables, 78
   Tofu Layered with Three
      Cheeses, 77–78
   Vegetarian Paella, 77
Tomatoes, 13, 38, 43
   Asparagus Quesadillas, 97–98
   Baked Rigatoni and Vegetables,
      124
   Bean Burritos, 96
   Black Bean Chili with Turkey,
      132
   Blackened Catfish, 59
   Chicken Fingers Parmesan, 41
   Chicken Pesto Pasta, 42
   Chili Con Carne, 138–39
   Couscous Salad Niçoise, 30
   Creamy Tomato Sauce, 40
   Fusilli Primavera in Spicy
      Peanut Sauce, 44–45
   Greek Salad with Shrimp,
      32–33
   Herbed Scallops with
      Tomatoes, 63
   Lamb Curry with Rice, 70–71
   Lentil Soup with Sun-Dried
      Tomatoes, 129–30
   Mexican Cornbread Casserole,
      126
   Pasta Primavera with Tomato-
      Basil Sauce, 40–41
   Pasta with Red Clam Sauce, 43
   Penne with Mediterranean
      Vegetables, 39
   Poached Sole with Italian
      Vegetables, 60
   Quick Cassoulet, 122
   Quick Tomato Sauce, 40

Salmon Bisque, 131
Sloppy Burger Sandwiches, 70
Stuffed Red Tomatoes, 75–76
Stuffed Tomatoes, 106
Sweet Pepper and Corn Soup,
    130–31
Thai Chicken Kabobs, 50
Tofu Layered with Three
    Cheeses, 77–78
Turkey and Sausage Jambalaya,
    54
Tuscan Chicken Legs with
    Spinach Fettuccine, 48
Vegetable, Beef, and Barley
    Soup, 128–29
Vegetable Chili, 125
Vegetarian Paella, 77
Wagon Wheels with Mexican
    Salsa, 79
Warm Pasta Salad with
    Chicken, 31–32
Zucchini Marinara, 106–7
Tortellini
    Cheese Tortellini Soup, 132
Tortillas, 94, 95–96
    Asparagus Quesadillas, 97–98
    Bean Burritos, 96
    Beefy Tortilla Stack, 96–97
    Pork and Cabbage Roll-Ups,
        96
    Spinach-Cheese Quesadillas,
        98
    Thai Tuna Wraps, 97
Truffles
    Dried-Fruit Truffles, 115
Tuna, 14, 63
    Couscous Salad Niçoise, 30
    Grilled Tuna Steaks with Chive
        and Dill Sauce, 88
    Thai Tuna Wraps, 97
    Tuna Noodle Casserole, 122
Turkey
    Black Bean Chili with Turkey,
        132
    buying, 16, 47
    cooking methods, 25–26,
        46–47, 81, 134
    defrosting, 46
    fat in, 16, 47, 53, 54
    in healthy diet, 14

herb blends for, 15
Italian Sausage and White
    Bean Stew, 137
leftover, ideas for, 50
marinating, 25–26
Mushroom-Onion Burgers, 86
Quick Cassoulet, 122
Savory Beef Rolls, 70
Sesame Turkey Cutlets, 53
spice rubs for, 83
Turkey and Sausage Jambalaya,
    54
Turkey Divan with Peaches, 55
turkey dogs, 54
Turkey Hash, 55
Turkey Meatballs, 39
Turkey Piccata, 54–55
Turkey Potpie, 123
White Beans and Sausage with
    Greens, 32

V

Vegetables. *See also specific
    vegetables*
    browning, 120
    canned, 13, 100, 105
    Chicken Vegetable Soup with
        Shells, 133
    defrosting, 21
    frozen, 13, 100, 105
    Ginger Chicken, 48
    grilled, uses for, 88
    grilling, 81, 85
    in healthy diet, 6, 9
    prewashed, precut, 8–9, 72
    Quick Pilaf, 101
    in salads, 28
    sautéing, 74
    in soups and stews, 127–28
    steaming, 21, 74
    stir-frying, 91–93, 93
    in well-stocked kitchen, 13–14
Vegetarian cooking, 72, 74–75
Vinaigrettes
    Classic Vinaigrette, 32
    Curried French Vinaigrette, 32
    Dijon Mustard Vinaigrette, 32
    Fruit Salad Vinaigrette, 32
    Garlic Vinaigrette, 32

W

Waffles
    Chicken and Waffles, 51
Wagon wheels
    Wagon Wheels with Mexican
        Salsa, 79
Watercress
    Warm Pasta Salad with
        Chicken, 31–32
White beans
    Crock-Pot Baked Beans, 136
    Italian Sausage and White
        Bean Stew, 137
    Quick Cassoulet, 122
    Red, White, and Green Pizza,
        78–79
    White Beans and Sausage with
        Greens, 32
Wraps, 88, 94–96
    Bean Burritos, 96
    Pork and Cabbage Roll-Ups,
        96
    Thai Tuna Wraps, 97

Y

Yellow squash, 85
    Penne with Mediterranean
        Vegetables, 39
    Pepper-Marinated Flank Steak,
        83–84
Yogurt, 17, 113
    Banana-Mango Mousse, 116
    Creamy Strawberry Sauce,
        109
    Dill Sauce, 61
    Italian Biscotti Parfaits, 112
    Peach Crunch, 117
    Poached Bananas in Vanilla
        Sauce, 116
    Summer Fruit Salad with
        Honey-Lime Dressing, 35

Z

Zucchini, 85
    Warm Pasta Salad with
        Chicken, 31–32
    Zucchini Marinara, 106–7

Conversion Chart

These equivalents have been slightly rounded to make measuring easier.

Volume Measurements

U.S.	Imperial	Metric
¼ tsp	–	1.25 ml
½ tsp	–	2.5 ml
1 tsp	–	5 ml
1 Tbsp	–	15 ml
2 Tbsp (1 oz)	1 fl oz	30 ml
¼ cup (2 oz)	2 fl oz	60 ml
⅓ cup (3 oz)	3 fl oz	80 ml
½ cup (4 oz)	4 fl oz	120 ml
⅔ cup (5 oz)	5 fl oz	160 ml
¾ cup (6 oz)	6 fl oz	180 ml
1 cup (8 oz)	8 fl oz	240 ml

Weight Measurements

U.S.	Metric
1 oz	30 g
2 oz	60 g
4 oz (¼ lb)	115 g
5 oz (⅓ lb)	145 g
6 oz	170 g
7 oz	200 g
8 oz (½ lb)	230 g
10 oz	285 g
12 oz (¾ lb)	340 g
14 oz	400 g
16 oz (1 lb)	455 g
2.2 lb	1 kg

Length Measurements

U.S.	Metric
¼"	0.6 cm
½"	1.25 cm
1"	2.5 cm
2"	5 cm
4"	11 cm
6"	15 cm
8"	20 cm
10"	25 cm
12" (1')	30 cm

Pan Sizes

U.S.	Metric
8" cake pan	20 × 4-cm sandwich or cake tin
9" cake pan	23 × 3.5-cm sandwich or cake tin
11" × 7" baking pan	28 × 18-cm baking pan
13" × 9" baking pan	32.5 × 23-cm baking pan
2-qt rectangular baking dish	30 × 19-cm baking dish
15" × 10" baking pan	38 × 25.5-cm baking pan (Swiss roll tin)
9" pie plate	22 × 4 or 23 × 4-cm pie plate
7" or 8" springform pan	18 or 20-cm springform or loose-bottom cake tin
9" × 5" loaf pan	23 × 13-cm or 2-lb narrow loaf pan or pâté tin
1½-qt casserole	1.5-l casserole
2-qt casserole	2-l casserole

Temperatures

Fahrenheit	Centigrade	Gas
140°	60°	–
160°	70°	–
180°	80°	–
225°	110°	–
250°	120°	½
300°	150°	2
325°	160°	3
350°	180°	4
375°	190°	5
400°	200°	6
450°	230°	8
500°	260°	–